BERMUDA
Today and Yesterday

1503 – 1980s

BERMUDA
Today and Yesterday

1503 – 1980s

TERRY TUCKER, O.B.E.

LONDON
Robert Hale Limited

BERMUDA
Baxter's Limited

First published 1975
Reprinted with revisions 1977
Second edition 1979
Third edition 1983

Baxter's Limited
P.O. Box 1009, Hamilton 5
Bermuda

Robert Hale Limited
Clerkenwell House
Clerkenwell Green
London, EC1

ISBN 0 7090 0843 0

Printed in Great Britain by
Redwood Burn Limited
Trowbridge, Wiltshire
Bound by W.B.C. Bookbinders Limited

CONTENTS

ILLUSTRATIONS

FIGURES IN THE TEXT

ACKNOWLEDGEMENTS

Bermuda News Bureau Photos, including jacket, by Staff Photographers of that Bureau by courtesy of D. Colin Selley, Director of the Bermuda Department of Tourism.

One of Walter Rutherford's famed photographs is reproduced to show the now-defunct Bermuda Railway.

The photos by Bernard Brown were donated by the late Bernard B. Brown of the Staff of the Bermuda Royal Gazette.

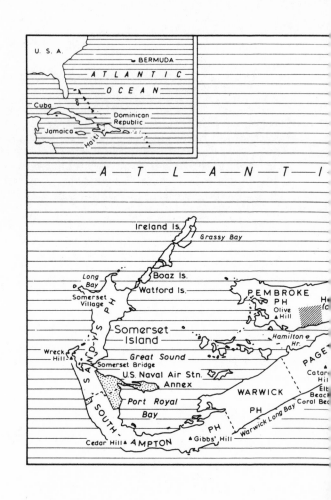

St. George's
Island

Fort St. Catherine

St. George's (town)

Sugarloaf
Hill

St
George's
Hbr.

Roberts Hill

St.
David's
Island.

U.S. Naval Air Stn.

Civil Air
Terminal

Coney Is.

ST. GEORGE'S PH.

Castle

Harbour

Nonsuch Is.

HAMILTON PH.

Harrington

Tucker's
Town

Shelly Bay

Sound

Knapton Hill

SMITHS PH.

Gilbert Hill

ONSHIRE

on

PH

Devonshire Bay

O C E A N

Hungry Bay

pe Bay

0   Miles   3

For
My Son, G.H. St George Tucker
to whom Bermuda is 'home'

1
The Unknown and Uninhabited Isles

Landfall – that climactic moment of travel – startles the senses as one approaches the isolated Bermuda Islands. Paradoxically, it is not the land, a meagre total of approximately 20 square miles in all, that rivets the traveller's attention, but the sea itself, of an incredible cerulean and aquamarine shot with purple above the underlying reefs, that dazzles and astounds. Bermuda is indeed the Land of Water.

Approaching from the air, one realizes instantly that this attenuated group, the Bermuda Islands, (usually referred to in the singular, Bermuda,) is a series of continuous islands, islets, rocks, banks and shoals emergent as the south-east rim of an otherwise submerged plateau. The water above this platform – a platform perched on the summit of extinct volcanoes – is so much shallower than the steep illimitable depths beyond, which descend to a depth of well over 5,000 feet within a mile or so of shore, that it radiates the brilliant colours of sub-tropical seas unpolluted by the sediment of rivers.

This whole submerged plateau of over 200 square miles, is like a giant immersed saucer with its curved south-east rim emerging a little above the water – while at the north the saucer rim forms a line of submarine reefs, with North Rock protruding to the north-east. All that now lies above the surface of the sea, a bare 20-square-mile area comprising some 120 isles and islets, is therefore set in a maze of rocks and jagged reefs that have been the doom of mariners who attempted to approach the shores. No wonder then, that the islands remained uninhabited until the seventeenth century.

Fourteen miles south-west of this Bermuda Platform is the Challenger Bank; still further south-west is the Argus Bank. These submerged banks are the eroded stumps of two volcanoes, above ocean level during the Ice Age.

GEOLOGY

Twenty thousand centuries or so ago when the first glacial epoch began, the level of the ocean sank, leaving the

Bermuda mountain, formed volcanically some 30-35 million years earlier, high and dry. Terrific wind storms ground up shelly creatures of all kinds into sand that blew into high dunes and, cemented by rain, hardened into the aeolian limestone which constitutes the Bermuda of today, but of ten or twelve times its present sparse area. Most of this as we have seen, now forms the shallowly-submerged Bermuda plateau.

The rim of islands, perched on the south east of this elliptical submarine platform, composed as it is of wind-blown shell fragments, is *not* therefore a true atoll though the description 'coral island' is sometimes erroneously attached to it. Corals have contributed only a thin veneer; living coral heads exist — thanks to the proximity of the warm Gulf Stream — on the reefs around the islands. These coral reefs help to protect the land from the erosion of the waves.

The richly-tinted soil has formed from the disintegration of the aeolian limestone; interbedded with the aeolianites are five fossil soils showing that numerous changes of level — alternate lifts and depressions — have taken place in the past, this in addition to the change, already noted, in ocean level. And although local soil has sand and lime content, it also owes its richness to climatic conditions and to decayed animal and vegetable matter. The porous nature of the rock allows water to percolate through to depth and prevents the formation of springs and surface waters — Bermuda has therefore no surface waters except in sounds and marshes.

This underground seepage water forms subterranean streams that eat out caves and caverns before emerging through the rock beyond the impervious area. Many caverns have been discovered beneath Bermuda's hills, with stalagmites and stalactites still in process of formation; and doubtless many more remain to be discovered in the older Bermuda rocks.

It was as recently as 1912 that proof positive was found of Bermuda's suspected volcanic base. A great bore was made near Gibbs' Hill in a search for fresh water. The first 360 feet was found to consist of limestone, the next 200 of decomposed volcanic calcareous material forming yellowish claylike rock, and below that, down to the very limit of the 1,400-foot boring, nothing existed but black volcanic rock.

In 1972, the Bermuda Biological Station for Research made another deep bore in order to determine more exactly the island's geological age. This important station, incorpo-

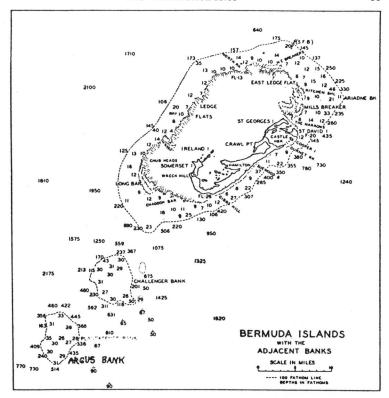

BERMUDA ISLANDS
WITH THE
ADJACENT BANKS
SCALE IN MILES
---- 100 FATHOM LINE
DEPTHS IN FATHOMS

rated in N.Y., owns 14 acres of land fronting Ferry Reach, St George's, and was formally opened in January, 1932.

We may say, then, that these islands are an eroded remnant of a layer of aeolian limestone, several hundred feet thick, whose land area was much larger formerly than it is to-day, perched on the top of an ancient volcano. The group is situated near latitude 32 degrees north, longitude 65 degrees west. The nearest land is Cape Hatteras, North Carolina, 570 miles west-north-west; the nearest point in the West Indies is 770 miles south west, and London is 3,445 miles distant.

Nowhere does the land rise as much as 300 feet above sea-level; nor, in any part of the islands, can one get as far as a mile from the coast. It is indeed the land of water; its climate, its history, its sociology, the habits, the temperament, the occupations of its peoples – all have been formed and moulded by the proximity of the ocean. Its pervasive presence makes young Bermudians reluctant to live elsewhere and draws, as a magnet, the hundreds of thousands of visitors who swarm to the islands every year to enjoy the sea and the oceanic climate it engenders.

CLIMATE

Not that this is a tropical island. Factually, it is sub-tropical — or, on the warm side of the warm-temperate zone. During January, February and March the average temperature falls below 64° F taking it out of the tropical bracket. The lowest temperature on record (taken at Fort George in 1955) was 41° F yet few places outside the tropics enjoy such warm winters where frost and snow are unknown.

In part this is due to the great current of warm water, the Gulf Stream, whose proximity we have already noted, which flows out of the Gulf of Mexico, passes thence between Florida and Cuba, along the eastern coast of the United States before deflecting eastward to the north of Bermuda diagonally across the Atlantic. Between these islands and New York its width is some 200 miles — a definite modifier of cold north winds.

Similarly in summer, when one might be apprehensive of unbearable heat, the ocean airs modify the temperature. The land is too small to remain in any part unaffected by the sea which warms the atmosphere in winter and cools it in summer. August is the hottest month but even then it is rare

---

(*above*) The Tropic Bird or Longtail (*Phaethon lepturus catesbyi*), one of the few varieties of the original breeding birds of Bermuda that continues to breed in the thousands each summer in crevices of the rocky coast, returning to the seas for the winter months. Its arrival, as its long white tail flashes while it wheels and manoeuvres in the sunshine, is hailed as the harbinger of spring. (*Photo by Bernard Brown*)

(*below*) Teddy Tucker, famed local treasure-diver, has, over the years, brought up much valuable treasure from Spanish ships sunk on Bermuda's coasts and reefs when en route to Spain with plunder from the Spanish Main, before Bermuda was inhabited. This gold cross, probably a pectoral cross, contains seven emeralds and may have been made by a primitive people. It was salvaged in 1955 and is only one of the many submarine treasures discovered in the twentieth century. (*Bermuda News Bureau photo*)

indeed for the thermometer to register 90° F. The hottest
day ever recorded was in August 1952 with a temperature of
92° F. But high humidity is admittedly enervating.

There are no wet and dry seasons. Rain falls throughout
the year, usually extremely heavily. It rapidly soaks through
the porous rock so that, except for sounds and marshes, there
is no surface water. Although the average rainfall is almost 60
inches a year, water conservation has always been a big
problem and helped determine early architectural features.
Another result has been the constant search for underground
water, the sinking of wells which soon yield brackish water,
and the construction of horizontal wells in the 1920s. It is
the extreme variability of climate, the rapid changes in
sunshine, wind, rainfall from day to day and hour to hour,
coupled with the fact that these changes are within a narrow
enough range to prevent extreme divergence between winters
and summers, that is part of Bermuda's charm. There is no
month of the year that cannot be enjoyable in the open air.
Not that one should describe these islands as enjoying twelve
months of summer; in the winter if high humidity happens to
coincide with a temperature that would appear moderate
enough in another region, the coolness can be quite penetra-
ting. Yet the sunshine is brilliant and the light unbelievably
clear at all seasons and the recorded hours of sunshine show
an average of over seven hours per day throughout the year.

Since there are no high hills, there is no protection from
winds, and many windy days with high towering clouds are
interspersed between periods of flat calm, when the weather-
wise fishermen are apt to exclaim: 'Ha! a weather-breeder.'

Somers' map 1609-10: When in 1625 Samuel Purchas published
William Strachey's letter giving a detailed description of the 9-month
sojourn in Bermuda of the castaways from the *Sea Venture*, he was
unable to include Sir George Somers' map which was missing. In
1948, this early Somers' map — or copy thereof — amazingly turned
up in the private collection of the seventh Earl of Dartmouth, and
was acquired for Bermuda by the Bermuda Historical Monuments
Trust. In Sotheby's catalogue of March 1948 the description of this
20½ by 13¾ inch map is: Coloured map of Bermuda, on vellum,
with coat-of-arms emblazoned, compass-rose, figures hunting, rowing
and fishing, and the figure of a boy on a turtle holding a banner
inscribed "Sumer Iles". In the lower margin are painted the arms of
Harington. No Harington holdings are recorded in Norwood's survey
which indicates this is an earlier map.

So, swift change and unpredictability spell an almost feminine charm. Slowly and painfully, an island lore evolved as to signs and seasons — one of the earliest being that the silk spiders spin their webs low at the approach of bad weather. Later they developed a shark-oil barometer, — the oil from a shark's liver, bottled, is a definite indication of coming storms since it clouds and thickens at their approach.

HURRICANES

Not that Bermuda is without one dramatic climatic happening; the group is within the hurricane zone. Hurricanes have influenced her history, her climate and her architecture. In fact, it was the results of one that led, fortuitously, to her colonization. Approximately 600 hurricanes spawn every 100 years somewhere in the huge bay of North America. The group of islands that is Bermuda, lying a thousand miles north of the hurricanes' usual breeding places and being but a mere speck upon the ocean, receives the impact of perhaps a twentieth of that number — many of which, indeed, reach no land whatever, and few of which are of major intensity. The old Bermuda doggerel, which even the children used to quote in reference to awareness of seasonal hurricane threat, runs:

JUNE	—	too soon.
JULY	—	stand by!
AUGUST	—	one *must*.
SEPTEMBER	—	remember?
OCTOBER	—	all over!

Hurricanes, i.e. tropical cyclones with wind velocity of over 75 mph, have been known to approach Bermuda from almost every point of the compass, but the large majority from between south and west. The maze of reefs surrounding the islands breaks the storm wave and protects the coast. The salt spray driven inland burns off the foliage, but also acts as nature's pruning fork and helps prevent the spread of blights. The extra rainfall that usually accompanies or follows the storm, and the clearing of humid sub-tropical summer into the clean blue sparkle of autumn, sometimes make the inhabitants feel that even a hurricane is not an unmitigated disaster. Especially as, by the time these latitudes are reached, the hurricane has usually lost some of its velocity. Those that have done great damage locally are naturally remembered and recounted in Bermuda's history. That September has usually been the worst month for such tempests is reflected in the folklore of the islands and its doggerel rhymes.

EARTHQUAKES

Despite its volcanic origin, Bermuda is, scientifically speaking, in a non-active seismic area and although mild tremors have been felt locally in historic times – mainly reflections of disturbances whose epicentre is many thousands of miles away – scientists definitely state that an earthquake with any serious effect is unlikely to occur; in modern times the world's earthquake shocks have been felt mainly around the margins of the Pacific in what may be termed a volcanic-cum-earthquake circle.

Interestingly enough, the terrible Lisbon earthquake of 1755, one of the world's worst disasters, was experienced as a tsunami on Bermuda's coasts, though at the time unrecognized as such. But a fairly severe shock was recorded 25th June 1664.

CONFIGURATION – PATTERN OF ISLANDS

The curved rim of islands protruding above the Atlantic, rather in the shape of a giant fish-hook, consisted of some 130 separate rocks, islets, islands – now reduced to 120 odd. Actually there are only seven principal ones (St George's, St David's, the Main, Somerset, Watford, Boaz and Ireland) so linked by bridges and causeways as to be practically regarded as one island, twenty-two miles long and from half a mile to approximately two miles wide.

The Main, the largest of these when regarded as a separate entity, comprises the whole centre and the greatest area of the group, and is about fourteen miles long by almost two miles wide at the widest point.

Eastward of the Main, smaller but far more important in Bermuda's early history, lie St George's Island, 700 acres, and St David's, originally of 510 acres. While westward of the Main arcs the remainder of the group, comprising Somerset Island, slightly larger than St George's Island, Watford, a mere 4 acres but a connecting link in the chain, Boaz of 30 acres, and Ireland Island – the narrow serrated point that pushes out into the Atlantic· at the extreme north west.

Where the encircling arms of the attenuated land enclose sounds, harbours, or bays, the water is dotted with smaller islands, islets, rocks. One thinks of Bermuda as an amphibean group the very atmosphere of which is unusually saline.

FLORA AND FAUNA

Since the islands rise sheer out of the ocean and have never been connected with any continental mass, it is obvious that, before the arrival of man, all life — insects, small animals, plants — was airborne on the breeze, carried by migratory birds, or as flotsam on ocean currents. Over the ages, these earliest arrivals gradually differentiated themselves from their original stock in adapting to totally new conditions and became entirely peculiar to the islands. These, since they are not found elsewhere in the same condition as in Bermuda, are considered *endemic*, while those that showed little appreciable change from their original stock are also referred to as *native*, though not peculiar to the region. In all, sixty-one of these 'true Bermudians' have been listed.

The most outstanding endemics were the cedars (*Juniperus bermudiana*) and palmettos (*Sabal bermudiana*) which heavily forested the islands down to the water's edge; the crab grass, and the little iris-blue bermudiana (*Sisyrinchium bermudiana*), also the maidenhair fern (*Adiantum bellum*) that seized crannies of rocky hillsides and was unlike any species elsewhere. They are the descendants of ancient wanderers cast on these shores such ages ago that they have differentiated their species.

Mangroves (*Rhizophora mangle*) and bay grapes (*Coccoloba uvifera*) had floated to festoon the beaches, the Spanish bayonet (*Yucca aloifolia*) pyramided its spear of white flowers between the coastal cedars, while mantling morning glory (*Ipomoea sagittifolius*) festooned other growths with its purple flowers — these were among many other plants also introduced by natural causes before the settlement of the islands, which grow wild and are native without being endemic since they are also found in such places as Florida.

The island group was a veritable paradise for wild life since man was not there to prey upon it. Though the range and variety was narrowed by isolation, whatever existed was prolific. Hence the dense forests, the swarming flocks of sea-birds, the rookeries of huge turtles along the beaches, the schools of whales and porpoises parading noisily past in spring and autumn on their seasonal migrations, the wide variety of fish teeming in the coastal waters, the land crabs that burrowed in the sandy soil, even herds of wild pigs rooted among the underbush — doubtless descendants of a few that had swum ashore from some early wreck on the reefs. According to Spanish records, hogs were set ashore in 1563 by Commander Menendez de Avila who had been given permission by Philip II to visit Bermuda in search of his shipwrecked son.

One of the sea birds that bred in hundreds of thousands — and still the most famous, though depleted, of those surviving — was a petrel unique to Bermuda, (the *Pterodroma* cahow) whose harsh cry 'Ca-*how*, ca-*how*' startled the earliest settlers. Another more noticeably flashing bird, which bred plentifully by the thousands in crevices of the rocky coast from March to September before returning to the ocean for the winter months, is the much loved Tropic bird (*phaethon lepturus catesbyi*) known locally as Longtail. Indeed, many other species of tern bred here before colonisation; the islands were vibrant not only with them but with the great flocks of birds pausing during the huge arc of their seasonal flights in April and October. The uninhabited islands, lying almost midway between the West Indies, the American coast and the shores of Nova Scotia, presented a welcome break during these vast migrations.

Necessarily there was small variety of terrestial wildlife beyond those already noted. A reptile, the skink, somehow reached these shores and evolved different characteristics from its ancestors. And several varieties of those flying mammals, the bat, managed to fly the 600 miles or more of ocean to reach these isolated shores. Land crabs burrowed deeply into the sandy soil.

At least there were no serpents in this Eden!

These were the unoccupied islands — known, feared and shunned for a hundred years — on which the English landed by chance on 28th July 1609; and only then as a reluctant alternative to a descent towards Davy Jones' Locker.

Yet never again were they left entirely uninhabited.

* * *

The pattern of islands still enchants those who arrive by air and those who sail blithely among them in the Great Sound. Incredulous visitors have been seen surreptitiously bottling the sea water in the vain hope of exhibiting its unbelievable colours on their return home.

Naturally, thousands of plants and trees have been introduced by man. The colour and variety of the vegetation are far greater than before the seventeenth century. Yet those people who are primarily interested in the original flora and fauna will be fascinated by the conservation project on Nonsuch Island where David Wingate, the Conservation Officer, is making a wildlife sanctuary for endemics.

2
The Shunned and Dreaded Coast 1503-1609

It was the Iberians who first became aware of this tiny dot in the Atlantic set within dangerous reefs, and who, in the early 1500s, named the group Bermuda. So many false statements are made as to the date of this occurrence, that it is as well to quote the testimony.

Moorish pressures within the Iberian Peninsula had early stimulated the Spaniards and the Portuguese to extend themselves into all the continents of the world; the Mexic civilization and the Inca Empire fell before the Spanish conquistadores. It was not until their domestic problem was resolved that the Iberians relaxed enough to lose their lead in that New World they had almost called into existence, and the lands overseas began in the seventeenth century to fall to the Dutch, the French, and the English.

Almost three hundred years earlier, England had begun her own attempt at expansion. The long series of wars between France and England from 1337 in the reign of Edward III down to 1453 in that of Henry VI (known as the Hundred Years War) eventually cured the English of attempting to retain European dependencies. But now, in the early seventeenth century, under the rule of the great Elizabeth, the urge to expand was once again upon the British, but this time in an entirely different direction – into Virginia, New England, and West Indian Islands where it was hoped to establish a new civilization.

A condition of the success of such ventures was that they should be undertaken in times of peace. That England was at war with Spain was one of the reasons for the failure of the first Virginia attempt. But the men of the Elizabethan age, retaining their buccaneering spirit into later reigns, would adventure again when peace was restored.

The Virginia Company of London, composed of gentlemen backers of these vast enterprises and led by that great empire builder and leading spirit in many of the mercantile and colonizing companies, Sir Thomas Smith, naturally expected a return on their heavy investments. But they were also motivated by patriotism and religion in attempting to create markets and English settlements on the other side of the globe. Most of the emigrants would be modest landless people out to improve their lot and to create a better life for their descendants. If the name Bermuda crossed their minds, it was of a place to be avoided like the plague, an uninhabited group with a fiercely dangerous coast subject to violent storms and peopled only by evil spirits. In fact, the Spaniards had dubbed the group Islands of Devils (*ya de demonios*).* No, it was definitely not included among the places to be colonized in those very early years of the seventeenth century when the permanent expansion of the English race overseas began. Even though the great Elizabeth died in 1603, the men were Elizabethans who carried through their great adventure into the next two reigns.

But what do we definitely know of the previous hundred years during which the islands were so execrated?

The first date we have in connection with Bermuda is the year 1503. In the Chateau de Ramezay in Montreal hangs a map marked: 'Carte de la Nouvelle-France, 1690.' Hereon Bermuda is represented in a rather odd little shape and against it are the words: '*Les Isles Bermudes furent de-couverte l'an 1503. Les Anglois y ont un establisement depuis l'an 1612.*' There is no reason to doubt that French cartographer; on the other hand, this is not proof positive since the map is late-seventeenth-century. The year 1612 is correct as far as *deliberate* colonization goes.

But of the next date we are entirely positive. We *know* that the islands were not only known but that they were called *Bermuda* before 1511. For it was in that year that Peter Martyr, (C 1457-1526) the Italian historian and diplomatic representative of the Court of Ferdinand and Isabella of Spain, published the first edition of his *Legatio Babylonica*, copies of which rare book still exist in three United States' libraries. A map in this 1511 edition has 'La bermuda' plainly inserted.

So there is our proof: Bermuda was discovered *certainly before 1511, probably in 1503* and named for its discoverer, Bermudez – a not uncommon name at that period. The Spanish historian, Antonio de Herrera (1549-1625) states that Bermuda was discovered by 'Juan Bermudez, *natural de*

---

*The islands are so designated on the Mappa Mundi of Sebastian Cabot published in 1544. See pp. 26-27.

la villa de Palos' in his ship *La Garza*. There is no record that he ever landed. But, interestingly enough, Palos was the very spot that Christopher Columbus had returned to so triumphantly only ten years earlier in his small *Santa Maria* after his successful voyage to the Bahamas, Cuba and Hispaniola. Was Juan Bermudez, that native of the same port, fired into emulation by his fellow-citizen's exploits?

After that earlier discovery, we know that in 1515 Juan Bermudez again sailed near the islands named for him, Bermuda. This time he had aboard his fellow countryman, Oviedo y Valdes (1478-1557) the Spanish chronicler who was appointed historiographer of the New World by Charles V. Although 'by reason of contrarie winds' it was impossible to approach the island, he speaks of their wanting to leave 'certaine hogs for increase' and describes the surrounding waters as teeming with fishes and multitudes of sea-birds. The isolation of the spot was what struck him most, he speaks of it as 'the furthest of all the islands that are found at this day in the world.' The first edition of this part of Oviedo's work was printed at Toledo in 1526.

At this time the homeward course of the Spanish treasure ships was up from Chili and Peru, through the Yucatan Channel and on to Havana. Then up through the Bahamas Channel with the Gulf Stream to latitude 33 degrees where, once safely past the dangerous reefs of the Bermudas, they made east for the Azores. All mariners regarded these shunned uninhabited islands as the last of their American perils which, once past, justified enough relaxation to enjoy by way of celebration aboard 'the wine of height', the liquor given on safely reaching a certain latitude.

Nevertheless, there were many unknown wrecks around these rocky shores described as a 'graveyard of ships.' And, on the south coast in Smith's Parish a rock about 70 feet above the sea bearing the date 1543 and always designated 'Spanish Rock', is of great interest to historians. The graven inscription consists of that date, a cross, and two indecipherable letters in a monogram. Nothing at all is definitely known about this appeal to heaven of some castaway whose fate and identity remain a mystery. But the repeated effort to tie its story with that of Camelo* is patently absurd since the

---

*Hernando or Ferdinando Camelo was a native of the Azores who in the sixteenth century offered the King of Spain to convey people to the uninhabited Bermudas. The proposal came to nothing.

lettering is definitely not his initials – resembling JR or FK – and, according to Spanish history, no settlement was ever attempted by him, though one had been proposed. Not only that, but the spot is not one which would have been selected by the leader of an expedition.

There is a chance that the epigraph is Portuguese rather than Spanish. To revert once more to the chronicler Oviedo, we find a statement that in July 1543 he witnessed a convoy of seven vessels leaving the harbour of Santa Domingo. One of these was a Portuguese ship returning to Portugal in ballast with thirty men aboard. Although at first the weather was good, she soon separated from the rest of the fleet, got caught by a northern gale that necessitated reefing the main sails and a warning from the pilot, Amador Gonzavez, of the dangers from near-by reefs. The ship struck submerged rocks on the north coast of Bermuda and ultimately became a total loss. The thirty men lowered the longboat and rowed four leagues to land. They were ashore in Bermuda for two months, during which time they made thirty trips to their stricken vessel and built themselves a boat to get away. They got back to Santa Domingo on 2nd November 1543 and reported that the desolate islands they'd been lucky enough to escape had supplied them with plenty of food but also shown evidence of earlier shipwrecks ... It may have been one of these Portuguese who chiselled the lonely rock; it has even been suggested that the lettering was RP standing for Rex Portugaliae, and perhaps implying a claim on the islands nobody wanted ... We shall never know, and meanwhile the name Spanish Rock seems likely to remain.

It was the following year that Sebastian Cabot, the Italian explorer, published at the age of seventy his famous '*Mappa Mundi*' a copy of which was preserved in the Bibliothèque Nationale in Paris. On this map Bermuda is simply marked as

SPANISH ROCK.

Ya de demonios, proof, if further proof were needed, of the evil reputation the islands bore, serving as they did as a navigational mark for the galleons returning to Spain, but warning them that many a vessel had sighted them to her doom.

A little more than half-way through the sixteenth century a French ship under a Captain Roussel was lost on the reefs and some of the crew were drowned. The survivors managed to patch up a ship out of the materials of their wreck, escaped to Newfoundland and thence back to France thus further confirming the old stories of a treacherous ironbound coast. The bones of a ship of approximately that date have been discovered by divers in the twentieth century.

The wreck of another French ship near North Rock in December 1593 under Captain de la Barbotière (name of ship not recorded) is usually referred to as 'Henry May's shipwreck' since he was the only Englishman aboard – having been transferred to her from the *Bonaventura* to carry dispatches back to his previous ship's owners in England – and since he left us the first clear description of the islands in English. With the uncertain navigation of those days, the pilots of Barbotière's ship had reported at noon on 17th December that they were safely past the ill-omened islands and at least 12 leagues to the southward of them. All danger being now obviously over, they demanded their 'wine of height' and it was while they were triumphantly toasting their immunity that the ship struck a rock to the north of the island and became a total wreck. More than half the crew was drowned. Twenty six men managed to row in a small boat and pull a raft the seven leagues to the shore, carefully saving their carpenter's tools, 'else I think we had been there to this day,' with which in the five months they were stranded here they managed to build 'a small barke of some 18 tons' rigged with the shrouds from their wrecked ship. On 11th May 1594 'it pleased God to set us cleare of the Island to the no little joy of us all.' Meeting with an English barque, May took leave of his 'deare friend Captain de la Barbotière,' and arrived back in Falmouth in August. His description of Bermuda as 'divided all into broken Islands' and being 'all woods – cedar is the chiefest,' the difficulty of finding drinking water, the abundance of tortoises, wild hogs, and 'great store of fowle and fish' is in the British Museum and was published by Hakluyt. (Unfortunately, this wreck is occasionally indicated by writers as the basis for Bermuda's coat of arms. But May's wreck led to nothing at all in Bermuda's subsequent history: it remained for a later and much more momentous shipwreck to be immortalized in heraldry.)

Another item was added to the black record against the dreaded Isles about 1595 with the wreck on the North reefs of the Spanish Caravel *San Pedro.* This is another of the ships whose bones have been discovered by intrepid twentieth-century divers.

An event that was to have long-range repercussions occurred in 1603 when a Spanish galleon commanded by Captain Diego Ramirez was driven in a storm on the northern rocks of Bermuda when en route home to Spain with the remainder of a fleet under Don Luis Fernandez de Cordova. The whole fleet had been scattered in the Bahamas Channel, and four of the cumbersome galleons became total losses. Ramirez was comparatively lucky – he struck rock on the Bermuda coast at a spot where he was able to force his ship through into what is now known as the Great Sound, and everyone aboard was saved, including Ramirez himself and his pilot Hernando Muniz. They remained on the islands for twenty two days, patched up their fairly undamaged ship and continued their voyage to Spain. As we shall see, there was a far more fateful shipwreck, that of the *Sea Venture* in 1609. The castaways from this would find traces of Ramirez' encampment and name the area Spanish Point – a name it still bears.

Ramirez eventually wrote a careful and detailed description of the abominated islands together with a map he had drawn of them, and labelled it 'Captain Diego Ramirez' own Report to accompany his map of 1603.' Later, the pilot's story was added and signed Erando (or Hernando) Muniz, sworn to 'by God and the Cross and signed with his name.'

Although Ramirez' report of some 200 words, which he sent to Don Bernardino de Avellaneda, was more favourable than previous descriptions had been, it did not at first arouse much interest in Spain. King Philip III had about all the territory he could manage in the New World, so why bother with the uninhabited Bermudas with their treacherous coasts? For Philip III was weak, childish in his form of piety, and incapable of governing the vast Spanish possessions. So although Ramirez made it amusingly obvious that the feared evil spirits of the islands had proved to be squealing hogs and vast flocks of squawking sea-birds, navigators still did not think the isolated islands worth investigating. Nevertheless,

Ramirez' account was to have vast repercussions in May 1611 when the President of the Board of Trade in Seville sent it to the Council of War, Madrid.

For when in 1603, James VI of Scotland ascended the English throne as James I of England he concluded a peace with Spain, his hereditary friend. Resumption of diplomatic relations meant that the Spanish Ambassador in London would keep the Council at Madrid well informed of English plans and expansions; and Spain possessed an extensive Secret Service. The neglected account of Ramirez' Bermuda adventures came to light when the time was ripe, for even if Spain no longer had the strength and initiative to extend herself further in the New World (though no one yet realized this and she was still feared) she certainly could not afford to allow the perfidious English to build a nest of pirates in her sea lanes. No, Bermuda must remain uninhabited. In fact, no nation wanted to approach that dangerous doomed coast which had borne its ill-repute for a hundred years.

At last we come to the 'in the beginning' of Bermuda's colonial history. It was on 2nd June 1609 that seven tall ships and two pinnaces sailed from Plymouth on the south coast of England and bent their sails for the far west. This was the Relief Fleet sent by the Virginia Company in London (The Company of Adventurers and Planters of the City of London for the first colony in Virginia) to the assistance of the settlers in Jamestown, Admiral Sir George Somers in Command. Sir George, of modest origins, a Dorset man who as a typical Elizabethan had buccaneered against Spain and become a famous navigator, was fifty five years old. His flagship, *Sea Venture*, 300 tons, was the largest of the fleet. Aboard her were the Governor-Designate for Virginia, Sir Thomas Gates; the Captain, Christopher Newport; the Reverend Master Bucke, Church of England Chaplain to the expedition; William Strachey, Secretary Elect to Virginia; and about 150 men, women and children who were intending to settle there. Somers' nephew, Matthew, was also on this expedition, but in a smaller ship, the *Swallow*.

The first part of the voyage went well. Sir George paced the heaving deck, kept an eye on the eight other vessels in his fleet, took his turn at the helm and set an example of hard work to his crew. And then, when they were off the Azores, a sudden storm scattered the whole fleet. Worse was yet to come: on Monday 24th July when the *Sea Venture* had been

more than seven weeks at sea, lost to sight of the other ships
and far from any land, a hurricane struck. It took eight men
to hold the steering gear, the rain fell in cascades, the sea
mounted towards the sky. The wind roared so loudly in the
rigging that the shouted orders of the ship's officers and the
little children's cries of fear, alike went unheard. Soon even
the shrieks of the north-east wind were indistinguishable
from the booming of the thunder. All sails were furled, cargo,
luggage, goods of all kinds were thrown overboard in a
desperate effort to lighten ship. At every moment it was
feared she would split in two, and now, as if all that were not
enough, she suddenly sprang a leak. There was ten feet of
water in her hold. Everyone on board worked desperately at
the pumps and took turns bailing frantically with buckets.

Sir George Somers, that indomitable 'lion at sea' (though
'lamb on shore') did the lion's share in saving ship. He stayed
on the poop for three days and nights struggling to hold the
stricken vessel on her course and keep her from foundering.
By Friday morning he knew by the way she wallowed in
mountainous seas that half an hour was all they could expect
before she sank. He was still at the helm when the impossible
happened: a rocky coast with trees bending to the blast
loomed through the spindrift, though they were many
hundreds of miles from their actual destination.

Sir George drove the waterlogged ship hard towards shore.
She struck on a submerged reef half a mile or so off the east
coast – and wedged there. Between ship and shore lay a
stretch of blessedly calm water. The hurricane blew itself out.
Presently they lowered the longboat and, after several
journeys, everyone was landed safely ashore . . . So here they
were, a hundred and fifty of them, in the terrible Bermudas.
But even devil-haunted islands were better than a watery
grave.

That was how in 1609 the English came by chance to a
place long ill-famed and execrated. Friday 28th July was the
day they landed – afterwards named Somers Day in honour
of the great man who is really the Father of the Colony, for
this was the event that led to deliberate colonization. Never
again were the Somers' Islands, as they were henceforth often
called, entirely uninhabited. Never again was the name
Islands of Devils used except as a sardonic joke. The
submerged reef where the *Sea Venture* grounded is still
marked on maps as Sea Venture Flat.

Bermuda is not a country to set up statues to its heroes. Nevertheless, there are many reminders today of the great men of the past. In the Bermuda Historical Society's Museum at Par-la-Ville in Hamilton hang the portraits of Sir George and Lady Somers by Paul Van Somer who had also painted King James I. These portraits were purchased by the Society from Somers' collateral descendants in 1932. Here also stands the sea-chest Sir George took with him on his voyages and his lode-stone, 'a mass of meteoric iron employed by Admiral Sir George Somers or Sommers circa A.D. 1600 for magnetizing his compass needles.'

A model of the *Sea Venture* tops the City Hall on Church Street, Hamilton, and near the South Shore in Smith's Parish is the carefully preserved crag known as Spanish Rock, that reminder of an unknown castaway from an even earlier wreck.

3

The Earthly Paradise

The reaction of the 150 castaways from the wrecked *Sea Venture* on finding themselves in a land of sunshine, without native tribes to combat, and where the total lack of aborigines meant that nature's store was not only untouched but that the fauna was entirely unafraid of man (therefore easily caught for food) may be imagined. Although, as far as the remainder of the world was concerned, they were below the horizon's rim for nine and a half months, and were lacking all the amenities of civilization, many of them would willingly have settled for remaining. Sir Thomas Gates, Governor-Designate of Virginia; George Yeardley who would become Governor there in 1619; William Strachey, Secretary-Elect to Virginia; John Rolfe, who was later, in America, to marry Princess Pocahontas as his second wife; the Reverend Richard Bucke, Church of England Chaplain to the expedition; the ship's Captain, Christopher Newport; and Admiral Sir George Somers himself — all knew that the whole adventure was being financed by the Virginia Company of London, a business organization with large amounts of capital invested. Therefore their prime duty was to continue on to Virginia whose colonization might help solve some of England's social and economic problems, and where the majority of the colonists might hope to better themselves.

They were not yet to know that of the seven ships and two pinnaces that had sailed from Plymouth in Devon on that June morning fifty-seven days earlier, they themselves would be given up for lost, the pinnace *Catch* had already sunk with

The Deliverance, in St George's — a replica of one of the two ships built by the castaways from the *Sea Venture* while they were marooned in Bermuda, 1609-10. The other was the *Patience* built by Sir George Somers in which he afterwards returned to Bermuda to fetch food for the Jamestown settlers, and in which his body was returned to England after his death in 1610. (*Bermuda News Bureau photo*)

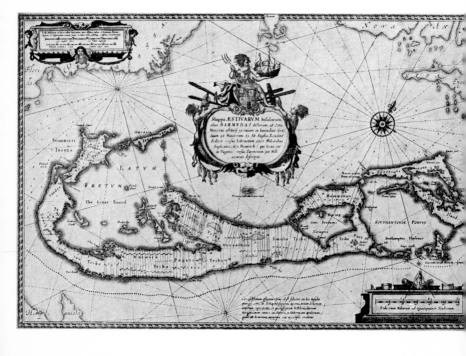

all hands, and that the *Falcon, Blessing, Lion* and *Unity* would make land on 11th August, the *Unity* with only ten sound men aboard out of seventy. The *Virginia* and *Diamond* would arrive at Jamestown days later with their masts gone and plague aboard. Last of all, the *Swallow* would stagger up the American coast in a sorry state – aboard her Sir George Somers' nephew, Matthew Somers, who, unlike his heroic uncle, turned out a ne'er-do-well.

Thus, from the very earliest days, and continuously thereafter, the history of Bermuda and that of Virginia have been deeply intertwined, so that thousands of visitors from America in this twentieth century eagerly seek the roots of the strong ties of commerce and family, friendship and tradition that still exist between the island group and their own country, particularly the south.

In Bermuda, that July of 1609, the fortunate survivors from the *Sea Venture* managed to go back and forth in the longboat to rescue tackle, guns, timbers, carpenter's tools, provisions, and leave the wrecked ship derelict. They found themselves on what was later named St George's Island but which at the time was dubbed Tortus for the vast quantity of turtle rookeries around the shores. Sir Thomas Gates had leaped ashore shouting: 'This is Gates – his bay!' – a spot still indicated by cartographers as Gates' Bay. And Sir George Somers set an immediate example of catching fish, collecting eggs, and indicating the vast store of fresh food swarming around them – turtles, birds, hogs – sufficient for an army.

But, necessarily, the story of that nine and a half months is of the attempt to continue their journey as they were bound to do. Within a month of the wreck, the *Sea Venture*'s longboat was closed in with hatches, fitted with mast and sails and despatched, under command of the mate, Henry Ravens, with seven other volunteers, to bring help from Virginia. She made one false start among the uncharted reefs, then got clear two days later, requesting that beacons be kept

---

Richard Norwood, making his famous Survey. (*Photo by Bermuda News Bureau of Diorama at Fort St Catherine*). Norwood came to Bermuda as a technical specialist in 1613. In 1614 he undertook to survey the islands and had made an initial survey before Governor Richard Moore left in 1615. Under Gov. Daniel Tucker he completed this during 1616-17 when he returned to England with what was the foundation of his famous map (*below*), referred to by Samuel Purchas. He made another Survey 1662-63.

burning on the high land where St David's Lighthouse stands to-day, to guide her safe return. Early maps mark 'Strachey's Watch' where William Strachey for two months kept the beacons burning, and 'Ravens' Sound' on the channel through which the valiant mate sailed away. But the longboat was never heard from again. The sea swallowed that small gallant company.

Meanwhile, on the very day Ravens sailed, 28th August 1609, Richard Frobisher, a shipwright, laid the keel of the *Deliverance*. She was built mainly from materials of the derelict *Sea Venture*, supplemented with planks from the endemic cedars. She was only 80 tons – little more than a quarter of the *Sea Venture*'s tonnage. Bermuda maps still carry the place-name Buildings Bay at the east of St George's Island.

But the pinnace that had far greater significance in Bermuda history was the one built by Sir George Somers himself and his immediate subordinates. When it became evident that Ravens was lost, it was clear that an 80-ton *Deliverance* would not carry all the survivors to Virginia so the Admiral offered to build a barque of 30 tons. This tiny vessel was built on the Main Island of Bermuda cedar, and was christened *Patience,* when both vessels were ready to sail by May 1610. And though the *Deliverance* then left for good, the little *Patience* played a greater part in Bermuda's subsequent story.

(There is a replica of the *Deliverance* in St. George's and the notice board against it refers also to the building of the *Patience*.)

The castaways must have worked hard through that autumn, the temperate winter and the spring to complete the two sturdy pinnaces in addition to building their huts and finding their own food. Sir George himself planted musk-melon, peas, onions, radishes, lettuce, sugar-cane – all the seeds originally intended for Virginia. They sprouted surprisingly fast but the August sun proved too hot for them. Here were 150 people of both sexes, all ages, and very varying levels of education and culture (Strachey speaks quite frequently of 'the commoner sort of people') learning to start a civilization for themselves, to work hard, to live simply, and to follow the example set them by their leaders. Gates knew the manner of salting and preserving fish, and went fowl-shooting. Their Admiral exemplified methods of pig-sticking, used hook and line to provide plentiful fish, built a small boat to encircle the islands so that he could draw an excellent map on vellum, and did his full share in building the *Patience.*

This Somers' map has had an almost miraculous history. Months later, when the castaways reached America, Strachey would enclose it with his 3000-word long descriptive letter to the members of the Virginia Company in London. The letter itself was doubtless eagerly read by every member including that remarkable woman, Lucy, Countess of Bedford, daughter of the first Lord Harington of Exton and friend of John Donne. Indeed, the letter may have been courteously addressed to her – though obviously meant for perusal by the entire Company – since it commences 'Excellent Lady' and she was a shareholder. Perhaps she retained the map while passing on the letter, for when Samuel Purchas, who inherited a mass of travel material from Richard Hakluyt, published Strachey's wonderful description of the wrecked *Sea Venture* in 1625 in his *Pilgrims*, he sorrowfully noted in the margin 'the map we have not' and in 1948 it turned up in the private collection of the seventh Earl of Dartmouth; and, at the base of the map, the Harington Coat of Arms is blazoned. This early MS map was being sold at Sotheby's and was, very fortunately, acquired for Bermuda.

And who can doubt that the Earl of Southampton, a member of the Virginia Company, showed this exciting letter to his 'protége', William Shakespeare? And that it inspired his last and most magical play?

Any of the dialogue culled from the first scene of *The Tempest* sounds the authentic note of the genesis of Bermuda's story. Very probably, then, it was the wreck of the *Sea Venture* that fired the poet's genius to write the story of a company wrecked on a lonely island. Internal evidence in the play indicates the scene as a Mediterranean isle; and the clue planted as to the story's origin – Ariel's reference to his having once been sent 'to fetch dew from the still-vex'd Bermoothes' – also sounds a geographical severance of Bermuda from Prospero's isle. But a poet is not tied by time or place, so although the locale is different it was almost certainly the shipwreck of the *Sea Venture* which Shakespeare thus immortalized.

Little wonder, when the castaways found that the dreaded spirits of the island were merely myriads of shrieking birds and herds of squealing pigs, they wanted to remain. Why, this was an earthly paradise – no frost, no snow, golden sunshine. Some of them indeed visualized it as an Eden where work could be entirely supererogatory. The uncertainty of their future, the delusion of complete freedom and biological equality soon led malcontents into making common cause against imposed authority in both boatbuilding camps.

The first mutineers were simply punished by banishment to a tiny island. They soon crawled back and were forgiven.

The ringleader of the second mutiny, Stephen Hopkins, was condemned to death by Sir Thomas Gates after a formal trial before the whole ship's company. But his impassioned plea for mercy for the sake of his innocent wife and children actually aligned Newport and Strachey on his side till, against his better judgment, Gates gave in and remitted his sentence. (Interesting to find that Hopkins behaved in an exactly similar fashion followed by the same abject pleas, after he reached America.)

But of course appeasement was taken for weakness and simply led to a third mutiny which embodied a plan to murder Gates and Somers, and set up a rebel government in the Bermuda Isles. This time no mercy could be shown and Henry Paine, their insolent leader, was instantly condemned to death − the sole leniency being that the sentence of hanging was reduced to death before a firing squad (as befitted a gentleman.)

Eventually the rebels were brought to heel and when on Thursday 10th May 1610 the 80-ton *Deliverance* and the 30-ton *Patience* at last set sail for Virginia (to conclude the journey begun on that sunny morning of 2nd June 1609 when Admiral Sir George Somers' fleet had set out from Plymouth on the south coast of England,) only two were left behind as deserters on the Bermudas: Robert Waters and Christopher Carter. (There were two men surnamed Waters.)

To-day so many people attempt to trace their ancestors' first arrivals in the New World, that it is of interest to give the names we happen to know among the 150 'gentlemen, adventurers, sailors, women and children' who were aboard that wrecked flagship: Admiral Sir George Somers, Sir Thomas Gates, Captain Christopher Newport, the Revd Richard Bucke, William Strachey, Sir George Yeardley, John Rolfe, Mistress Rolfe, R. Rich, Robert Walsingham, Richard Frobisher, Nicholas Bennit, Francis Pearepoint, William Brian, William Martin, Richard Knowles, Stephen Hopkins, Samuel Sharpe, Humfrey Reede, James Swift, Silvanus (or Silvester) Jourdain, Thomas Powell, Edward Eason, Mistress

Eason, John Want, Mistress Horton and her maid Elizabeth Persons, Henry Shelly, Jeffrey Briars, Richard Lewis, William Hitcham, Edward Samuel, Henry Paine, Henry Ravens, Thomas Whittingham, Christopher Carter, Edward Waters and the Robert Waters mentioned in the previous paragraph. (Also, according to Capt. John Smith, two American Indians.)

All of these continued the broken journey to Jamestown either in the *Deliverance* or the *Patience*, with the following exceptions:

Jeffrey Briars, Richard Lewis, William Hitcham, and Edward Samuel died in Bermuda, this last, killed by Robert Waters; Henry Paine had been executed for mutiny; Henry Ravens and Thomas Whittingham were lost at sea together with six un-named sailors in attempting to get help; and Carter and Robert Waters remained as deserters.

One new addition to the passengers was a baby boy born in Bermuda to Edward and Mistress Eason, and christened 'Bermudas'. The other baby born in the islands was a little girl to John and Mistress Rolfe. She was christened 'Bermuda' but died, and was buried by Master Richard Bucke. Mistress Rolfe herself only survived a short time after the arrival in America; her widower was the John Rolfe who later married Princess Pocahontas, the young Red Indian princess who had reputedly saved the life of Captain John Smith in Virginia in January 1608 when she was twelve years old.

In addition, one change of name occurred when Mistress Horton's maid, Elizabeth Persons, was married in Bermuda to Thomas Powell, the cook.

Some of these names are perpetuated as place-names on the Islands.

On 10th May 1610 these two small sturdy vessels left Bermuda, crossed the deep blue waters of the Gulf Stream and within two weeks – on 24th May to be exact – reached Jamestown. But if their arrival, sunburned and well-fed, was a startling sensation for the Jamestown settlers, the appearance of that settlement was a horrible shock to the newcomers. Of the 500 who had settled there, only 60 desolate people were left. Many of them had starved to death, others had been killed by Indians. Their plight was desperate. It was only new supplies brought in by Lord De La Warr that enabled them to remain, plus the supplies from Bermuda.

Sir George Somers then offered to return to Bermuda where there was so plentiful a supply of turtles, hogs and fish, to fetch more food for the starving colony. He took the

Patience he himself had helped to build, let nephew Matthew Somers captain her and sailed on 19th June 16]0 for the islands. A second pinnace, commanded by Captain Samuell Argoll, started with them but was forced back by bad weather; in fact, both vessels were blown back onto the American coast causing Argoll to give up the voyage while *Patience* continued on alone.

They found Waters and Carter alive and well; all started collecting stores for Virginia. But by now Sir George was utterly exhausted. He died on 9th November 1610 at the age of fifty-six on that island at the eastern end of Bermuda where they had first landed so fortuitously in July of the previous year, – an island ever since called St George's both in his honour and for the Patron Saint of the Mother Country. Officially, too, Bermuda was henceforth often referred to as the Somers or Summers Islands.

Matthew Somers left Virginia and returned to England aboard the *Patience* with the body of his heroic uncle in a sea-chest for ceremonial interment in Dorset. But the heart of this great adventurer, who had once served with Sir Walter Raleigh, was buried at St George's in the grounds that to-day are called Somers Gardens. Matthew later died in a debtor's prison in England after wasting all his inheritance from Lady Somers in 'riotous and disorderly living'.

When the *Patience* disappeared eastward over the horizon, Robert Waters returned to England, but Christopher Carter again remained; and this time Edward Waters, and the late Admiral's personal servant, Edward Chard, stayed also—in order to hold the islands for England. They chose to live on the south side of Smith's Island, and here they made a garden.

For nearly two years these three lived in the lonely islands with only themselves, the ship's dog, and the wild life for company. And since the islands had not been completely depopulated since that fateful shipwreck of 28th July 1609, that is the accepted date for the beginning of Bermuda's history as an inhabited place. And, later, 28th July was officially designated Somers' Day.

It must have seemed an endless two years, during which they sometimes wondered whether the *Patience* had reached England, and whether, if so, there would be enough enthusiasm to send settlers out to make a colony.

Actually, the arrival in England of the *Patience* from Bermuda with Somers' body, and of Sir Thomas Gates who had sailed from Jamestown in July 1610 with the long descriptive letter of the Bermuda adventure written by Strachey (by now appointed 'Secretaire of State' to the Virginia Council in America by Lord De La Warr) together with Somers' map, aroused tremendous interest in London. Admiral Sir George Somers who had been born of modest parentage 24th April 1554 (according to Lyme Regis Parish Registers) and had been knighted in 1604 by King James I, had come home at last after all his adventuring to be laid in his native Dorset earth. His body was buried with full honours on 4th July 1611 at Whitchurch Canonicorum. In Captain John Smith's *History of Virginia* we read: 'This cedar ship [*Patience*] at last with his dead body arrived at Whit Church in Dorsetshire where by his friends he was honourably buried, with many vollies of shot, and the rites of a souldier.' (Incidentally it should be made clear that Captain John Smith was never in Bermuda.)

His Will, which had been made 23rd April 1609 when he was 'intending to pass the Seas in a voyage toward the land called Virginia,' was proved on 16 August 1611. It makes interesting reading. There were bequests to the poor of Whitchurch and of Lyme Regis. Since he had no direct descendants, the other legatees were the children of his brother John – John, William, Toby, Mary 'and others'; Nicholas and Matthew, sons of brother Nicholas Somers, deceased; and Sir George's widow, Dame Joan. His brother John was named as Sole Executor.

Although, as we have noted, Strachey's official account was not published for fifteen years, it doubtless circulated among the Virginia patentees in England with its lively description of the flora and fauna of the islands and its confutation of the 'divil' population theory. In the meantime, an unauthorized work was rushed through the press ('Printed by John Windet and to be sold by Roger Barnes in St Dunstanes Church-yard in Fleet-Streete, under the Diall') in 1610. It was called, *A Discovery of the Bermudas, otherwise called the Ile of Divels* and was by 'Sil. Jourdain' who had sailed from Jamestown for England July 1610 in the same ship as Gates when the latter was despatched to fetch further supplies for Virginia. Both accounts stress the abundance of natural food in Bermuda; of fish Jourdain says: 'And fish is there so abundant, that if a man steppe into the water, they will come round about him: so that men were faine to get out for fear of byting.'

Inevitably, the Virginia Company sought to extend their

charter to include these newly named Somers or Summers
Islands as the Bermudas were now often called. This
extension of jurisdiction was granted by King James in a new
Charter dated 16th June 1612, the third Virginia Charter.
Two thousand pounds was paid towards the establishment of
this new colony and it became the property of George
Berkeley, Richard Chamberlain, Sir Dudley Digges, Jerome
Heyden, Sir Baptist Hicks, Robert Johnson, Richard Martin,
Robert Offeley, George Scott, William Wade, John Wolsten-
holme; also Henry, Earl of Southampton, William, Earl of
Pembroke, William, Lord Paget, William, Lord Cavendish, Sir
Robert Mansell, Sir Edwin Sandys; and Sir Thomas Smith as
Governor of the Company.

And in the meantime, 9th May 1612, a small ship, *The
Plough* had been despatched to Bermuda with the first
permanent settlers — sixty of them, under the first appointed
Governor, Richard Moore, a ship's carpenter, who proved a
practical and wise choice.

But it was not found expedient to run two colonies under
one company, and by 1614 the Virginia Company gave up its
jurisdiction over Bermuda. In June 1615 an offshoot of the
Virginia Company was formed as The Somers Island
Company and was granted a separate Charter by King James.
Among the rights granted in this Charter was that of calling a
General Assembly with power to make laws, provided that
these were not contrary and repugnant to the laws of
England. The amount of land in Bermuda had been over-
estimated so a tract in Virginia was included in the grant. The
actual area at that time was approximately 19¼ square miles
or 12,400 acres. This Somers Island Company ran Bermuda
from London for sixty-nine years, choosing its Governors,
sending magazine ships with supplies and in return asking for
pearls, whale-oil, tobacco, silk, and, above all, ambergris, —
that intestinal by-product of the spermaceti whale which
floated on warm sea currents and was cast up on the sea-coast
in warm countries and that was so invaluable in the
manufacture of perfume that it sold in London at over £3 an
ounce. This was a lodestone that attracted colonists whose
reward for the finding was 13s 4d per ounce.

Unfortunately, the stories that circulated regarding the
islands excited delusive expectations. The reports were not
wilful misrepresentations but the natural resources which the
castaways described as inexhaustible were merely nature's
untapped stores which soon would be depleted in the using.

Alas! Work would be an unescapable reality, even in Eden!

The *Plough* arrived in Bermuda, after a smooth Atlantic crossing of nine and a half weeks, on Saturday 11th July 1612, sailed into St George's Harbour between St David's and Smith's Island (named for Sir Thomas Smith one of the greatest of empire builders and Governor of the Company) and landed everyone on the south side of Smith's Island where their first act was to kneel down in a service of thanksgiving conducted by their chaplain. (The large majority of these colonists adhered to the Church of England. Indeed, in the early days of the Somers Island or Bermuda Company, all clergy had to take an oath of allegiance to that Church.) While they were kneeling in prayer, a boat with Carter, Chard and Waters rounded the point. The Narrows, 17 yards wide, by which *The Plough* was eventually anchored, is still marked as the strip of water between Smith's and St David's islands.

These men had worked industriously in their lonely exile but were desperate to get away by the time the newcomers arrived since they had come across an enormous mass of ambergris, 180 pounds, and had quarrelled over its ownership. Now they attempted to make a deal with Captain Davis of *The Plough* to smuggle the ambergris aboard and not deliver it up to the Company. But Governor Moore circumvented their plans, punished them, and shrewdly used the precious find of ambergris as a magnet to stimulate official interest by only shipping part of it at a time home to England where it fetched some ten thousand pounds. This naturally kindled delusive fantasies among the investors of untold wealth floating in on many a tide.

The Company's commission to Governor Richard Moore contained instructions concerning the religious government of the islands, orders to fortify, and to build storehouses. The land was to be planted with corn, sugar-cane and other necessities and the manufacture of salt from sea water proceeded with. Individual settlers on public lands were to be allotted a quarter of an acre for house and garden — double that area for a married man with family. A skilled workman was to be paid twenty pence a day by the Company while a labourer could expect up to twelve pence.

Governor Moore at first established his little settlement on the southern side of Smith's Island where Waters, Carter and Chard had raised their produce and built their huts. So here on this 61-acre island was the first seat of government and the first experimental plant-culture station. After remaining

here for a few weeks and making rock ovens in the hard
limestone, the whole settlement transferred to the 700-acre
island to the north of them where the whole Bermuda
adventure had originally started, marked Tortus Island on Sir
George Somers' map but now named St George's in his
honour. The great green turtles, nesting around the beaches,
provided them with ample flesh and a multitude of eggs. This
animal played a great part in history, helping to make
possible the course of colonization; it could be pickled or
even stowed alive on deck, so that in fact all early activity
round tropical and semi-tropical waters in the New World was
dependent on turtle as its safeguard from the horrors of
scurvy and other deficiency diseases, due to lack of fresh
vegetables, and to reliance on spoiled kegs of beef aboard
ships. (Colombus had acknowledged the debt in so naming
the Tortugas!) But with the coming of the great depredator,
man, the rookeries began to disappear. Those in Bermuda
were among the first to go. Governor Moore wrote of them in
1612:

'Turkles there be of a mighty bigness: one turkle will serve
or suffice three or four score at a meale, especially if it be a
shee Turkle, for she will have as many egges as will suffice
fiftie or three-score at a meale; this I can assure you, for they
are very good and wholesome meate, none of it bad, no, not
so much as the very guts and maw of it, for they are
exceeding fat, and make as good tripes as your beastes bellies
in England.'

Both William Strachey and Silvanus Jourdain had reported
equally enthusiastically on them in 1610, the former remark-
ing that they found 500 eggs at a time 'in the opening of a
shee Turtle.' And the shell of one as large as a dining-room
table was found in the shifting sands of the South Shore in
the late nineteenth century.

The immense number destroyed in those early years
caused their rapid decrease. This is proved by the fact that in
August 1620 an act was passed by Bermuda's first Parliament
'against the killing of over young tortoises' referring to them
as 'so excellent a fishe' and of the danger of 'an utter
destroyinge and losse of them.'

But to return to the founding of St George's Town on the
south side of St George's Island in the year 1612 — this was
'the prime towne' and remained the capital of Bermuda for
203 years. To roam its picturesque narrow alleyways to-day
(they were required to be twelve feet wide) is to breathe the

very atmosphere of early Bermuda history. The town lies partly along the water-front of a commodious harbour and partly on the slope that runs northwards from the water.

They had left behind them the 'small cabbens of palmatta leaves' on Smith's Island and at first similar cabins were built in St George's; in the stoutest of them cedar saplings were used to make a frame while sides and roofs were neatly thatched with the tough palmetto leaves. But these did not stand up very well to the high winds and hurricanes ('Hunraken' is supposed to have been the Guatemalan Indians' god of stormy weather) which the early settlers were beginning to expect every third year or so. Soon, spacious cedar cabins were being built – stout enough to last for their children and their grandchildren. Many of these cabins were on stone foundations and most were palmetto-thatched. Even Government House and the first Church were insubstantial buildings which suffered from the cyclonic tropical storms of this part of the world to which the settlers were becoming accustomed. The one of 1612 was particularly disastrous to all Moore's early buildings.

But Governor Moore's most urgent business was to fortify the country against the Spaniards and roving free-booters. He actually managed to build eight or nine simply-designed wooden forts, mainly low down and close to the water to suit the gun-range of those days – and one more solidly of masonry.

This circle of forts protected the entrances into St George's and Castle Harbours, and included St Catherine's Fort (at first called Sandys Fort) at the north-east of St George's Island; Warwick Fort on a rise behind the little town; and Danvers or Gates Fort at the south-east point of the same island. 'Pagit's' Island early had two forts – one at the north called Cavendish Fort, the other very close to the old Ship's Channel at the extreme south east tip – and across the narrow channel that it guarded, one-acre Governor's Island faced towards it with its own small fort. A little further into the Channel, Smith's Island boasted a battery. Further south, on the tip of Cooper's Island stood Pembroke Fort; Charles Fort on the island of that name and King's Castle – of stone on Castle Island – completely protected the entrances to Castle Harbour. Moore selected positions strategically important to the colony of his time.

Many succeeding governors strengthened, rebuilt, refortified, re-named the existing forts and re-located others, so that, looking at those that remain, some of them in ruins, some developed and continuously added to, it is misleading to give an exact date for their erection. To-day they are a fascinating study. St Catherine's, originally planned by Governor Moore, is a product of the seventeenth to the twentieth centuries; our cover shows it as it appears now. Warwick Castle or Fort was built to protect the town's water supply in the rear of the settlement and was later termed the Western Redoubt. (It is now misleadingly known as the Gunpowder Cavern.) Moore's most detailed fortification was on Castle Island – this is probably the one he built of masonry – and there are picturesque ruins there to-day of the King's Castle that developed from his original structure. Simple Gates' Fort (once Danvers) is now a small stone-block fort, well worth a visit.

Perhaps the most fascinating traces of very early forts are found on Paget Island. At the south-east tip are traces of the original wooden fort's foundations blasted in the rocks, and similar traces are clear on tiny Governor's Island opposite. But, to-day, huge Fort Cunningham commands the highest point of the island with its ramparts, and its labyrinths far below the surface. For long after the danger from Spain had passed, wars with Holland, France and the United States meant that Bermuda had to be defended from every other power. At least twice – during the American Revolutionary War, and the War of 1812 – America planned to seize Bermuda.

Gradually, too, as her population spread into the remainder of the islands, defence was needed for every part of the coast. So that eventually not a yard of water that encircled her but was within the range of her guns and Bermuda became the Gibraltar of the West.

It is the fashion to sneer at such vast expenditure compared with their lack of defensive use. But this is arguing from a false premise. Many times the island might have been raided or even seized – Lafayette urged this on America in 1777 – had there been no preparedness for defence. And though, as is almost inevitable, strength for resistance lagged behind the need, yet at least the threat of armed resistance existed even from the earliest days and, by its very existence, warned off intruders.

But to return to Governor Moore and those first forts that he erected; it is fascinating to find that he at least had the satisfaction of firing a cannon from King's Fort on Castle

Island at two approaching Spanish ships. The ancient record runs: two ships arrived 'sounding with their boat which attempted to come in; but from the King's Castle, Master Moore made but two shot, which caused them presently depart.' 'Howsoever, certaine it is that upon that shott, both the shyps . . . finding the ordnance to speak more loud and hottly than they expected . . . cut their main sails, cast about and made away.'

The escape of the young colony was providential, for their sole barrel of gunpowder had been overturned in their haste. Moore publicly gave thanks to God for the deliverance.

Local legends proliferated over the centuries that this arrival of Spanish ships indicated a previous burial of treasure which now was to be retrieved. Stories of 'treasure trove' are always popular. (Even the cross Ramirez had raised to help other castaways locate drinking water was at one time considered a pointer to Spanish gold.) Though why it should be interred merely to be sent for and dug up again was never satisfactorily explained. Many spots in these islands have been the scene of prolonged and bootless digging.

The truth lay hidden till the twentieth century in File 'Santo Domingo 272' in the archives of the Indies at Seville, visited by our local historian, Dr Henry Wilkinson, in 1926. Here lie all the definite facts of Spanish intentions towards Bermuda, what she actually managed to do, and how far she failed. The story reveals everything that was planned and suggested from the time of Ramirez wreck in 1603 to King Philip III's last laconic decision in 1615. And the visit of those two ships to make a reconnaissance of Bermuda's defence works, before advising a full-scale ejection of the whole English population, is the crux of this fascinating story. Miss I. A. Wright, the Archivist in Seville at the time of Dr Wilkinson's visit, reported that no search had ever been made there for information about Bermuda and there was no Index. However, she found the bundle of relevant despatches written over 300 years earlier tied loosely together.

Even ill news travelled more slowly 360 years ago than it does to-day. And to the Spaniards the rumour that the heretical English had, in 1609, landed on these uninhabited Islands of Devils, used merely by the Spanish treasure ships as a navigation mark, was indeed ill news – but it did not circulate in Spain till 1611. Philip III, King of Spain, was somewhat irked to learn that the perfidious English had landed there within fifty miles of his galleons returning from the Caribbean and the Spanish Main; he longed to chide his admirals for having left even this insignificant island, open as a sally-port . . . To read all despatches in this voluminous file makes one realise the efficiency of the Spanish Secret Service, and of Ambassador Don Diego Sarmiento de Acuna in London. Space forbids more than a few extracts being given fron these important letters.

The first is from Don Francisco de Varte Ceron, President of the Board of Trade at Seville, to an official of the Council of War at Madrid which was busy investigating reports of an English landing at Bermuda in 1609; the investigation had been instigated by Philip III's Council of State.

This letter is dated 24th May 1611:

I now answer your letter of the 1st of this month, in which you advised me that information had reached the Council of War with respect to a statement made by an Englishman who had put in at Corunna, to the effect that the English have landed at Bermuda for the purpose of settling it and fishing for pearls. [He has had a great many Englishmen questioned and continues] but they say they have not heard that their country has sent settlers to Bermuda . . . Even so, I am inclined to accept as true the statement of the Englishman who put in at Corunna because an Englishman who came to Cadiz said that the flagship of an English squadron had been lost at Bermuda, that her survivors had built a pinnace there, and, on returning to England, had talked much of the great wealth of pearls at that island, with the result that many people were minded to go and settle there and a number had banded together for that very purpose, . . . I would be of the opinion that a ship should be sent out with a skilled pilot and an able soldier to ascertain whether the enemy had landed there and whatever else can be learned in this matter. I suggest that the ship be sent as a fast despatch-carrier to the Indies and that there she be given secret instructions for this single voyage. *A description of the island of Bermuda is sent herewith, and the report on the island made by the pilot Hernando Muniz, who ran aground there eight years ago with Captain Diego Ramirez and spent twenty-two days on the island. . . .* It would be highly important if enemies have not occupied the place that His Majesty's subjects should do so, and, if the enemy has taken possession, that efforts should be made to eject them from there before they can fortify themselves.

Attached to this was a lengthy deposition made and signed by Ernando (or Hernando) Muniz, 'pilot on the Indies route, wrecked in La Bermuda with Captain Diego Ramirez about eight years ago.' He describes the many very large cedar trees 'on the fruit of which they lived for 22 days they were there . . . there are also many palms, resembling dates, which produce a wild berry providing sustenance for a great number of hogs.'

Captain Diego Ramirez' own report and his rough sketch-map of the island accompanied the pilot's deposition and give a complete picture of Bermuda at this period as seen by Spanish eyes. They killed thousands of birds 'so fat and good every night the men went hunting . . . 4,000 could be killed at the same spot in a single night.' No doubt he was speaking of the cahow whose numbers were later so terribly reduced that the cahow was almost exterminated.

The result of these reports was that a Captain Diego de Avila was given a sealed despatch from His Majesty to be opened when forty leagues at sea. This secret despatch, dated December 1611, commanded Captain Diego de Avila under sealed orders to go to reconnoitre Bermuda. But the weather turned foul, he had a mutiny aboard, and although 'he came into the altitude of Bermuda' he disobeyed his instructions, for which he was afterwards condemned to death.

(Interesting to note that though at the moment England and Spain were not at war, the former is referred to in these despatches as 'the enemy'. Evidently a seventeeth-century version of the cold war! And we remember that in Queen Elizabeth's reign the Spaniards and Portuguese declared that they had an exclusive right to North and South America and that no one else ought to plant colonies or even trade there; but to this claim the Dutch and English would not submit.)

A letter from the Spanish Ambassador in London to King Philip dated 30th May 1613 reports that two vessels left England for the island of Bermuda at the end of January, that one had returned with good reports˜of both the climate and the land and that 'about 250 persons had begun to settle in that place.' He made adverse comments on the settlement in Virginia 'hunger and savages may have finished off that colony.'

The Duke of Medina Sidonia who, in 1588, had been commander of the famous 'Invincible Armada' despatched by Philip II against Elizabeth and England, wrote to the President of the Council of War on 20th June 1613 and two days later penned a lengthy missive to King Philip III. In the former, he urged that 'to uproot them (the English) from that place is what is truly desirable and therefore, although the counterweight of the peace with England be so heavy, I *do not know that by that peace we could concede that they occupy or settle what is so wholly His Majesty's as that island.*' He urged five ships of the Flanders squadron and veteran infantry to go immediately 'and bring off those people from the island. The English confirm that they are about 200 there and in shacks . . . Delay will make it more difficult. If the secret is half kept everything is so readily available, little money will be required. If sought, even if taken off the altar it will not be found lacking for this purpose.' And he concludes: 'I propose to remove these people without doing them harm (*unless they defend themselves*) and send them off to England.' In his letter to the King, he offers to summon Ramirez to assume the undertaking and urges that action be taken quickly 'to cut this thread before the English take deeper root there . . . because the place is what they may well desire with very good havens from which to over-run everything on the route of the fleets and armadas, because, although not within sight of this island, everything that comes from the Indies must pass to south or north of it.'

The draft reply from the Council of War (2nd July 1613) asks for a careful map of Bermuda made by Ramirez, and suggests assembling 150 or 200 soldiers, and in the meantime the Council wrote pressingly to the King with a resumée of letters and despatches to date. 'New advices have confirmed that English pirates were fortifying themselves in Bermuda, the Council was of the opinion that it was advisable forthwith to send forces sufficient to expel them from there.' This despatch to the King was followed by a second on 6th July 1613 urging that it was 'imperative to send out, once and for all, an expedition strong enough to expel from the islands of Bermuda the English who, it is understood, are fortifying themselves there . . . Not only is it detrimental to our reputation that they do so in a quarter so much Your Majesty's own – and in such plain view of all – but also the

---

Crystal Cave – the largest of Bermuda's caverns. East and north-east of Harrington Sound, at least ten well-known caves lie in close proximity. Stalagmites may be seen standing up through the sea water. They ceased to grow with the sea's invasion of the cave, but the downward-growing stalactites still continue their slow lime-charged pattern. Wherever large-scale quarrying takes place, unknown caves are being discovered. (*Bermuda News Bureau photo*)

day they establish a footing and fortify themselves there, being to windward of all the Indies, they can do very great damage in proportion to the strength they may possess.' And they urged sending five ships and a caravel with 1,000 men, 600 soldiers and 400 seamen, and to augment the number of ships if necessary, again suggesting that Ramirez go on this enterprise since 'he has a full knowledge of Bermuda as his report shows.'

His Majesty's reply made in July 1613 is a cool procrastination. 'It does surprise me that in all the years since the Indies have been discovered, no one should have thought to make certain of this island; and that now so much importance is ascribed to it without even knowing for sure what enemies are there; and too the month of July, proposed for this enterprise was already well advanced before the recommendation was laid before me and is now passed. Clearly, this won't do!' Therefore the King suggested merely that Diego Ramirez proceed to Havana and *reconnoitre Bermuda on the way* . . . 'if the English fortifications presumed to be on that island are not there he is to forgo the enterprise until he shall have reported.'

On 1st September 1613 the Council came back to the King's veiled reprimand with the excuse that 'ever since the

---

(*above*) Rape of the Gunpowder-Magazine. (*Bermuda News Bureau photo of Diorama at Fort St Catherine*) On the night of 14th August 1775, during the American Revolutionary War, the little Government Gunpowder Magazine on Retreat Hill north of St George's was rifled of one hundred barrels of gunpowder which were rolled down the hill to Tobacco Bay and despatched to an American schooner off the coast. Unaware that this raid had taken place, General George Washington on September 6th wrote an urgent letter 'To the Inhabitants of Bermuda' begging for this same gunpowder – but the letter never had to be delivered. The Gunpowder Magazine, which had been built by George James Bruere, has long been utterly demolished.

(*below*) Gates' Fort flying the Stuart Flag. Governor Moore built eight or nine forts at the east end. At first of wood they gradually, with successive governors, attained strength and stability. No exact date for their erection can really be given since '1612 onwards' describes the development of most of them. Gates' Fort was named for the Deputy Governor of Virginia (who had leaped ashore when the *Sea Venture* foundered, crying, 'This is Gates, his bay') and maintains an early simplicity. (*Bermuda News Bureau photo.*)

Indies were discovered it was always understood that
Bermuda was uninhabitable land, its coast so dangerous, with
such powerful currents and such heavy winds almost all the
year round that not only has no one returned to enter there
but all have shunned the place ... The English gained their
knowledge of Bermuda from a vessel accidentally lost on the
coast and are settling there ... (Since) the pirates had
fortified themselves in Bermuda, it seemed advisable to
dispatch forthwith an expedition strong enough to expel
them.'

In case the King again temporized by suggesting further
reconnaissance, the Council stressed that full reports from
Diego Ramirez and others were already on file and that
Ramirez had made the map requested by His Majesty. They
knew for certain by now that some 200 persons were living in
shacks and huts in the island 'but there is no certainty that
the English have constructed fortifications.' The Council
moderated their demands sufficiently to allow that now
September had arrived it might be too stormy to attempt
anything that year, therefore it might be 'advisable and
necessary to dispatch a sloop to reconnoitre and two caravels
of 30 or 40 tons not to get further information concerning
the island but to approach cautiously, coast its shores
endeavouring to see whether they have erected any fortifications, in what place and situation, and entering into
communication from the caravels with whatever people may
be seen on the shore ... Let them be ordered to return to
Spain with their information ... in order that the English
may be attacked promptly before they can fortify themselves
more strongly.'

His Majesty's reply, penned on 13th September 1613
briefly indicated that two caravels or other light vessels could
be sent to reconnoitre the island.

On 5th October 1613, the Ambassador in London wrote
to King Philip with the latest gossip regarding Bermuda. He
stated that 'they have built a fort there which is entrenched
and has some guns, and 80 persons both men and women.'
And he reported that a ship had just arrived from the island
with valuable ambergris aboard – 74 pounds of it. 'Bor
Maestre Mour, (Moore) who was a carpenter in this city, is
Captain and Governor ... Don Thomas Esmit (Sir Thomas
Smith) is President of the Council and Board of Merchants
who have been and still are promoting these settlements,
Virginia and Bermuda, at their own cost.'

In fact it soon became evident that by now higher expectations were held of the future of Bermuda than of Virginia.

By February of 1614, the Council of War for the Indies was still pushing the King for decisive action — 'there should be dispatched without loss of an hour's time an expedition strong enough to drive the English out of Bermuda ... Your Majesty will decide whether to omit the reconnaissance of the island by the two caravels.' There was also a lot of humming and hawing as to whether expense could be saved by basing the punitive expedition on Havana rather than on Spain.

And then at last we come to the two ships that approached Bermuda and were chased away by two gunshots from Governor Richard Moore at King's Castle on Castle Island. The Council of War at Madrid sent a long despatch to King Philip dated 9th May 1614 sadly recounting

It appears that these two ships reached Bermuda on its south side on March 14 ... Captain Domingo de Ulivari determined to reconnoitre ... drew in to land until he was in 8 fathoms and saw smoke signals ashore for which he steered along the south coast. He found this smoke issued from two forts. One of these looked new, built of masonry. The other, which is higher, is built of timber ... In both these are some ten or twelve pieces of artillery ... When one of the two ships and a boat approached the shore, two English launches came out to inspect them, and when they were about a musket shot off, they were invited to come aboard to talk. The English would not do so nor would they go beyond the range of their fort's guns. The forts fired on our vessels, so they withdrew and continued their voyage.

That, at long last, is the full story of the two Spanish ships that were indeed repulsed by Governor Moore — that they were ships coming in for buried treasure was a romantic and absurd myth that at last has been exploded by search of the Archives at Seville.

With this report to King Philip, the Council of War again pressed for a full expedition to be sent against Bermuda in March of 1615 if it could not be managed earlier. 'Merely for having dared to settle lands belonging to Your Majesty an effort should be made to chastise them and drive them thence, but he (Don Diego Brochero) believed this undertaking should be deferred till March of next year.' In reply

Philip charged the Council to make the necessary prepara-
tions for the following year, and on 14th May 1614 he
received a further long-winded appeal from them for
immediate and expensive action.

The conclusion of the whole matter was expressed by King
Philip III in one laconic paragraph:—

'As the Council will be aware of the state of my treasury
and of the very large provisions which have so recently been
made from it, the Council must try to find some way of
accommodating the needs of the Fleet out of those grants
already made.'

So the expected Spanish attack on Bermuda did not
materialize. Moore had done better than he knew.

But his intense preoccupation with defence works un-
avoidably led to a neglect of agriculture and precipitated a
famine. Although small supply ships put in from England,
they also brought new colonists and the level of provisions
grew woefully low. A chance frigate that put in with meal
aboard luckily saved the famished islanders but unhappily
also put rats ashore that speedily became 'one of Pharoah's
plagues' almost bringing colonization to a standstill. Starvation faced the settlers, many of whom began suffering from
scurvy, so Moore perforce slowed down on the necessary
construction works and sent a gang of colonists to Cooper's
Island to gorge themselves on cahows and fish; surfeit was
almost as fatal to them as abstinence had been.

A last straw to Moore's devoted administration must have
been when the Minister, the Reverend George Keith, accused
the Governor from the pulpit that 'hee did grinde the faces of
the poore.' When Moore challenged him to prove his
assertions he fell on his knees for forgiveness and the
Governor while raising him up swore that such libellous
statements would be punished with death in the future.

The Adventurers in England had little insight into Moore's
difficulties and he determined to return to present his side of
the picture before his three-year appointment was quite over,
leaving six men to run the government in turn until a new
governor could be officially appointed.

He had been promised a special coinage by the Company.
Early in the seventeenth century — but after Moore's time —
when this brass coinage did at last arrive it was in four
denominations: II^d, III^d, VI^d, XII^d. These bear a hog on the
obverse in allusion to the wild hogs that had been found here
by the *Sea Venture* castaways; and, on the reverse, a ship

corresponding to that flagship with the cross of St George at every mast-head. Naturally enough they became known as Hog Coyne or Hog money. They have the distinction of being the earliest British colonial currency, and are now extremely rare – and valuable. Specimens may be seen in the collection of the Bermuda Historical Society.

So Richard Moore and his good wife left the little colony in which they'd worked so hard. Before their departure Bermuda received her first consignment of potatoes for planting – a vegetable which was to mean much to the colony over the centuries and which was introduced to America from these islands.

Eventually, the proprietors in London showed their gratitude to Mrs Moore. After her husband's death (he, poor man, died on Sir Walter Raleigh's ill-fated Guiana expedition) they made her a grant of shares in the Somers Island Company in recognition of the three years she and her husband had laboured to establish the colony.

And in the meantime, the six jolly temporary governors – a month each at a time – were having a high old time in Bermuda. The sound of the clang of pewter drinking-mugs was heard instead of that of hoes, pickaxes and shovels. The two clergy, George Keith and the Revd Lewis Hughes, were at loggerheads, and the latter was imprisoned for opposing the lax rule – 'Revels and perpetuall Christmas (was) kept in the Sommer Islands.' No cargo of tobacco, ambergris, or other produce was sent home to the Adventurers who had, so far, sunk £20,000 in the Bermuda Venture.

The rats were rampant, everything that Moore had tried to put in order was in disrepair. Total ruin faced the little colony. Yet as long as well-stocked cellars and convivial drinking companions remained, the jolly temporary governors lived from day to day, oblivious of the future. Something would turn up!

The islanders had already learned to make a strong potent liquor from palmetto sap – they dubbed it 'bibbey' in allusion to the sound a duck makes when gulping water. Its use, over the years, was to land many a man in the stocks or pillory.

And something *did* turn up. A Flemish ship was wrecked on Bermuda's western coast, near a hundred-foot-high hill still marked on our maps as 'Wreck Hill.' A messenger rushed to the Governor shouting: 'Good news!' On which the Governor asked eagerly whether a fresh supply of liquor had arrived. 'No, Sir, – but next that, the best news in the world, – treasure is found at the Flemish wracke.' In great excitement – 'We are all made men!' – they hastily repaired thither, but only recovered £20 which the Governor pocketed for his own trouble. For many years the spot was called Flemish Wracke – now used in its abbreviated form as Wreck Hill.

But there obviously had to be an end to such a period of unbridled licence. The 'gamboleinge times' of the six acting governors must be ended before total ruin engulfed the whole colony. Even Elysian fields must produce some blooms.

Only the forts and the church remained to remind the settlers of all Governor Richard Moore had attempted. And to-day the traces of the earliest forts, and the ones developed from his beginnings take our minds back to his desperate struggle; tiny Gates' Fort still flies the Stuart flag, first flown when James VI of Scotland became James I of England and quartered the Arms of Scotland with those of England in all flags and ensigns, thus in 1603 bringing into existence the first Union Jack – the Red Cross of St George on a white field, combined with the White Diagonal Cross of St Andrew on a blue field. (The flag does not contain the Red Cross of St Patrick since union with Ireland was not effected till 1800.)

St Peter's Church is also a reminder of those early days. Originally known as *The* Church, it is considered the oldest Anglican Church foundation outside of Britain for within its walls are remains of the church built in 1619 after Moore's church of timber and palmetto had been blown down in a hurricane. That is not to say St Peter's predated the Anglican Church in Jamestown which was built within James Fort in 1607. This has been expertly reconstructed as an exact replica in the twentieth century. But although St Peter's has been rebuilt, enlarged, reconstructed, gradually over the centuries, it is not a mere replica but a church in continuous use; the changes of 1713-14, down to the reconstruction in the present century, have retained some of the ancient fabric within its walls – and the plaques thereon provide a survey of Bermuda history.

From 1612-1825, Bermuda was included in the Bishopric of London, a very early see founded centuries before Canterbury. But no Bishop of London ever visited the Colony and though they ordained men for the ministry of the Bermuda Church, difficulties of communication made their control remote, — so that the early Governors of Bermuda were ex officio 'Ecclesiastical Ordinary' and, as such, administered the local church. (It was not until 1825 that Bermuda was included in the ecclesiastical jurisdiction of Nova Scotia, and the following year that a Bishop — Inglis — visited Bermuda, consecrating all the parish churches and graveyards. In 1839, Newfoundland and Bermuda were separated to form a new diocese. And then, in 1925 Bermuda was further separated to have her own bishop under the appelate jurisdiction of the Archbishop of Canterbury.)

We may hope — and presume — that their powers of adjudication in ecclesiastical matters never crossed the minds of the six jolly deputy governors! But in any case, a cloud no bigger than a man's hand was observable at last, to the most reluctant intelligence, to be looming above even an earthly paradise — the necessity to work if they were not all to starve to death.

4

Struggle for Survival

Richard Moore had been despatched to Bermuda by the Virginia Company in London. Now the offshoot of that Company, the Somers Island or Bermuda Company, elected Daniel Tucker to be Governor of Bermuda in February 1616. He arrived in March that year in the nick of time to save Bermuda from ruin and starvation. During five hard-pressed years in Virginia he had learned the salutary lesson that an adequate food-supply is the first requisite of a colony. He had to combat the rats, the jolly governors, and the habits of sloth and dissipation engendered by their lack of discipline. The picture that has come down to us is of a bad-tempered man who put the fear of God into the islanders, who made them rise at dawn to start work and belaboured them with blows as well as words when they slacked off, and whose temper and disposition for the day could be detected even in the angle at which he wore his hat!

Faced with the conditions that he found on his arrival, and pressed as he was by the Proprietors in England for the produce of the land — who can blame him?

He set all the loafers to work, had a man hanged for saucing him (judged by the jury to be guilty of mutiny), had ground cleared for crops, and despatched a ship to the West Indies to fetch plantains, sugar-cane, figs, pines, cassava and paw-paws. The ship — the *Edwin* — also returned with a cargo which would affect the island's entire history — 'an Indian and a negar,' the second Negro to be seen here (since Ramirez distinctly refers to one ashore from his wreck for the twenty-two days of their stay); but this importation of 1616 was the first of his race to remain — and the seeds of dual race complications were planted. Before this colony was twenty years old, more and more negroes were brought to Bermuda from the slave plantations in the West Indies, and slavery became a part of Bermuda's way of life.

White victims of wars and economic conditions, Red Indian captives from the Indian raids, and Negroes sold by their chieftains in West Africa for work-gangs in the New

World, were all enslaved. The Negroes quickly outbred and outnumbered all others.

Meanwhile, the rats swam from island to island like an invading army, devouring all the crops, eggs, young birds, and invading the houses where they ate not only all provisions but even clothes and shoes. The Governor took drastic action by setting traps and poison and having the islands burned twice over. He also made the settlers hunt them at night with dogs. By May of 1617, a year after his arrival, Tucker was able to report he was keeping the number down. That arrival of a runaway frigate so welcomed three years or so earlier by the hungry colonists had proved an expensive boon with its unintended cargo of equally hungry rats. When at last they were completely conquered, Governor Tucker ascribed it to his unsparing war upon them but the Revd Lewis Hughes declared it a miraculous answer to his public prayers. In either case, the plague had been so bad that for a time the Company discontinued the practice of sending out more colonists.

Trial by jury and the regular holding of Assize Courts were held from the first month of Tucker's term of office. Times were harsh and a man – Paul Deane – was hanged in St George's for stealing 20 penny-worth of cheese. But law and order once more came to be respected, and he had seen the First Criminal Code of Virginia administered there by Sir Thomas Dale. Dale's Code listed 20 crimes punishable by death and many more by whipping. Governor Tucker brought a copy of Dale's Code to Bermuda with him.

Tobacco-growing was decided upon as the prime product of the colony. Moore had sent the first consignment of Bermuda-grown tobacco home to the Proprietors, and though Tucker despatched even more, he was long-sighted enough to warn against total dependence on any one crop and thus over-specialisation. To vary their occupations he sent for a special ship for whaling since whale-oil would be a valuable product both for the islanders and the Company. But though the whales were so numerous in the seas around Bermuda that the noise of their spring and autumn migration past the coast disturbed the colonists in their beds, they were not at first very dexterous in the hunt. Later it was to become an exciting way of life for many Bermudians. The flesh gave welcome steaks, the oil was the usual illuminant, footwear was made from the hide – nothing was lost. All this in addition to the barrels of oil despatched to England. But

Governor Tucker's main concern was with the food supply
and therefore crops in general. For this inclination he was
sneered at as a mere gardener.

By far the most important event under his administration
was the islands being surveyed and divided up into tribes and
shares. A man called Bartlett had commenced this big job in
Moore's time but had fallen out with the Governor and gone
home. He returned briefly a second time with as little result,
this time returning to England in the ship he arrived in. The
Bermuda Charter specified that a fourth part of the islands
was to be set aside for defraying public charges, and the
remainder divided into 8 tribes (the origin of 8 of the present
9 parishes,) each tribe to contain 50 shares.

This important job fell, almost accidentally, into the hands
of an Englishman who turned out to be Bermuda's outstanding genius of the seventeenth century. His name was
Richard Norwood. Actually he had come to Bermuda in
1613 at the age of twenty-three mainly because there was
some talk of pearl-diving off the coast and he had invented
and used a diving bell so was regarded as a technical expert.
When the pearl-diving came to nothing, he commenced a
survey of the coastline for Governor Moore. Now Governor
Daniel Tucker called upon him in 1616 for a detailed survey,
the division of the land into 8 tribes (to be named for the
principal shareholders) sub-divided into fifty 25-acre plots. St
George's Island, St David's Island, Longbird, Smith's,
Cooper's, Coney and Nonsuch Islands, including a small
eastern portion of the Main Island, were to remain general
un-allocated land. Norwood calculated that the remainder
divided into 25-acre strips would leave a small overplus. In
this he was correct.

The ancient record says: 'The first tribe to bee Eastward
was then called Bedford Tribe, now Hamiltons [i.e. Hamilton
Tribe or Parish, *not* the City of Hamilton]; the second,
Smith's Tribe; the third, Cavendish, now Devonshire; the
fourth, Pembrooks; the fifth, Pagets; the sixth, Mansils, now
Warwicks; the seventh, Southampton; the eighth, Sandys.'
The persons whose names have been perpetuated were: James
Hamilton, second Marquis of Hamilton; Sir Thomas Smith or
Smythe; William Cavendish, first Earl of Devonshire; William
Herbert, third Earl of Pembroke; William Paget, fourth Lord
Paget; Robert Rich, second Earl of Warwick; Henry
Wriothesley (pronounced 'Rocksley') third Earl of
Southampton; and lastly (the farthest west) — Sir Edwin
Sandys.

Those were the eight tribes that we now call parishes. Our ninth parish is, of course, St George's, where the whole development started but which was not considered a tribe.

Richard Norwood, in his immense task, had the help of Charles Caldicott. There were some 120 islands to be surveyed, all densely covered with cedar forests and without roads. The final survey, begun in the summer of 1616, was completed by May 1617, and the resultant map, published in London in 1622, five years after Norwood's return to England, has been engraved by several cartographers (including John Speed in 1631, Abraham Goos 1626 and Hondius) and served as the basis of all land tenure to the present day.

Before Richard Norwood sailed for England with all the data for his map in May 1617, he was involved in what became known as the scandal of the overplus. The fact was, Governor Tucker was due three shares from the Company; if the survey had continued straight ahead from east to west inevitably the expected overplus, the Governor's perquisite, would fall at the extreme west end. But at a middle stage of the work, the Governor suddenly ordered Norwood to begin working from Sandys eastward, the reason given being that the rats had not yet attacked that part which therefore could easily be laid out. Norwood complied. The overplus which he had correctly anticipated, now fell in a specially luscious vale between Southampton and Sandys which Tucker immediately claimed as his bonus. Feelings ran high and when, undeterred, the Governor proceeded to build himself a fine house on this 200 acres the Rev Lewis Hughes denounced him bitterly as building a 'flauntinge' cedar mansion for himself while leaving 'Gods house . . . but a thacht hovell.' Even the Somers Island Company in London seemed likely to deprive the retiring Governor of the overplus and the house built at their expense. But in his last term of office he managed to send a huge consignment of tobacco from Bermuda, and appeared himself in London to state his own case. The result was that he retained the by then famous house (on the property later designated The Grove) and a little less than half the overplus property – a large and beautiful slice of land.

After his retirement he returned to live, and die, in Bermuda. He was buried at Port Royal 10th February 1625. His brother, also from Milton, Kent, and the brother's son, later settled in the islands. The huge Tucker clan of Bermuda had begun – and with a vast head-start.

Richard Norwood proved his innocence of any complicity in the overplus plot, if plot there had been. He remained away from Bermuda for twenty years during which time he wrote several learned books on trigonometry, on navigation, on fortifications – books which went through many editions and continued being published for over half a century. That no one had ever ascertained the exact length of a degree or of a nautical mile led him between 1633 and 1635 to measure the meridian altitude of the sun at the Tower of London and the centre of York City, and the exact ground distance between his observation points. This was 150 years before the use of the theodolite. Thus he made another mark on the then inexact art of navigation – an inexactitutde that meant ships often were unable to locate the Islands.

In 1637 he returned to Bermuda as a schoolmaster, bringing his wife and four children. His first school was probably in Devonshire Tribe, but later he built his own school on his estate in Pembroke. This estate is still called Norwood – the beautiful house on it to-day was built about 1711 by the husband (Saltus) of Richard Norwood's great-grand-daughter, but there are no remains of the school house.

(The last Saltus, named Samuel, left the property to his junior partner, Henry Darrell, and the remainder of his estate as a foundation for a school for white boys – Saltus Grammar School. At the entrance to Norwood, Henry Darrell erected the notice that so intrigues visitors to-day: 'Where tramps must not, surely ladies and gentlemen will not, trespass.')

In 1662, when Richard Norwood was over seventy, the Bermuda Council implored him to make a second survey of the islands. The book he made to accompany his new map was called the Domesday Book of Bermuda. The original manuscript map is in the Bermuda Archives. He received the magnificient pay of £50 for this survey and that not till 1668. At his death in 1675, in his eighty-fifth year, it was found he was still writing – now on music and art. Bermuda had been fortunate indeed to have this intellectual giant bestriding the seventeenth century, spending over forty years of his long life in these islands. His career is all the more amazing when one realizes that he had been obliged to leave school – the famous Berkhamsted School in Hertford-shire – before his fourteenth birthday.

But to revert momentarily to Governor Daniel Tucker: the place in Bermuda that still bears his name, Tucker's Town, a beautiful residential area on the eastern limits of the Main Island, is, somewhat ironically, a twentieth-century development. But it has carried that name for more than 350 years because he had intended to build a settlement there and a few roads were laid out in his time. These were to serve people connected with the fortifications on Castle Island.

Since Tucker had returned to London somewhat hurriedly, an Acting Governor, Kendall, was put in his place. But the most significant happening of this era was the arrival in 1619, as governor, of Captain Nathaniel Butler.

Governor Butler cast a wintry eye on the state of the fortifications which he described as 'little better than scarecrows.' As a matter of fact, each succeeding governor was to be critical of his predecessor's defence works, so that increasingly the forts were re-inforced, brought up to date and some re-located as the range of gun-fire increased. He also saw to it 'that Captain Daniel Tucker, the retired governor, received his three-sevenths of the overplus with his home, though Butler had reservations about the latter, protesting to the Company in London that Tucker was thus receiving 'such a seat, such a house, fit only for a governor.' But his objections fell on deaf ears.

The new governor had arrived in October 1619 and must have been discouraged that two hurricanes struck the islands in November – one of them wrecking the *Warwick* in which he had arrived, the second tearing up 'by the roots' the watch-tower Governor Moore had built as a look-out (known as the Mount), and blasting all the crops. The following year, Governor Butler rebuilt it 7 feet higher than before, with a field-gun mounted at the base to be discharged as a warning to all the forts when any enemy ship was descried on the horizon. Fort George is now on this site.

By this time lath-and-plaster shacks with unglazed windows, crowned with palmetto thatch or the newer wooden shingles, had succeeded the earliest wooden huts. (The first record of a stone *residential* building was not till 1665, and it was much later before they began to be at all general.) Every two or three years, violent storms or hurricanes damaged or blew down a good proportion of them. But, providentially, there had been no loss of life on shore.

Butler pressed on, finished the Church in St George's and salvaged everything usable from the wrecks. But the spring of 1620 saw another famine due to the hurricane-blasted crops.

And now the Bermuda Company was complaining that the tobacco crop they were receiving was of a very inferior quality. The poorest leaves were carelessly packed in with the better, so that the whole arrived in London in a completely rotten condition. Carelessness and high humidity were both to blame.

By now, the population had increased to fifteen hundred persons. During Butler's administration – and from time to time for many years afterwards – more and more Negroes were brought to Bermuda from the slave plantations in the West Indies where they had been taken by the Spaniards to replace the vanishing Caribs. Inter-tribal wars in Africa had led to various Negro chieftains selling their war prisoners to the Spaniards and Portuguese. In Governor Tucker's time a few had been introduced to dive for pearls, and, by their skills, occupied a considerably better position than those who were to come later. Now they also were used in agriculture but since there were no huge plantations in the sense there were in America, they came into direct contact with the Bermuda families who owned them and, in many cases, a reciprocal loyalty developed. The coloured Bermudians of to-day – or 'black' as the latest trend has it – are mainly the descendants of these, who were not aborigines as some mistakenly suppose. Most of the outstanding white families are descended from early English settlers. To-day, there is also a large number of Portuguese, most of whose forebears were introduced, mainly from the Azores, from the late nineteenth century onward to help develop Bermuda agriculture. These three cultural strands form the main basis of the island's present day residential population.

The most momentous event of Butler's governorship was the convening of the first Bermuda Parliament on 1st August 1620. This is an outstanding date in Bermuda history. The first Colonial Constitution in the British Empire was instituted in Virginia in July 1619 and this was followed by that of Bermuda in 1620. Bermuda's first Legislature met in the Church at St George's on 1st August 1620 and has been in continuous existence from that date, making its own laws and with a very short Constitution stating that Bermudians were free denizens with power to make their own laws not contrary to those of the Mother Country, but with the Monarch exercising powers of disallowance. Since, as we have seen, Bermuda had no inhabitants when colonised, all English laws in force in England on 11th July 1612 when Moore

arrived as first governor came automatically into force in
Bermuda, and are still in force except in so far as they have
been supplemented, repealed, or amended by Acts of the
Bermuda Legislature.

Procedure in this first Parliament was simple, the seating
arrangements being approximately the same as in Virginia.
The Governor and Council sat behind the Secretary at one
end of the Church, while the latter acted as Speaker and
faced the burgesses, each tribe having elected two. A member
wishing to speak simply doffed his hat and stood. His
Excellency the Governor, Captain Nathanial Butler, his
Council, the Secretary, the Baliffs, the Clerk and the
Burgesses all assembled within the newly-finished simple
frame church at St George's on 1st August 1620. The three
hundred and fiftieth anniversary of this great occasion was
celebrated with pride and thankfulness at the same spot (now
called St Peter's) in 1970 when His Royal Highness, Prince
Charles, the Prince of Wales, read the speech from the Throne
at the request of Queen Elizabeth II.

Little change has been made in Bermuda's Constitution
over the years, until the sweeping New Constitution which
came into effect 8th June 1968 and under which Parliament
convened 14th June 1968. (We shall come to the details of
these twentieth-century events in their due place.)

We have the complete record of Governor Butler's
memorable speech of some 2,000 words in 1620. He
reminded them not only of their duty to God, and their
allegiance to the King, but of the folly of attempting to cheat
the Adventurers in England, or of 'choseing and electinge
your owne Governor here.' He spoke at length on defence
and fortifications 'to provide against the attempts of all
forraigne enemies . . . otherwise I see not with what comfort
we can plant tobacco, and take paines to make it good (as we
ought to doe), unless we provide to keep it when we have it.
Me thinks, that every married man that hath a childe borne
to him here should be ready to keepe it a freeman: and ther
is noe earthly means to doe it better than by this . . . You
heare by this barke that is newly come in unto us from
England of the rumous and likelyhoode of great warres in
Christian-doome. If it should so fall out that any soudaine
breach happen between England and Spaine (and who knows
how sone this may be?) ther is not any place that it will
break out upon soner than upon this. The pirates, likewise,
have a longing eye after these Islands, and knowe well how

behousefull they would be for them; let us therefore so provide for ourselves that come an enemye when he will . . . we may be able to give him a brave welcome.'

After all his practical advice – and war with Spain would indeed break out again in 1625 – Butler also spoke of the ideals they should hold. His words, indeed, have such universal application, that some of them were incorporated into the speeches made in St Peter's Church in 1970. He reminded them that 'we come not hither for ourselves only, and to serve our owne turnes, or any mans els in particular, but to serve and regard the public . . . we are therefore to riddle ourselves from all base desires of gaine; we are to despice all private interests, thus farre at least, as to cause them to give place to the generall.'

Various rules were made to be observed by the members, some of which read rather amusingly to-day. 'In speakeinge against any man's speach, the partie spoken against was not personally to be named, to shunne thereby heates of contention and the giveinge of distastes one to another. *Noe revilinge nor nipinge speaches wer to be used upon any occasion whatsoever.*'

Of the 15 Acts passed in 1620 and 1623, some were already concerned with conservation ('Against killing over-young tortoises'; 'against the unjust killing of swine'), others dealt with the care and disposal of the aged, sick, and impotent, and one passed in 1612 was succintly labelled 'Against non-residents'. And, in case the reader should be misled into thinking the second act mentioned was an early version of our present Social Security, it must be admitted that this law was passed because 'there can be found noe greater disease and canker to a new settled plantacon than the stuffinge it with idle and unprofitable persons whose bellies for the most part are extraordinarylie cravinge and there mouthes as ravenous . . . such [have] bene throwne in and forced upon us . . . It is enacted and concluded by the

President Henry Tucker House, St George's, takes its name from the President of the Council, Secretary of the Treasury and Acting Governor who owned it and lived there from 1770 to his death in 1808. He was the eldest son of that large family at The Grove, Southampton, whose portraits are on exhibition at Tucker House. This is now the property of the Bermuda National Trust. (*Bermuda News Bureau photo*)

full consent and authority of this present generall Assemblye that from hence forward all such over aged, diseased and impotent persons . . . [who] rest and remayne here as drones and horsleaches living upon the sweate and blood of other men . . . that all such shall presently be shipped backe againe unto the place from whence they came.' This may sound brutal but the islanders were having a struggle for survival and could not allow themselves to be used as a disposal unit for the off-scourings of society. Practical laws as to bridge and road building were also passed in this epoch-making first Bermuda Assembly of 1620, and, (stung perhaps by what the Governor had said about being 'honest and discreat' in their dealings with the Company 'and soe to mix our owne good and proffitt and theirs together') they made strict laws 'against making up rotten and unmerchantable tobacco' for shipping to England.

Governor Butler decided that St George's needed a Towne House or Sessions House as it was unsuitable for the church to be used for both secular and religious occasions. He therefore proposed building a 'fayre house of hewen stone' eastward of King's Parade, and thus balancing the church to the west. It was to be solidly built of limestone blocks – the first building entirely of stone to be erected in the islands – and would thus save the rapidly-depleting cedars and would outlast the wooden buildings. This was begun in 1620, completed in three or four years, and served until 1815 as the place for the meetings of the General Assembly, and as a Court House. Simply and solidly built of hard irregular blocks of limestone quarried from the earth, set in a primitive mortar of lime mixed with turtle oil, and with plain heavy walls several feet thick, this building, now known as the State House, still looks as if it might well stand for centuries longer. Originally, there were two upper floors, or decks, with little headroom, meant for storing supplies of gun-

---

St George's Town and Ordnance Island. One of the oldest settlements in the Western Hemisphere, it was founded in 1612, and remained the capital till 1815. The 1¾-acre island immediately off the Square was two separate islands, Gallows Island and Ducking Stool Island, till 1799 when a canny Scot, Simon Frazer, acquired them for a song, joined them together and sold them to the War Office in 1814 as a military storehouse for more than £14,000. (*Bermuda News Bureau photo*)

powder. The flat roof began leaking after several hurricanes early in the eighteenth century and by 1732 the top floors had to be removed. The ground floor was a single room 32 feet by 22 feet where the Members of the House of Assembly and the Council then met together, though they voted separately. Bermudians are proud of this their earliest and oldest stone building, so in the 1970s it has been restored to its original condition though its function has altered. For after Hamilton became the seat of government, the Free-masons obtained the use of the simple dignified old building at a token rental of one peppercorn per year. Nowadays there is always a colourful ceremony when the Governor accepts the rental on behalf of the colony.

When the Book of Laws of the Bermuda Company was sent out in 1622, the cover carried the design of the coat of arms that had been granted to it: 'Argent, on a mount vert a lion sejant affronté, Gules, supporting between the fore-paws an antique shield, Azure, thereon a representation of the wreck of the ship *Sea Venture* (A.D. 1609) all proper, together with this motto *"Quo Fata Ferunt"'* (Whither the Fates carry us.) The motto was taken from line 7 of Book III of Virgil's *Aeneid*: '*Incerti, quo fata ferunt, ubi sistere detur, contrahimusque viros*' (an appropriate text describing how Aeneas and his party set forth to found a new settlement in an unknown land.) These Arms were originally granted to the Bermuda Company in reference to the wreck of the *Sea Venture* leading to the colonisation of Bermuda. The earliest known use of these Arms was this on the Company's Book of Laws printed in 1622. It was also engraved on Norwood's map of Bermuda, and became the coat of arms of Bermuda itself. (Later, in 1684, when the Company's Charter became forfeit to the Crown, the Public Seal was adopted bearing the device of a Graving Dock with ships. This design was never popular. Authority was eventually granted by Royal Warrant 4th October 1910 for Bermuda to use Armorial ensigns corresponding to the Arms granted to the Bermuda Company so long ago. And the Bermuda flag is the Red Ensign with this same coat of arms on the 'fly'.)

The struggle for survival that continued as governors came and went was in a sense a three-corner affair between the Company, (members of which had sunk £200,000 in the venture,) the Colonials and the unfortunate governor between the two. The islanders' grievances against the Company included the fact that they were only allowed to

Armorial bearings on the reverse of the ancient seal of the Bermuda
or Somers Island Company which received a Royal Charter in 1615.
The device shows on a shield the *Sea Venture* being wrecked on the
Bermuda coast with the motto '*Quo Fata Ferunt*'. When the
Bermuda Company was dissolved in 1684 the Royal Arms (modified
with each new reign) were used instead on the Public Seal till 1833,
when a new seal was sent from England bearing the device of a
graving dock. This remained in use till 1910 when the islands
celebrated their 300th anniversary and obtained Royal warrant for
the Bermuda Coat of Arms to revert to this ancient design.
(Photographed by Frederick Hamitlon)

trade with the Company ships which therefore had a
monopoly; that they did not get all the supplies they needed;
the tobacco could not compete in quantity or quality with
that grown in Virginia yet it was, at first, the staple crop, half
of which had to be paid over to the Company as rent.
Finally, as we have seen by some of the earliest laws passed
locally, there were strong objections to the type of people

sent out to the colonies – between younger sons of the gentry who sometimes considered themselves too good to work, and the dregs exported from slums and prisons, the honest sturdy colonists had a hard time of it. As did the governors in keeping order.

A jail was built in St George's in 1620, while stocks, pillory, and whipping post stood near the Sessions House. There were various sites for ducking stools around the coast – mostly used as a punishment for naggers of the female sex, men having to commit a far more heinous offence to merit the same punishment; and a gibbet or gallows stood conveniently on one of the two small islands close off-shore from the town, one being called Gallows Island, the other Ducking Stool Island, names which sufficiently proclaimed their purpose. (The two islands are to-day known as Ordnance Island; they were built into one towards the end of the eighteenth century.)

The ancient records of the Assizes of the early seventeenth century give an illuminating glimpse of the social life of the time. Offences for which people – including children – were indicted included such acts as stealing a potato valued at 3d, ears of corn, an instrument for striking fish, a gelded hogg valued at 10s, a cheese, a pair of shoes worth 5s, pair of sheets priced at 4s, an axe valued at 6 pounds of tobacco, a tablecloth. Other offences mentioned were railing against the Governor's authority; behaving irreverently in church; neglecting to receive Holy Communion; allowing Bibbey to be 'inordinately drunk' in their houses; refusing, as a married couple, 'to live together according to the ordinance of God'; playing at unlawful games as dice, cards, ninepins and such like; frequent resorting to 'tipling houses'; attempting escape from the colony; treason; un-natural offences; assault; absence from church; debt; melting down 'coyne of Gould and Silver'; 'suspition of incontinence'; letting loose of 'swyne that should be kept in sties'; burglary; exporting cedar wood; concealing finds of ambergris; hiding tobacco; the acting of any stage play of any kind whatsoever; being 'notorious cursers and swearers'; breaking the Sabbath by 'making an apron upon that day'; profaning the Sabbath day by fishing; leading 'an uncivil life and calling her neighbour an old Bawd and the like'; arson; conspiracy; scandal; murder.

The punishments covered an equally wide range:- to be censured; to stand in the church two Sabbath days bearing a paper on the breast proclaiming the offence; 'to make a publique acknowledgment in the parish church where she lives before the whole congregation' (this usually for incontinence); to be burnt in the hand or branded; fined in tobacco; ducked at a ducking stool a stated number of times; placed in the pillory for a certain number of hours – sometimes with one ear nailed to the post; confined in the stocks near the Sessions House porch; condemned to penal slavery; compelled to labour on the public works; ears cut off; declared infamous; banished; stood in a sheet in the church porch; lashed on the bare back at the Whipping Post 'till the blood came'; placed astride a piece of ordnance 'being fully laden and so discharged'; jailed; hanged. (Paul Deane who stole one Holland cheese was hanged 'at the common place'.)

Governors occasionally were a law unto themselves as at the Assizes of March 1626 during Captain Woodhouse's administration. One Margaret Heyling, wife of John Heyling of Southampton, was accused of stealing her neighbour's turkey in the middle of the night. The jury of twelve men found her Not Guilty – whereupon the Governor committed *them* to prison and fined them 20 pounds of tobacco each! However, eventually this was reversed.

It is no use pretending that men and women were equal before the law. 'One William Robinson and his wyfe for divers discord were censured, he to be bound to the good behaviour and she to be ducked 3 tymes in the sea.'

Even more extreme was the case of Henry Otwell who was presented by the Churchwardens of Pembroke Tribe for 'beatinge and abusinge his wife with unsufferable blows and vile speeches. Upon examination . . . it did appear they were both faulty and therefore were censured, upon the first mis-demeanor on either side the husband to be bound to the good behaviour and the wyfe to be ducked.'

It was, needless to say, a far harsher age. Nevertheless, this grim picture presents but one side of the coin. There must have been many people living simple, happy, hard-working and frugal lives as unaffected by the Assizes as the majority to-day is uninfluenced by the Supreme and Magistrates' Courts. In fact the very Act which was drawn up 'Against Unlawfull Games' (dyce, cards, tables, shove groats or shove ha'penny, closh-quoyts) mentioned specifically the evil of playing these for any sum or sums of money, tobacco, or other things, and *'except for honest and healthful recreation.'*

And the game of bowls was played in Government House grounds with saker (cannon) shot used as balls. Life was a struggle but the climate was a healthy one, the children thriving in the golden sunshine and balmy air. And though the soil was in places scanty, a profusion of mulberries, wild olives, baygrape, and a thousand other plants grew everywhere. Cedars were huge enough to yield planks over twelve feet long and nearly a yard in width. The palmetto that grew so readily was useful in a multitude of ways for mats and chairseats, cordage and mattress supports, hats and fans. Hogs and turtles were still there and good eating. And the incredibly brilliant seas around were a storehouse of obtainable food. But the islanders had realized at last how hard they would have to work merely to stay alive, and to protect themselves against invaders. Their main crop, tobacco, was exposed to competition from many quarters and was crushingly taxed.

The seven principal islands have already been indicated (Chapter I), and now, long before this, most of the little islands had been named – some for a great man in the Company, for a local character, for its fancied resemblance to some familiar object, for fish or birds, for the reigning King or for the dead great Queen, or merely for its transient owner. Coney Island named for the plentiful fish around its shores bore that name long before its American counterpart, or before the local governor of that name; Longbird Island, Henn Island, Elizabeth Island, Tucker's Island, Darrell's Island, Pearle Island, Somerset (for Somers' seat) The Staggs, Castle Island for the fort Moore built there, Charles Island for King James' son afterwards Charles I, Gurnet Rock again for abundant fish, Gibbet Island, Bird Rock, Bird Islands, Brother Islands for two grouped together like twins, and, later, all the smaller islets in the Great Sound named for the letters of the Greek Alphabet: alpha, beta, gamma, delta and the rest of it. Lovely Nonsuch on the fringe of Castle Harbour was named for that opulent Royal Palace at Cheam, begun by Henry VIII and later a favourite residence of his daughter, Queen Elizabeth – some 130 islands in all, later reduced to 120 odd.

The Tribes, as we have seen when Norwood made his map, were already named for the great shareholders in the Company in London but they soon also acquired local popular designations – Sandys being known as Mangrove Bay, Southampton as Port Royal, Warwick as Heron Bay,

Paget as Crow Lane, Pembroke as Spanish Point (in allusion to Ramirez), Devonshire as Brackish Pond, Smith's as Harris's Bay, and Bailey's Bay for Hamilton Parish. Naturally many other names have been given to islands, capes, bays and rocks over the years for transient owners or their vagaries, and may be traced from map to map.

As if the islanders' lot was not difficult enough, the second half of the seventeenth century saw them suffer from a wave of that terrible delusion of the age — witchcraft. The witchcraft mania that swept so many countries presents a horrifying example of mob-hysteria, of the demoralizing effects of fear, and of the ability of man for self-delusion. The microcosmic happenings on the small stage of the Bermuda Islands were an amazingly true reflection, on a minute scale and at a slightly later date, of the same events in the distant Mother Country. It was also a part of the wave that was to break on Salem.

The islanders had naturally brought with them such superstitions as were current in their native land; but such beliefs remained tolerant and quiescent till goaded by persistent witch-hunts. In England the sporadic outbursts of witchcraft under Queen Elizabeth had become something far different under the witch-obsessed abnormal King James whose book *Demonology* became a textbook for witch-hunters.

For the first thirty or forty years of Bermuda's settlement, the harmless crones who concocted simples from Bermuda plants, muttered incantations and charms over their neighbours' sick children, goats, shotes* and hens, were not regarded as evil women to be 'presented' at an Assize Court. They'd never heard of a pact with Satan even though as early as 1622 the Bermuda Company, complying with the new law of James' Parliament, had instructed churchwardens to present 'whosoever hath or seemeth to have any familiar consultation with the Devil' at the next Bermuda Assizes.

It was to a simple and credulous community of 1,500 people that, just before the turn of the half-century, a strange influx of people was introduced: Scottish prisoners from the defeats of the Royalists Armies. King James had been succeeded on that distant throne of England by his son, Charles, in 1625. It was with astonishment the colonists

*Shote or shoat was a provincialism for a young pig and is a term still occasionally used.

belatedly received the news that King Charles had been put to death in 1649 by some of his own subjects and that a Commonwealth had been declared under Cromwell.

When this news reached Bermuda, Charles II was pro- claimed as King, orders from Cromwell's parliament were flouted, and all the people who sided with the Common- wealth were exiled to an island in the Bahamas under a staunch Puritan, Captain William Sayle. However, the Royalists in Bermuda were forced to knuckle under when the Long Parliament declared Bermuda to be in a state of rebellion and prohibited all trade with the islands. And though Sayle returned to Bermuda — and was twice governor — the islanders in general rejoiced when in 1660 Charles II did indeed ascend the throne and was proclaimed locally a second time at this belated news of the Restoration.

It had been in 1650 and 1651 that batches of Scottish prisoners captured at Dunbar and at Worcester, arrived from time to time in the colony. The uneducated, the rank and file, poor bewildered Celtic peasants, were sold as slaves to Bermuda and to the other plantations. They had witnessed the frightful cruelties of the witch-hunts in England and Scotland of the last few years and so were engrossed in this mass hysteria.

Captain Josias Forster was appointed at this time to his last term of office as Governor of Bermuda, and was fascinated by the impact of the Celtic prisoners' beliefs upon the islanders. Searching for signs of witchcraft naturally produced immediate results, and he took part with zest in their trials and persecution. The trials took place in what is now the State House, the poor deluded women and half- crazy men were 'swum' in the narrow ribbon of water between the islands off King's Square and the wharf. Hanging took place on the eastern one of those two islands — Gallows Island, now a part of Ordnance.

No one was safe whose neighbour's turkeys or cows died after they'd been 'over-looked,' — or whose child pined away soon after a friend's visit. People were accused of oozing under doors in spirit form, of attending witches' sabbats, of giving suck to imps and familiars, of bearing 'sympathetic wounding,' of preventing butter from 'coming' in the churn, of causing miscarriages, of casting an Evil Eye, of adminis- tering love potions.

The first of these trials was that of Jeanne Gardiner in 1651, who was tried, 'swum' and hanged. Dreams and hallucinations were accepted as evidence and even such brilliant minds as that of Richard Norwood were intrigued by this belief in organized witch-cults. In all there were twenty-two trials for witchcraft in Bermuda in that second half of the century, resulting in five hangings of which one was that of a man. The ancient MS. volumes in the Archives still bear the entries of various governors empanelling juries of women to search the bodies of the accused for the Devil's Brand or the Witch's Marks. The last case occurred in the Quarter Court Records for the year 1696, but long before this the trials had begun petering out, to non-convictions, then to no further prosecutions.

At the time the Quakers, then a disapproved-of sect in Bermuda, were courageous enough to condemn the idea of a deliberate pact with Satan as a revolting delusion. In particular, the Quakeress wife of Governor Florentius Seymour made no secret of her opinions. And gradually the laws were modified in the Mother Country.

The Church ascribed all the tribulations of the era to the mighty hand of God in punishment, reproof or warning, and days of penitence and prayer were set aside after such disasters struck, but it was from St Anne's Church, Southampton that, according to legend, on wild nights men would begin scurrying forth, even before the sermon was ended, (and at times eagerly accompanied by the minister himself) to capture 'a turtle in the net' as a ship on the reefs was heartlessly described. Indeed, Bermudians took early to piracy and occasionally indulged in the more indefensible sin of wrecking. The Assize Court Records for December 1652 outline such a case to which the Grand Jury adds the sorrowful footnote that this Plantation had once enjoyed the reputation of being a merciful and loving people. And Governor Richard Coney, later in the century, shocked at the behaviour of the islanders towards a stranded French vessel which they set on fire to be able to loot, complained bitterly that he was unable to obtain evidence since 'they are all of them akin both by consanguinity and villainy.'

The reign of Charles II was characterized by a social permissiveness and moral deterioration that later spread to Bermuda and which help explain some of the disorders in the community. So that when the news of the Great Plague of London (1665) reached the islands, a day of Humiliation and Prayer was set aside in July 1666. In January of the following year Governor Florentius Seymour issued another proclamation 'whereas wee have understood that the eminent City of London hath undergone inexpressible damage by the dreadful furie of ffire . . . all which callamities have bin derived from the aloud crying sines that have bin practised therein . . . we having (if not in England yet in these Islands) even out-dared our Heavenly Maker by our Sabbath breaking drunkenness . . and such like abominations . . . for all which we may justly expect the like or more dreadful Judgement from the sinne-revenging Almighty to be poured out uppon us spedily' — and set aside another day of prayer and humiliation 'to divert all manner of judgment from us and all ours.'

Such was the thinking of the age.

It was no wonder then that a day of Hurricane Thanksgiving should have been set aside early in the century when they regarded the loss of crops and buildings as direct punishment from God and were only too thankful that all lives had been spared.

As tobacco proved a more and more unrewarding crop, Bermudians turned increasingly to the sea. As directed by the Company, they had early attempted to set up salt pans but atmospheric humidity prevented rapid enough evaporation. Full of the spirit of adventure they cut down more cedars, built swift craft and sailed nearly a thousand miles south to seize a tiny uninhabited island where the sun's heat would be more intense yet continuous trade winds would prevent humidity. They first sighted the islands (discovered in 1512 by Ponce de Leon) called Grand Key in 1668 and a few years later had seized the 10-square mile uninhabited Turk's Island (so called from the giant cactus with its huge blossom like a man's head that alone broke the monotony of 'rugged rocks and burning sand') and built huge shallow salt ponds from which they raked salt from April or May till October. For a hundred years Bermudians had possession of this tiny island as a colony of their own, taking blocks of Bermuda aeolian limestone south with them to build their houses and a church, and returning laden with salt which they traded up the American coast in exchange for food — then home to Bermuda to plant their winter crops of corn and onions. Several times they were to be dispossessed by raiding Spaniards and once by a French flotilla from St Domingo but each time they regained peaceable possession with the unrestrained liberty of gathering salt. These predatory attacks on the salt-rakers entailed the Bermudians in the expense of arming their vessels, and once in despatching an expedition to eject the Spaniards. In 1766 a residential agent was appointed 'by his residence on the spot to ensure the right of the islands to His Majesty.'

It was a great blow to the Bermudians when, in 1799, the Turk's Islands were annexed by the Bahamas Government and many protests were made to the Bermuda House of Assembly. However, Bermuda did not regain possession of them and they passed through various stages of government and later annexation to Jamaica, but are to-day, by the choice of its people in 1962, a British colony. Bermuda still feels an affinity for the little island it once owned and populated, and has frequently sent assistance after its devastation by hurricanes. The names on the church walls and tombstones are those of Bermuda families.

However, towards the close of the seventeenth century, the salt-raking at Turk's was a god-send to the Bermuda settlers, and the salt trade remained their hub of commerce for the next hundred years. 'Salt, Cedar, and Sailors' was the descriptive phrase for the Bermudian way of life. But their preference for shipbuilding, whaling, fishing, saltraking, piracy and privateering inevitably led to neglect of agriculture and they became dependent on food supplies fetched from the mainland of America. A dangerous dependence for the future.

As far as the Bermuda (or Somers Island) Company was concerned, their hopes for the Colony had proved delusive, while, on the other hand, the strict monopoly these proprietors claimed (that it was a private inheritance enclosed to the use of the purchasers) was impossible to maintain. Unintentionally, the islands had early gained a reputation as a source of wealth that was entirely false. The tenants on the spot began sending petitions to Charles II for redress against the Company and at last, in 1684, proceedings under a writ of *quo warranto* resulted in the forfeiture to the Crown of the Company's Charter. It had outlived the Virginia Company by sixty years.

So now the government of Bermuda passed to the Crown, but the inherent rights of the inhabitants to make their own laws remained undisturbed and the island did not become a Crown Colony. The Governors were now appointees of the Crown but the island became far more independent since by this time most of the shares of land were owned by the people who lived here and local affairs were largely in their hands, claiming as they did a measure of self-government surprising for so small a body of people under a distant monarchy. No longer with the Company's ships to rely upon, but feeling at last that the islands were their own, the struggles of Bermudians, so far from the world's markets, were intensified. St George's, their one town, at the end of the seventeenth century consisted of three-score cottages thatched with palmetto leaf. Some of these were the now dilapidated early wooden shacks, others their hastily erected replacements, lath and plaster cottages. Throughout the islands there were eight churches sharing four ministers to serve 679 houses in the entire countryside. By this time the total population was 5,889 of whom 4,152 were white and 1,737 were of Negro descent from the few who had been brought in from 1616 onwards. In 1681 they had plotted, during the absence of their masters in Turk's Island, to take over the Colony. This naturally resulted in measures restricting their liberty.

It was obvious by now that stronger houses would have to be built to withstand the frequent hurricanes. The solid State House built 1620-23 of the hardest limestone set an example of what could be done. It would endure for hundreds of years. It still stands today.

5

Lean Times

Probably it was from 1684 onwards, when they lost the support — however irksome — of the Company, that Bermudians developed the stubbornness, independence and self-reliance that characterise them to-day; also their love of the sea and of hard adventuring. Quite prominent Bermudians did not hesitate to share in the spoils of piracy with such lawless characters as Thomas Tew of Newport, Rhode Island, who came to Bermuda in 1691. Letters of Marque, however obtained, covered a multitude of sins and such a hair's breadth divided piracy from privateering that one did not enquire too closely into that flimsy legality; King James himself described privateering as 'a splendid theft'. After all, the greatest of Elizabethan seamen, Sir Francis Drake, dead only thirteen years before the Bermuda adventure began, was regarded by England's enemies as history's most spectacular robber. Yet his glorious expedition around the world was a great privateering adventure, redeemed by romantic enthusiasm and devotion to the country he was thus serving.

So when Thomas Tew arrived, armed with some sort of privateering papers, five Bermudians let him buy shares in their fine 70-ton sloop, *Amity*, entirely ignoring his notorious reputation as a bloodthirsty pirate. He enlisted forty-five men as crew and is credited with resorting to open piracy which included boarding several Arabian ships and looting them of £100,000-worth of plunder. On his return to Rhode Island, his Bermudian partners hastened to America to receive their fair share of the spoils which he had buried till their arrival.

As for such windfalls as news in 1687 of a Spanish caravel, richly laden, and wrecked off San Domingo — every available Bermuda boat crammed on sail and skimmed rapidly southward to salvage over £47,000-worth of silver bullion. And then cheated the Crown out of the 50 per cent legally due! The meagre 10 per cent reluctantly handed over was mainly spent in strengthening the island's fortifications against French attacks.

Such strokes of luck were the exception. After the collapse

of the Somers Island Company (which the settlers rejoiced at
since they wanted the benefit of the Crown's control rather
than what they designated 'the oppression of Egyptian
task-masters') the record of the next 150 years is one of
struggle, hardship and often extreme privation, spiced with
reckless adventuring, treasure-hunting, piracy, privateering,
wrecking, smuggling, and the excitement of occasional
short-lived wealth. Even wars beyond the horizon, while they
cut off the islands' supplies and disrupted their carrying
trade, also gave opportunities for adventuring and privateering, stimulating Bermuda's growing ship-building, and the
pride taken in the sea-worthiness and speed of the sturdy
cedar craft.

Probably the islanders were 'feeling their oats' now they
were free of Company control; for Governor Richard Coney,
who had been sent out by the Company in 1683, and then
ordered to remain at his post under the new regime, could
not but notice the unrest and sedition on the island. Royal
decrees and legislation were by now endeavouring to outlaw
piracy; local governors were ground between the upper and
nether millstones of what ought to be enforced and the
driving necessities of local people. Besides, as Governor
Butler had confessed in the 1620s, it was not always easy to
distinguish between pirates and honest men.

In 1595, Sir George Somers himself had, in those his
younger days, gone on raids in the Caribbean. In fact at that
time it had often been a case of gallantly fighting England's
enemies single handed and at overwhelming odds. But now
the scene had changed. Such notorious men as 'Blackbeard'
(Edward Teach) were lawless murderers, out to attack any
rich prize, to torture, maim, kill, irrespective of country or
origin and merely to enrich themselves. Madagascar became a
citadel of piracy as did some West Indian islands; but though
Bermuda was threatened with a similar fate and lost sloops
captured off the coast by Teach, it never did become a
piratical base and neither he nor Henry Morgan landed here.

Even the harsh word 'pirate' was beginning to be avoided
in favour of the newly-coined 'buccaneer' — a more pleasing
euphemism derived from reference to the 'boucan' or
wooden gridiron used by bands of rovers, mainly French, to
cook meats out of doors native fashion in the West Indies.

Bermudians had profitable dealings with some of the
smoother of such characters, Thomas Tew and George Dew
for instance, when it suited their purpose. They also

contributed at least two colourful members to this rogues' gallery themselves: John Bowen and Nathaniel North. Both of them made their headquarters at Madagascar and afterwards in Mauritius. The former was a son of Anne née Norwood, (daughter of the famous Richard Norwood) who had been presented on suspicion of witchcraft at the Assizes of 1651; Captain John Bowen is reputed to have lived in high hilarity in Mauritius and to have been buried there, if not with a stake through his heart, at least under a highway.

So it seems rather hard on Governor Coney that when he appealed to a certain Captain Bartholomew Sharpe, (who sailed in most opportunely with his 10-gun sloop and 100 men,) to help reinforce authority over the obstreperous Bermudians, that the 'beloved Commander' should just then have been seized by Captain St Lo on behalf of the Governor of Nevis. It appeared that Sharpe was to stand trial in that island on a charge of piracy in the South Seas. He was acquitted for lack of evidence, backed by Coney's letter of thanks for preserving the King's peace in Bermuda! It was almost impossible to know where you stood since privateering was eminently respectable and piracy, unfortunately, so often its concomitant. That Coney could be reproved both in England and by the Bermudians themselves was indeed ironical. The unfortunate governors must often have felt that the islanders played both sides against the middle.

As for smuggling, it was taken for granted. Most homecoming ships put into some small inlet on the excuse of seeing a wife or settling some private business, before making official entry into St George's Harbour. No one turned informer at such evasion of customs duty, for everyone was in it. In fact, they could not have existed without such stratagems. Poverty was widespread.

But although all this activity at sea led to a deplorable neglect of agriculture, even privation could not be allowed to prevent the re-building of homes and public buildings all of which, except the State House, were in a deplorable condition by the end of the seventeenth century. Colonel Richard Coney had complained that Government House, built with such pride by Governor Moore on the western side of King's Square, leaked in every room. So now, just before the turn of the century, when Governor Samuel Day took office, it was decided to re-build St George's in the soft aeolian limestone, that hardens after quarrying, of which the islands are composed. The building known to-day as the

Confederate Museum, opposite St Peter's Church, was built by Governor Day as Government House. But though the building still stands, it was used for Day's intended purpose for a very short period indeed.

The pattern of narrow alleys being left as originally laid out, St George's now took on a permanent air as, by 1703, the next governor, Benjamin Bennett, required every lease-holder to re-build in stone or forfeit his lease. Where picturesque Bridge House now stands facing west, the town bridge then spanned a creek — long since filled in — that ran up to the present Somers Gardens. This re-building project not only preserved the town but saved the rapidly thinning cedars, and was planned to cover 27 acres eventually. Perhaps 'planned' is an inadmissible word in this connection since the winding lanes that delight the visitor to-day run higgledy-piggledy. They were often blocked by wandering livestock, and the only torch used by the occasional after-dusk pedestrian was that of a lighted palmetto frond expertly rolled. The Old Rectory behind St Peter's, the Tucker House on Water Street, and many another home belong to this era.

The struggling Colony was devastated by unusually

(*above*) The Old Rectory, St George's. North of St Peter's Church, at the end of Broad Alley, stands this delightful old building in which can be traced the earliest construction of the original half-timber walls. These were afterwards replaced with stone but show in the wall-plate where the uprights once stood. Parson Alexander Richardson (1730-1805) known affectionately as The Little Bishop, was the man for whom it retains its ecclesiastical designation. He was rector of St Peter's from 1755 till his death, with the exception of 6 years spent in St Eustatius, and many stories are still recounted of his eccentricities for he was an Irishman whose lively personality made him a legend. He married twice, his second wife bringing this home with her, ever since known as The Old Rectory. It is now a Bermuda National Trust Property. (*Bermuda News Bureau photo*)

(*below*) St Peter's Church, St George's. The original place of worship in St George's was constructed in 1612, a stone church being erected seven years later. St Peter's is considered the oldest Anglican Church in the western hemisphere in continuous use, having been repaired, enlarged, refurbished over the centuries; its fabric contains examples of seventeenth, eighteenth, nineteenth and twentieth-century work. It is indeed 'our town's treasure' as was claimed for it over a hundred years ago. (*Bermuda News Bureau photo*)

frequent and severe hurricanes in the early years of the eighteenth century, particularly in 1712. Most of the churches, including St Peter's, had to be practically re-built. Even the solid Sessions or State House suffered badly in 1726, the jail was demolished and all crops failed, while the palmettos were dashed to ribbons. By now there were over 8,000 inhabitants in the islands and they were beginning to appreciate the edict as to all houses being built with a view to permanency, especially since they had to withstand these strange Witches' Brew of storms that suddenly descended upon them without apparent rhyme or reason.

Consequently, one of the industries that suffered was that of palmetto-plait. From the earliest days (and down to the eighteenth century in some cases) houses and churches were thatched with palmetto. Cordage, baskets, hats, fishing lines were made of the tough leaves. During the eighteenth century it was the main support of many poor families. There is a legend that one of the first fine lace plait bonnets was sent to Queen Anne – at any rate for a time they became the rage in England and remained so until fickle fashion turned to leghorn hats. This export of fine plait meant a great deal to Bermudians and the industry continued during the eighteenth century. One of the names associated with the industry is that of Martha Hayward née Carter, a St David's islander, (grand-daughter of the Christopher Carter cast away on the *Sea Venture*) who lived in what is still called the Carter House. Born in 1677 she lived to the incredible age of 114 years . . . After the fashion passed in England, where it lasted for a quarter of a century, a coarser plait continued to be used for local farm-hats and for use of convicts on the hulks in mid-nineteenth century. They sold them at 1s each. Fans made of a palmetto leaf were obtainable till the 1920s, and even to-day, on Palm Sunday, the congregations in the churches receive a small cross made from the palmetto.

Of course the whale fishery also suffered during this almost continuous series of gales and hurricanes, while the

---

Two views of narrow alleyways in St George's lined with houses with solid outside chimneys and the push-out blinds that gave rise to the local saying: 'His ears are out on blind-sticks'! Banana trees and palms may be glimpsed over the pastel walls and against white-roofed cottages. The solid simple architecture has stood up to many a hurricane. (*Bermuda News Bureau photos*)

An early print of St George's Town showing the church, in which the first Bermuda Parliament convened on 1st August 1620. Opposite can be seen the house built by Governor Day *circa* 1700 as Government House (now known as Globe Hotel or Confederate Museum). The creek, filled in when it became 'noisome', ran up past what is today called Bridge House. The pillory is in the foreground. The inset at top right shows the State House (built *circa* 1620-23) on a hillock eastward of the town.

forts and public buildings were badly damaged. Much as Bermudians had wanted to be free of the impositions of the Bermuda Company, they also missed its support; in 1727 they sent a petition to King George II explaining their plight. In reply, the whale fishery was freed to them, thus giving impetus to the failing whaling industry.

But in addition to the devastation caused by hurricanes, there were plant diseases that brought the inhabitants to the verge of starvation; worst of all, epidemics of yellow fever, small pox and typhus decimated a population that understood neither the cause nor the cure. No one at that time considered mosquitos at all dangerous – they were referred to as 'harmless flies' – and, as yellow fever epidemic succeeded epidemic from the 1690s through 1779, 1796, 1812, 1818, 1819, 1837, 1843, 1853, 1856, 1864, 1867 and 1879, official investigations laid the root cause to a miasma of the atmosphere, abnormal tides, freak meteorological phenomena, the visit of a comet, or the use of previously infected clothing or bedding. In the earliest recorded visitation, nearly 800 persons died and only six members of the Council survived. No wonder the whole small population was aghast. In the yard of the Church at St George's can be found graves of those 'died of the prevailing fever' and on the plaques inside the Church, sad records as to the second battalion of the second regiment losing 120 men out of 148 in 1864.

The almost constant naval and military struggles of the eighteenth century kept the islanders on the *qui vive* for invaders, and before that – as early as 1687, Governor Sir Robert Robinson had attempted to organize a local militia in readiness against attacks by pirates. He brought the strength up to 780, with arms and ammunition and two troops of horse. During 1690-91, the Militia Act called for every man from 15 to 60 years of age to appear at every muster with muskets and bullets, and a good sword.

In 1701, a company of soldiers belonging to the 2nd Foot was sent from London, but was made into an Independent Company on reaching Bermuda; the following year, since war had been declared against France, the Militia was strengthened, a troop of Horse Grenadiers was raised uniformed in scarlet, and 600 trusted slaves were provided with lances. Local vessels drove off privateers and the general alarm was twice sounded. Although peace was proclaimed in 1713, two years later the Militia was once more alerted as England and

Spain were again at war.

Some of the local uniforms worn may be seen today at the Bermuda Historical Society's Museum in Hamilton; they are quite strikingly smaller than would be necessary nowadays — doubtless due to the short rations on which the islanders were forced to live. The Militia Acts were renewed at intervals during the eighteenth century as emergencies arose, but the end of the Seven Years War in 1763 and reforms in the British Army spelled the end of the Independent Company, and saw Bermuda furnished from England with a Company of the 9th Regiment of Foot 'in place of the Independent one lately reduced.' A new military era had begun. But though from 1778 there was a flow of regular troops and a regular garrison there were also local Militia Acts until 1813. The Bermuda Regiments that sprang out of them came much later.

Despite all these struggles some kind of trading had to be carried on. The salt industry on Turk's flourished and 13,000 bushels of salt were transported to America. On the other hand, solitary fishing boats had to be forbidden to fish off the reefs where they might be seized by French men-o'-war. And during the whole century, little shops in St George's or 'in the country' carried on with the silver-smith's art. The early colonists had brought silver-plate from England; later pieces were salvaged from Spanish wrecks and seized from French ships in the eighteenth century wars. People who were hard up would sell their old silver at 3s per ounce. The silver-smith — of whom some 25-30 are known to have worked in Bermuda, — would sell his finished product at 8s per ounce. There are some very valued collections of this home-made silver ware in the islands made by such men as William Adams, Philip Ball, William Barker, Thomas Bennett, Thomas Blatchley, Zachery Bolitho, Samuel John Canton, Thomas Dixon, Joseph Gwynn, George Hutchings, Samuel Lockwood, David Glegg Ming, Peter Pallais, George Samuel Rankin. Most of these silver-smiths worked in or before the eighteenth century though a couple continued into the nineteenth century when the fashion for hand-made silver passed. Eleven of the silver-smiths were born in Bermuda.

In all these early years of the eighteenth century there was considerable friendship and trade between Bermuda and Virginia, both by now firmly established outposts of empire. In 1699 Williamsburg had succeeded Jamestown as Virginia's capital, and here English customs, culture and fashions were dominant; as was the Anglican Church. Bermudians felt equally at home in either colony and many family ties joined the two. In fact, those in both colonies who looked back over their first hundred years of development, could not fail to be struck by the many parallels between Bermuda and Virginia: the latter's House of Burgesses had first met in the Jamestown Church in 1619, while Bermuda's Assembly had, as we have seen, held their first Session in the Church in St George's the following year. Both colonies were at first largely agricultural though, by the eighteenth century, the islanders had turned, far too exclusively, to maritime pursuits. Finally, they shared the same criminal code (the First Criminal Code of Virginia) drawn up in and for that colony by Sir Thomas Dale with the assistance of William Strachey and brought to Bermuda by Governor Tucker. If it sounds brutal to say that more than twenty crimes were punishable by death and many more by whipping, one must realise that the same code could be administered with a light or heavy hand, and that in England itself the death penalty could still be applied to 160 offences. History must be considered in its context and in perspective.

Despite poverty and hardships in Bermuda, governors had early decided that some pomp and ceremony were necessary in a new society in order to bolster authority with a background of tradition. A governor 3,000 miles from his base must be able to show how firmly his power derived from royal authority; otherwise his position would soon become untenable. Hence the Royal Salutes, the official ceremonies, the State Functions of the old country revived and blossomed in the new, alongside the very real simplicity of the way of life. When Colonel Benjamin Bennett arrived as the new governor in 1701, he brought with him the Silver Oar, emblem of Admiralty Jurisdiction, which was meant for use in the Admiralty Court. But it soon found other uses, was Bennett's personal property with his name engraved upon it, and in the absence of a Mace was considered as such and was ceremoniously borne before him into Council and placed on the table as token of authority. (The present Mace is of silver-gilt and was made by Garrard and Company in London in 1920 when Bermuda was celebrating the tercentenary of the institution of Parliamentary Government. It is the symbol of authority of the Speaker of the House and is carried before him by the Serjeant-at-Arms and placed on top of the Clerk's Table.) The Silver Oar itself was bought by the

Bermuda Government in 1721.

Such pomp had been mostly in abeyance during the years of the Commonwealth when even local names were shorn of their *Saint*-hood! St Catherine's Fort lost its prefix, and St George's for a time became merely Georgestown. The criminal code had been considerably tightened. But now, even in ecclesiastical affairs, it was recognised that good social standing did no one any harm, so that the seating in church was strictly 'according to degree', with the women carefully segregated from the men and a formal table of precedence worked out.

After the passing of the Puritan régime, people gradually became more tolerant and punishments slightly less harsh – though it was still obligatory to attend the lengthy church servies and defaulters were fined. There was some relaxation as to games, sport, dancing. By the 1730s the State House was used as a ballroom in celebration of the monarch's birthday. But drunkenness brought many a man to the stocks or pillory and 'Itche of the Tounge' still received stern moral correction. But who are we of the twentieth century to judge such standards of the past when to-day on the leader page of Bermuda's morning paper, the following notice is prominently displayed in a square box:—

NOTICE 1973 (July)

Anyone found scandalizing my name will be prosecuted to the fullest extent of the law.

(Signature in full.)

Indeed the phrase 'scandalizing my name' is a not-infrequent twentieth-century local expression.

The coloured people had multiplied so rapidly by natural increase that, as early as in the Company's era, further importation of them had been forbidden. In Bermuda, there were no huge cotton plantations as there were in the Southern States, they came into direct contact with the family instead of with an overseer, their work was mainly that of the household and garden, so that their lot was far easier. They were, indeed, in much better case than the unfortunate exiled prisoners from the Civil War in England, or even than indentured servants. Slavery in fact included white bondsmen and Red Indians in addition to the Negroes and was proving very much of a two-edged sword – terribly impoverished householders still had to keep and feed the old

who were past work and the young children; and when the
men of the household were away at sea or at Turk's Island,
the burden fell upon the women-folk.

A few were 'Crown' slaves assigned to wait on the
governor. When these were past work and there was therefore
no one responsible for them, (as there would be in a private
family,) they might be officially assigned to some already
over-burdened household. In at least one case where the
dismayed recipient protested he could afford no more
dependents he was cited for contempt. In fact, the economic
problems of the colony were partly caused by the ever-
growing menace of slavery and the sheer pressure of
population – compared to facilities – where, in time of
continental wars, there was not enough food to go around.

On the other hand, there was often mutual trust and
dependence. As we have seen, many of the slaves bore arms
in the militia, were taken in sloops to sea, were taught
mechanic trades. Some were freed by Wills, others in
gratitude for special help, as was the case with Governor John
Bruce Hope whose adored wife, Charlotte, died here on
Christmas Eve 1726. The broken-hearted widower bought the
Crown slave who had waited on his wife, in order to free her.
Hope had arrived in 1722 and was the first to occupy the
large official residence, behind its imposing pillars, north of
the town – the new Government House. The pillars still
stand to-day, but the small house now used as St George's
Rectory is all that remains of that once-proud building. At
first the grounds comprised 300 acres, a park stretching south
into the town; later it shrank to 25 acres around the
governor's house. The present Somers Gardens were originally part of the park and here to-day may be seen the tomb of
Charlotte Hope near the spot, noted earlier, where the heart
of Sir George Somers was buried.

To-day, in the Colonial State papers can be read all the
detailed careful accounts this charming and chivalrous
governor, Hope, sent Whitehall as to the life in Bermuda: the
appearance of the islands; the method of housebuilding (both
roofs and walls from the aeolian limestone that formed the
island); his dismay at the blights and worms that destroyed
the once-plentiful oranges, lemons, dates, mulberries, tobacco
plants, paw-paws, plantains, pineapples – so that by now the
inhabitants were living almost entirely on fish – and the
methods of conserving water. He remarked on how many of
the menfolk were lost at sea so that the preponderence of

women in the islands was 3 to 1, in a total population of 8,270, of whom 3,500 were coloured. When Hope left Bermuda, he had laid the body of his beloved wife to rest within the enclosure of what was then Government House grounds.

As we have seen, most of the slaves in Bermuda were descendants of African Negroes transported to the West Indies by the Spaniards to take the place of the rapidly-vanishing Caribs. A few were themselves descendents of Carib Indians. For most of them Christmas-tide, and especially Boxing Day, was a time of merry-making, when troupes of them danced barefoot in the sunshine, whirling merrily down the narrow Tribe roads which had been left as boundaries of the shares by Richard Norwood and which ran in straight lines from shore to shore. They are still public right-of-way to-day. These troupes of dancers called themselves 'Gombeys' from the African word for their rustic drum, a goat-skin stretched across a hollowed tree stump. At first they danced the traditional dance mimes of Africa and merely added a coloured ribbon or a flower to their hair-do and daubed paint on their faces. Later, they enacted newly-learned versions of Biblical stories, and their costumes evolved through a period of wearing model boats and homes on their heads to the present-day elaborate robes with gauze masks and peacock head-dresses. The same distinctive unforgettable rhythm has survived. You may hear it to-day.

Whether they sang the old Bermuda doggerel or not, ancient Bermuda jingles have survived. Such couplets as 'All the way to Mangrove Bay, There the old maids go to stay' or 'All the way to Spanish Point, There the times are out of joint' were used derisively of the different parishes but are not properly *Calypso* which was never a Bermuda word, being used for the work-rhythm song of the cane-fields — non-existent locally.

Small gifts of coins were thrown to the troupes as they danced in front of houses or in each small settlement, if not, singing, 'Sail away — no money here', they careered onwards.

But life consisted mainly of living from hand-to-mouth in hope of better times. That a proportion of the slaves were unhappy in their servitude is evidenced by the revolts they staged and by the fact that at night, when opportunity offered, they rifled their neighbours' larders and hen-roosts. Slavery was indeed a double-edged blade.

One of the biggest of these rebellions occurred in 1730

when the Independent Company had been sent to the Bahamas to quell trouble there. Some of the slaves in Bermuda thereupon seized the opportunity to foment a general scheme of poisoning their masters (described in the Assembly as an attempt 'to extirpate the white people and Christianity out of these islands'.) By order of King George II in Council, the garrison was returned to Bermuda in 1732.

In the meantime, the abortive plot had been dealt with, and a slave, Sarah Bassett, burned at the stake as a ringleader, (in strict conformity with the law at that time for her offence of *Petit Treason*) near an old well on Point Finger Road, Paget. She had been convicted of attempting the lives of her master and mistress, Mr and Mrs Thomas Foster, and that of a Negro girl called Nancy, by administering Rats' Bane and Manchineel root. A broiling June day saw her execution – since when in popular parlance, a 'Sairy Bassett day' describes a sweltering one . . . The accepted misconceptions on this story are numerous: Sarah is popularly represented as a harmless old crone, burned for witchcraft when the punishment should have been hanging. But as a matter of fact, the witchcraft trials were a thing of the past, that was not the offence for which she was charged, and even to equate 'witches' with 'old crones' was an entire misconception. Poor Sarah must have been a vigorous and capable woman.

Thirty years later – in 1761 – a much more general mutiny of the slaves was plotted. Their excitement and whisperings betrayed them, and the bachelor governor, William Popple, nipped the incipient upheaval in the bud. The (British) 'Annual Register' for 1762 carried this note headed New York, January 18: 'By Captain Snellen, who arrived here on Friday last from Bermudas in 24 days, we learn that between 600 and 700 Negro men and women were on the list as conspirators in a late plot; and that the island in general was so fatigued in taking up and apprehending the suspected and keeping guard as to make but slow progress in trying them; but all that were brought to trial have been condemned'.

By this time the slaves were almost equivalent in numbers to the white population. And the inevitable consequence of such upheavals was that their position in the community worsened; however great the threat of invasion, they were no longer trusted to bear arms as they formerly had been. For at least a century the evil of too many slaves had been recognized – in another seventy years both white and coloured would be infinitely relieved at the prospect of emancipation, even though it brought its own problems.

It was in 1738 that the first of the aristocratic Popple family arrived in Bermuda as governor. This was Alured (early form of 'Alfred'), elder brother of that William whose activities during a slave rebellion have been already noted. Alured Popple brought with him a library of a thousand books, (scientific and pseudo-scientific – some dealing with witchcraft), an instrument for night observations, a microscope, a bath tub, a navigational instrument, a telescope, a pipe organ, and the first sedan-chair seen in the colony, which proved so suitable for St George's alleyways that the leading families soon adopted them.

Bermuda had starkly lean public funds. There were few police, no real highways, but fortifications, pathways, bridges and ferry had to be kept up and the administration maintained. All this on the small total revenue of £750 a year in Alured Popple's time. The revenue was partly derived from a small levy on shipping, a tax of £2 a year on horses, a liquor duty, a tax on real estate, some rents from the Crown Lands that had once been the Common Land of the Company, – and a shilling a year levied on all bachelors of twenty-one or over! Sometimes the unfortunate governors were out of pocket, though they were paid partly from the Exchequer in London.

Two famous names are connected with eighteenth-century Bermuda, Bishop George Berkeley and George Whitefield. Berkeley conceived a romantic and impractical scheme of 'founding a college at the Bermudas for the Christian civilization of America', as head of which he was to receive £100 a year! To prepare for Bermuda – which he was never to reach – he made a temporary home for himself, and his newly-married wife, for nearly three years in Rhode Island. The promised support for his scheme never materialized and in 1731 they returned to England. A hundred years or so after Bishop Berkeley's death, a school, St Paul's, was opened in Bermuda in his memory, and though it was a short-lived enterprise the sale of its lands led to the founding of the Berkeley Educational Society which in 1897 founded the Berkeley Institute, a now well-known school.

The other famous personage, George Whitefield or Whitfield, one of the founders of Methodism in England, spent his life in constant travel and incessant preaching. He made seven evangelistic journeys to America and in March 1748 came thence on an 11-week visit to Bermuda. His earnestness and eloquence reduced his congregations to tears, and one out-door sermon drew a crowd of 1,500 coloured persons. He was as outspoken on their besetting sins as he had been to the white congregation in Brackish Pond (Devonshire) Church, and they were disappointed that he told them to obey their masters. Most of his sermons were preached in the Presbyterian Church in Warwick, a celebrated edifice to-day.

The war with Spain of 1739 led to a general European war, and then followed the Seven Years War (1756-63.) And though by now 80 Bermuda vessels and more than a thousand Bermudians were wholly engaged in the salt trade – mostly with Turk's Island – and had in addition developed a very good carrying trade, both of which were partly disrupted by these wars, yet there were compensations. For the islanders began privateering in earnest from the beginning of the eighteenth century. A small flock of them was often at sea under such captains or owners as John Trimingham, Francis Jones, Richard Jennings, Samuel Stone, William Joel, William Richardson, Lewis Middleton. This last had a salute of eight guns tendered him on returning to St George's with prizes astern. Soon the inflow of prizes put those who owned sloops, were in the ship-building business or personally went privateering, into a more flourishing condition. So that, from now onwards, large simple houses of distinctive architecture began to dot the countryside. Walsingham had already been built, and the Globe Hotel in St George's, Somerville in Smith's, the Bridge House, the Tucker House, and the Old Rectory in St George's, Norwood, Oleander Circle, Palmetto Grove, the Bridge House (Sandys' Rectory) in Somerset, Verdmont, Orange Grove, Tamarisk Hall, Inwood, Tankfield, Mount Wyndham – all remain to remind us of eighteenth century Bermuda. While such houses as Clermont, Rocklands and Belair were built early in the 1800s.

But, as ever, there was another side to the picture. The incoming ships brought prisoners and food was so scarce that at least a third of the people had neither flour, corn or rice and lived almost entirely on the fish they managed to take. And the epidemics of smallpox became of terrifying proportions. Both Burt's Island and Marshall's Island in the Sound are reminders of those days for they were set aside as quarantine stations, and were named for the people in charge of the isolation cottages on each. Here inoculation was introduced and practised by Dr John Drake, Dr George Forbes, and the latter's son, Dr Francis Forbes.

In 1764, soon after the Seven Years War had ended, a governor arrived who was a model of hard-working frugality, who imported the first ploughs to Bermuda urging the islanders to grow their own foods, who himself started grape-culture on 60 acres of land near his house north of the town, and who built a small cottage-like magazine to hold the gunpowder which was so dangerously housed in the town itself. His name was George James Bruere.

He realised the economic condition of the Island was at a low ebb. The palmetto plait industry languished. Whaling was not as repaying as had been anticipated, though this hazardous calling always had enthusiastic followers and a perfect Whale House with its huge outdoor ranges built in 1759 may still be seen on Smith's Island in St George's Harbour where the Eastern Whaling Company held an acre of land. And the salt-raking at Turk's, a necessity for Bermuda's very survival, had been again attacked by the French who destroyed buildings and carried captives to Cape Francois. The Bermudians again asserted their rights as colonizers of Turk's and, for the time, the trade was rehabilitated.

So engrossing were all these maritime pursuits and as carriers in the coastwise and West Indian trade that no attention was paid to agriculture which was left to the incompetent and the aged, so that three quarters of supplies had to be obtained from America. Even the cedars were becoming increasingly scarce, used as they were for ship-building and furniture – including the ubiquitous cedar-chests that graced every home.

Bruere was a simple and kindly man with a large family of children who accompanied him to Bermuda. He was intensly loyal to his king, George III, and was determined to do his best for Bermudians. The job wore him out and broke his heart. He was eventually to die in St George's in September 1780 – after sixteen years of unavailing struggle.

But who could have foreseen the American Revolutionary War? Or that it would have had any effect on tiny Bermuda?

6

American Revolution (1775) and the War of 1812

The Seven Years War was over when George James Bruere arrived as Governor of Bermuda. An expensive though successful war for England, establishing her supremacy in North America, it benefited the colonies in the New World while loading Great Britain with an enormous debt and a land tax. It seemed reasonable to the English taxpayers and to the Home Government that the American colonies should, uirectly or indirectly, pay something towards the upkeep of the military organizations necessary to enforce the peace there. A tax was levied which the American colonists resisted on the Constitutional grounds that it had been imposed solely on the authority of the English parliament. Armed resistance led to the outbreak of the American Revolutionary War in 1775, under George Washington, a 43-year old Virginian landowner of English stock. Ultimately, the French, Spaniards and Dutch sided with the secessionists — only too glad to revenge themselves on Britain for losses in previous wars.

We have to remind ourselves of this expanse of the struggle in order to understand tiny Bermuda's involvement. Actually, although it is considered a fight between the Thirteen Colonies in America and Great Britain it affected all the colonies in the New World and was apprehensively watched from Quebec to the West Indies. But none was more economically involved than Bermuda whose very life line was imperilled. Starvation could easily stare them in the face since their carrying-trade was their life blood as, due to their neglect of agriculture, their own products were slight except for the salt from Turk's Island, so that they had to range the Seven Seas to obtain the stock-in-trade for bartering.

It followed that pre-occupation with commercial trans-actions often over-rode other considerations. They were proud to consider themselves part of a great Empire whose Navy safe-guarded them, but by now they were first and foremost Bermudians accustomed to constant intercourse with America and the West Indies. True, in 1762, the

Bermuda Government had asked the Imperial Government to send Royal Naval ships to protect the islands from French privateers, and Commodore Samuel Hood had been despatched in 1767. Since then there had been a succession of Admirals on what began to be termed The North American and West Indies Station as the strategic value of Bermuda began to be realized. But as yet there was no naval establishment – no dockyard – to service them.

Governor Bruere decided Bermudians were unmanageable and obstinate. In this category as leaders of the different factions in Bermuda he placed first 'the two families of Tuckers.' Briefly, the vast Tucker clan was as divided in its loyalties as were the remainder of the islanders. The senior member, Colonel Henry Tucker of the Grove, Southampton, (the land once sequestered by Governor Daniel Tucker as the Overplus) had four sons and two daughters. His youngest son, St George, whose house in Williamsburg is still called The Tucker House, had been educated at the College of William and Mary in Virginia, and now openly championed the American Cause as did his brother Thomas Tudor Tucker who would eventually become the Treasurer of the United States. Another brother, Dr Nathaniel Tucker, settled in an English practice and wrote poems of his native country. The eldest brother, Henry Tucker, Jr, an ardent loyalist, lived in St George's at what is now called The President Henry Tucker House, was President of the Council, Colonial Secretary, Colonial Treasurer, Provost Marshall General and King's Receiver. He married Frances, daughter of Governor George James Bruere and was recorded as a man 'of spotless integrity.'

As if all these quite naturally divided loyalties among his immediate family were not enough to make old Colonel Henry Tucker's position difficult – he himself being a 'middle of the road' man who certainly did not want a break with Britain but was anxious not to see Bermudians starve – his loved daughter Frances married cousin Henry Tucker of The Bridge House, Somerset, (now used as Sandys Rectory), eldest son of Chief Justice John Tucker who had built that elegant home near Somerset Bridge. Somerset Henry, as he was called in differentiation, sided with the revolting colonists and most probably headed the local party that betrayed the gunpowder to George Washington thus double-dealing the British.

His cousin and brother-in-law, 'President' Henry Tucker in

St George's, never allowed bitter political differences to defeat family affection. Nevertheless these difficulties no doubt enhanced his melancholy cast of mind. He and his Fanny begot ten sons and one daughter in the house on Water Street, St George's, (well worth a visit to-day for its portraits and furniture of the period) but he felt Bermuda had become 'but a sad place' and one by one he sent all his children to England though 'it almost sinks me into the grave' as he wrote to brother St George in Virginia. The beautiful face of his daughter, Anne, painted by Raeburn, still looks down on us from the walls of the National Gallery in London.

But his father, old Colonel Henry at The Grove, still continued to play an important role in Bermudian affairs. In 1775 he was sent to the Continental Congress at Philadelphia as Chairman of a delegation to beg the Americans to continue accepting salt in exchange for provisions. But they would have no more of that exclusively – gunpowder was their prime necessity. The old Colonel returned sadly to Bermuda, – to his son-in-law who would provide it with gusto, and to his own son and namesake who would see the island starve first.

The islanders were also divided. Those who were unable to manipulate events often protested the doings on either side of Councillor Thomas Jones, Thomas Dickinson, Chief Justice Jonathan Burch, John Esten, Sam Harvey, George Bascome, Richard Jennings, Cornelius Hinson, the Gilberts, Darrells, Triminghams, Pruddens, Albouys, Dills, Coxs.

Those who felt intensely loyal to Britain held meetings of protest in the central parishes against making any overtures to Congress whatsoever. They would have been dismayed had they known that, despite his assertions before congress of complete loyalty to King George III, on his return to Bermuda old Colonel Henry would confer with Somerset Henry as to what should be done.

Theoretically, Bermuda was strictly neutral in the struggle but factually, despite the positive loyalists and the many of divided minds, the island as a whole behaved more as an ally of America, since they struggled to retain economic relations with the Thirteen Colonies throughout. Nevertheless they had no wish to separate from the Mother Country.

One dramatic incident is vividly remembered in Bermuda, . . . It had been a still and sultry night. When dawn broke over the islands on that 15th August 1775 a low heavy bank of clouds hung motionless above the northern rim. An old man, by chance in Tobacco Bay on the north shore of St George's Island at an early hour and who, perhaps, had seen Cap'n Morgan's whaleboats stealthily returning from some excursion to that distant smudge of a ship, hull down on the horizon, shook his head forebodingly. Already he had heard whispers about what had gone on the previous night. Now he muttered: 'This day's deed will ever be a dark cloud hanging over us.' Legend has embalmed this story in a tradition that such frequent cloud-formation is the remorseful spirit of Old Morgan, unable to find rest until the descendants of the gunpowder-betrayers are brought to justice.

The ship on the dawn horizon was the 14-gun American frigate, *Lady Catherine*, despatched from Rhode Island under Captain Ord on purpose to obtain the gunpowder, so desperately needed by George Washington's army, from the magazine Governor Bruere had built for its safety.

The dark hours of the previous night had been a time of unwonted activity in usually somnolent St George's. Only four members of the House of Assembly had turned up that afternoon, and, unexpectedly, St George Tucker had come down from Virginia and was seen walking on the Parade with the Chief Justice. The heat was oppressive and His Excellency retired early – to be awakened at dawn with the horrifying news that the roof of the powder magazine had been broached, the door unfastened from within, and 100 kegs of gunpowder stolen.

Afterwards it appeared they had been rolled across the grass and down the hill to Tobacco Bay where Somerset Henry had collected whaleboats under charge of a Captain

---

The Sessions House stands on the highest eminence of the City of Hamilton. The large chamber in its upper storey is reserved for the use of the House of Assembly; the Supreme Court holds its sessions below. The original building was an unpretentious two-storey edifice which was not ready when the Seat of Government was transferred to the town of Hamilton (formerly Crow Lane) in January 1815. Consequently the members met till 1818 in the small Town Hall on corner of Front and Court Streets (which became the City Hall in 1897 and now houses the Department of Tourism). Many ornate additions have been made to the Sessions House since 1818, including the terra cotta facing and the clock tower which commemorates Queen Victoria's Jubilee (1887).

Morgan, and had even supplied more gunpowder on his own account to be sailed out to the frigate. (Tobacco Bay lies half a mile westward of the Fort St Catherine pictured on our cover.)

When Bruere awoke to the news on the 15th August, he was distraught with horror. His own son was an officer in General Thomas Gage's army — and the other had been killed at Bunker. His whole loyalty — his whole duty — was to the Crown. If he had not been fiercly angry at this betrayal, he would have been less than human; yet, on the strength of it, historians have described him as 'bad-tempered'! At the moment of discovery, with the *Lady Catherine* still in sight, he issued a hasty proclamation: 'Save your country from ruin which may hereafter happen! The powder stole out of the magazine late last night cannot be carried far as the wind is so light. A great Reward will be given to any person that can make a proper discovery before the magistrates.'

This powder is reputed to have been used to compel British troops to evacuate Boston 17th March 1776.

Bruere made frantic efforts to obtain a sloop to send despatches to General Gage in Boston — but suddenly and unaccountably, none was to be found fit to sail! The Assembly met on the 16th and put a good face on things by voting a Reward of £100 to any persons who could find the perpetrators. To this Bruere offered additional Reward and a free pardon for any who would turn King's evidence. Neither was ever claimed. The Continental Congress lifted the embargo against provisions for Bermuda, and opportunities were made to ship salt to the Americans. To those who had won their way it was a matter of sheer survival.

In those days of slow communication, George Washington was unaware of the successful mid-August gunpowder steal when on 6th September 1775 he penned a lengthy letter 'to the Inhabitants of the Islands of Bermuda' from Camp Cambridge three miles from Boston, in which he begged for a

---

Blockade-runners in St George's Harbour, American Civil War (1861-65). St George's was the port of transhipment for blockade-runners laden with cargoes of war-materials from England bound for ports of the Confederate States and returning thence with cotton. The ancient town was crammed with seccessionists, spies, adventurers, money and liquor! To Bermuda, as a colony, no benefit accrued from the trade. (*Bermuda News Bureau photo*)

supply of gunpowder since 'we are informed there is a very large magazine on your Island under a very feeble guard,' – and promising that 'the whole power and exertion of my influence will be made with the honourable Continental Congress that your Island may not only be supplied with provisions, but experience every mark of affection and friendship which the grateful citizens of a free country can bestow on its bretheren and benefactors.' Captain Abraham Whipple at Rhode Island was entrusted with this mission, but as events turned out the powder was already long gone when he arrived and the letter was never presented in Bermuda. (Nor, incidentally, was George Washington himself ever in Bermuda, despite legends to the contrary.)

Ironically, the marks 'of affection and friendship' several times included plans for the seizure of the islands. These were projected in 1776 by Silas Deane, a secret agent of the Continental Congress, and by Lafayette in 1779 and 1780 who suggested he would '*toucher à la Bermuda et y establier le parti de la libertie.*' And in the Treaty of Commerce between France and America signed 6th February 1778, plans were alluded to for the capture of Bermuda by the American navy with the stipulation that these islands, if conquered, should be allocated to America, and the West Indian Islands to France.

The American Continental Navy had been founded in October 1775; when first it carried the struggle for independence to sea, some 2000 privateers, some of them Bermuda-built, carried letters of marque. Originally these privateers had become expert when preying upon Britain's enemies. Now the tide flowed the other way, and the new Continental Navy, eager for major action, undertook tasks beyond the range of mere privateers – and no longer against Britain's foes. The new navy consisted of some 27 small men-of-war few of which survived the Revolutionary War. In the event, quite a number of vessels were eventually captured by privateers based on Bermuda and condemned here. Bermuda remained under the British flag and a large proportion of Bermudians were stedfast in their allegiance to the Crown. At the coming of peace in 1783, the US Navy dissolved, to be resuscitated in April, 1798, with the establishment of the Navy Department.

At the time of the American Revolutionary War Bermuda's population numbered some 10,000 of whom just over half were descendants of the original British settlers, the remainder descendants of imported Negroes. By this time, the British stock in American colonies had increased to three millions. When the Continental Congress was ready to consider Bermuda's plea for continued bartering of supplies, the population figures of the islands were prudently raised to 15,000!

Most of the islanders were not in favour at first of privateering against American ships as they did not want to cut off their own supplies, but Governor George James Bruere and, in his turn, his son, George Bruere, urged them to destroy the commerce of those fighting against England and to abandon illicit trade with them. Actually it was the loyalists from America who had taken refuge in Bermuda, notably Bridger Goodrich, from New Jersey, who cruised so successfully against the King's enemies that in one winter he captured and brought in 36 vessels as prizes. Later, privateering became popular among the Bermudians themselves and they became committed to a more loyal course.

George Bascome, that clever St George's lawyer, was afterwards to declare 'poor little Bermuda observed a strict neutrality,' though this was far from being the case. While old Colonel Tucker, despatched to London as the Colony's agent from 1779-1784, also protested loyalty to a rather disinterested Colonial office, but, ironically, changed his own wavering point of view for an imperialistic one! But when, in 1786, the staunchly loyal party in Bermuda raised a committee of enquiry into the still-rankling question as to the gunpowder theft, producing some evidence for the Council and House of Assembly, such an investstigation was dismissed as 'frivolous'. The small gunpowder magazine, centre of this story, was long since razed to the ground; its remains lie beneath the hill leading down to Tobacco Bay. The old restored fort now labelled 'Gunpowder Cavern' had nothing whatever to do with this incident and was not used as a gunpowder depository till 100 years later.

This terrible century in Bermuda saw one of the periodic scourges of smallpox in so virulent a form that 300 people died in Hern Bay alone in 1780. And in October of that year, a hurricane that is considered by far the most terrible tropical storm of modern times – 'the Great Hurricane' – struck the islands, driving 50 ships ashore, blowing houses down and uprooting the cedars. St George's town, which bore the brunt, by now consisted of a little over a hundred stone houses and four small shops in which simple clothing and ships' chandlery fought for pride of place with general merchandise. Near famine followed on the heels of the hurricane . . . much of the eighteenth century had been a story of hard times, hurricanes, epidemics, disaster. But at least we can associate the 1790s with the introduction of the oleander from South Carolina. To-day it would be hard to picture the Bermuda landscape without these riotously-blossoming shrubs.

After the Revolutionary War was over, with the peace signed at Versailles in 1783 acknowledging the independence of the United States of America, American ships were still brought in to St George's as prizes because, though professedly neutrals, they were trading with France with whom Britain was at war. Wealth began flowing through the island from this privateering – a sport as rewarding as, and slightly more legal than, the earlier piracy and wrecking. Sea captains began building substantial houses throughout the countryside from the proceeds of these exploits; shipowners after depressing struggles again found much employment in the carrying-trade between US ports, Canada, the West Indies. And forty new vessels were built of the indigenous cedar in one year alone, 1789. But the local population had declined steeply immediately after the war, since it not only took some time to recover the carrying-trade but – a staggering blow – Turk's Island, so long a Bermuda dependency and centre of the salt trade was finally lost to the Bahamas in 1799.

A survey of Bermuda was prepared by a Select Committee of the House of Assembly (probably between 1783 – 1808): this contained lists of freeholders in every parish, the person in possession, acreage, value of land, of timber, of houses and other improvements. It was 120 years since Norwood's second survey, and for the myriads of people to-day who are seeking genealogical material, these surveys are of inestimable value.*

Another definite step forward was the arrival from London of Joseph Stockdale with his wife and daughters, bringing the island's first printing press and starting a newspaper at St George's in January 1784. '*The Bermuda Gazette and Weekly Advertiser* forerunner of the present daily *Royal Gazette* was issued from a house in the lane NW of St Peter's Church, still called Printer's Alley in his memory. In the basement of the St George's Historical Society, a printing press of that period

(* Survey circa 1783-1802, pub. Bermuda Historical Quarterly 1946).

is on display. The early issues carry references to his attempts at setting up mail delivery. His newspaper flourished despite the fact that there were less than 6,000 white people in Bermuda and not all of those were literate. At his death in 1803, his daughters carried on the newspaper, one of them marrying the printer. That first issue of all carries the terms of the treaty between the new United States of America and Great Britain.

St George's was still the centre of activity. The only link between that island and the main, was the old horse-ferry at Ferry Point and Coney Island. There was, indeed, a village springing up around Crow Lane in Pembroke Parish; this would be called Hamilton in honour of the governor from 1788 to 1794, since it was incorporated as a town the year before he left office.

All the doings of the French Revolutionary Wars began to be reflected in the new local newspaper and made Bermudians cognisant of the need to be alert to the chances of invasion and their duties to support the local Militia, to whom detailed instructions were issued in May 1793. A sloop and a gunboat represented Bermuda's own small navy. Consequent on all these alarms, Admiral Sir George Murray began turning Bermuda into an important naval establishment by using it as a resort for ships of war, raising a flotilla of local vessels at St George's, and recommending the home government to establish a Naval Dockyard at the extreme western undeveloped end of the group. In October 1795, the Legislature gave its support to this proposal, Ireland Island was selected and in 1809 the Imperial Government purchased that island, and the tremendous labour of building the Dockyard was commenced the following year. This began a new era in Bermuda, English taxpayers' money flowed into the islands and there was local employment in jobs there for many years after the Dockyard was completed.

For the actual construction work, artificers were sent out from England to direct slave labour and later the naval authorities advocated the use of convicts as labourers on the fortifications and other Imperial works. More than 1,600 of these men were eventually housed in hulks off St George's, off Ireland Island and in buildings on Boaz Island. More than 9,000 of them served part of their sentence here before the system of penal exile was abolished in March 1863. Unlike Australia, where the convicts were allowed to settle, none of the men was discharged in the islands so that it never became a convict settlement as such. The one strange exception was that of a man called William Facey, who had been condemned for a boyish prank of stealing one of his father's horses, and who not only was allowed to remain after his sentence was served but became an outstanding and responsible citizen. He ran a livery stable in Bermuda and the first regular overland communication (by coach) between Hamilton and St George's in the 1840s, which also carried the mails.

Of the 9,000 convicts who served part of their prison sentence at Bermuda over 2,000 left their bones here, – most of them victims of yellow fever epidemics. The Naval Cemetery at Ireland Island had to be enlarged several times, convicts and others being buried there till 1849, after which Watford Island was used till 1854 when permission was asked of the Admiralty to bury yellow fever patients on Long Island in the Great Sound. These pathetic isolated cemeteries still bear witness to the terrible scourge of yellow fever of which there was so much ignorant fear that to touch the dust above a grave was supposed to be dangerous. Bermuda was swept by it at least nine times during the nineteenth century.

It is difficult now to realise that as late as up to the time of the naval occupancy in the early nineteenth century there were no roads and but a few inhabitants on Ireland Island; it was a jungle of cedar and sage, over-run by wild swine, and the few houses were still wooden, thatched with palmetto, long after houses of the local lime-stone were usual in the rest of the colony. From 1809 the construction of a vast complexity of buildings went steadily on to standard English Admiralty plans. The name of the island itself had doubtless been derived from that of a John Ireland whose name appears on MSS. of 'affaires from Somersett' in the 1620s.

At the beginning of this nineteenth century with Union of Ireland and Great Britain effected, the Union Jack as it now exists was displayed in Bermuda. To-day, at such places as Gates Fort, the Stuart flag, combining the crosses of St George and St Andrew, is flown to emphasize their early history.

Thomas Moore, that sentimental Irishman, is always remembered as the true poet of Bermuda though he spent but three and a half months here, January to April 1804, in the surprisingly incongruous job of Registrar to the Court of Vice-Admiralty. But such poems as –

But bless the little fairy isle!
How sweetly, after all our ills,
We saw the dewy morning smile
Serenly o'er its fragrant hills, —
Oh! could you view the scenery dear,
That now beneath my window lies,
You'd think that Nature lavished here
Her purest wave, her softest skies,
To make a heaven for love to sigh in,
For bards to live and saints to die in!

endear him to all Bermudians.

Unfortunately, tourist resorts like Bermuda are apt to flavour stories of the past to suit visitors; the web of extravaganza woven around Tom Moore's visit is patently absurd. He was twenty-four years of age, a writer of pleasingly amorous verse, and irresistible in society. He was entertained by Admiral Mitchell in Cumberland Lane (now Old Maid's Lane) St George's, next to the Marshall of the Vice-Admiralty Court, William Tucker and his bride of seven months, Hester Louise, barely 17 years of age. At their later home, Rose Hill, (on whose site the St George Hotel was later built) she eventually bore her husband a quiver-full of children and died young. Undoubtedly Tom Moore was also entertained by them, just as he was at Walsingham, the home of the Hon. Samuel Trott, where he immortalized a calabash tree (still standing in the grounds.) This house is now advertised as 'Tom Moore's' — a misnomer which leads to underestimation of its age. Charming Walsingham is well worth a visit as one of the very few houses remaining from the seventeenth century. An earlier Samuel Trott, kinsman of the Earl of Warwick, erected it circa 1665 partly of lath and plaster. Moore's visit was a brief but memorable incident 140 years later.

Moore wrote thirteen romantic song-poems while in St George's. Always fond of classical allusions, he addressed some of them 'To Nea' — 'Neaera' being the synonym for 'sweetheart' in Horace, Virgil and Tibullus. But in his letters home of the same period he is declaring himself wholly heart-free and always insisted that 'Nea' was merely a poet's conception of what a woman should be, an idealised blend of perfections. One well-known Ode immortalized the sight of a young woman embracing a baby: 'On seeing an infant in Nea's arms,' 'the first ambrosial child of bliss.' Unfortunately, twenty-five years later, a young Englishwoman, Susette

Harriet Lloyd, visiting Bermuda, wrote a book in which she described Hester Louise Tucker dead long before, as the one and only 'Nea'; her eldest son, by then the Reverend Richard Tudor Tucker, as 'the first ambrosial child of bliss' – and much other consequent nonsense. The fact is that Richard Tudor Tucker was born in July 1805, and Tom Moore, disgruntled with his Bermuda job, had left forever in April of 1804 . . . The whole romantic myth was as insubstantial as a dream!

Although Moore had 'a generous contempt for money' his position as Registrar was impracticable as at that time it earned a mere pittance. Unfortunately for him, before sailing he placed his Bermuda affairs in the hands of a local deputy who embezzled £6,000 for which Moore was held responsible since he nominally retained the post till 1844. Ultimately a compromise was effected on this figure but in the meantime poor Tom Moore fled to Italy with Lord John Russell to avoid arrest in England . . . His lovely descriptions of Bermuda scenery are worth remembering.

During most of the period from May 1803 to June 1812, the British Empire was standing out against the tyranny of one man intent on European and ultimately world, domination. Napoleon Buonaparte. An odd reminder of his world threat is found on the part of St George's Island least visited to-day, (yet once, when the Old Ferry ran from Ferry Point via Coney to the Main, as the only link with the remainder of the Island Group, the route followed by hundreds of people every week in the year,) – the western extremity of St George's island. For here, alone and solitary and somehow incongruous, stands a Martello Tower dating from 1823, exactly similar to those built around English and Channel Island Coasts to withstand invaders. Nearby is an ancient fort from early colonial days.

Meanwhile, since England was straining every nerve to preserve world freedom, she regarded it as a stab in the back when the United States, taking advantage of her pre-occupation in the struggle with France, declared war on England 18th June 1812. This declaration of war was seen as a mere pretext for the United States to attempt to seize Canada while England was heavily involved elsewhere.

But it is the repercussions in Bermuda with which we have to deal – If, thirty-seven years earlier, Bermudians had been confused and divided during the American Revolutionary War, the new war found them standing firmly with the

Mother Country, despite the great hardships the war brought. It also sparked off the last revival of privateering the islands were to know. The Royal Navy was bringing in a succession of prizes to crowded St George's Harbour and Bermuda's swift cedar privateers proudly added to that number. The enemy captured 40 Bermuda vessels valued at £200,000 but, on the other hand, the close of the war found the islanders in possession of 43 foreign-built ships which, added to their own depleted tonnage, gave them a merchant marine of more than 70 vessels.

This war provided one of the occasions when once more the Franco-American Alliance laid plans for the capture of Bermuda. An American fleet was assembled off New York for the purpose of seizing these islands. A casting vote at the Council of the United States changed the order for the squadron to that of attacking instead a merchant-ship fleet homeward bound for England from the West Indies.

At first, in the naval actions which took place in the autumn of 1812 and spring of 1813, the Americans were uniformly successful. By June 1813, there was a swing of the pendulum when HMS *Shannon* (38 guns) captured the *Chesapeake* (44 guns) off Boston Light in a decisive engagement lasting only 15 minutes. The commander of *Chesapeake*, James Lawrence, who was mortally wounded, was related to the Cox family of Bermuda, and another officer was William Cox of the same outstanding clan and son of a Bermudian who had settled in America. To continue the Bermuda connection: the following year Thomas Tudor Tucker, born at the Tucker House on Water Street, St George's, (and named for his uncle, the Treasurer of the United States) commanded HMS *Cherub* in an engagement off Valparaiso when the USS *Essex* was captured.

There were many actions with losses and successes on both sides of which news was always anxiously awaited in the islands. And then, early in 1814, six British frigates arrived bringing the 7th Fusiliers and three other regiments. Amidst intense local excitement a brigade of troops disembarked near little Devonshire Dock on the north shore of Devonshire Parish. Legend relates that the local lassies danced on the green sward with the men who came ashore. Impatiently they waited here two whole weeks for the wind to shift so that the fleet could negotiate the usual Narrows en route for the open sea, but a prolonged succession of S E winds made it impossible. So the decision was made; they risked the deadly

North Rock Passage. This intricate and tortuous channel through nine miles of needle-like reefs had never before been attempted except by a small frigate. A Bermudian, J.N. Hayward, offered to pilot the fleet out, the extreme clarity of the water enabling him to avoid the reefs.

A young major of 27, Harry Smith, later to become Lieutenant General Sir Harry Smith and a close friend of the Duke of Wellington, was in HMS *Royal Oak* and wrote at length of the thrilling adventure of that bold experiment on the way to the sack and burning of Washington, plans for which had been laid at Mount Wyndham leased by the British Admiralty from 1812 — 1818 for use as Admiralty House.

Nowadays it is fashionable to write of such expeditions and the destruction of the United States capital as acts of vandalism. But it was a bold and courageous act of war and, though most histories neglect to relate what had led up to it, it was in fact retaliation for the American looting of York (now Toronto.) It was a combined operation by Sir George Cockburn afloat and Major-General Robert Ross — who did not survive the expedition — ashore.

On 3rd September 1814, the general order issued by Vice-Admiral Alexander Cochrane 'after the successful expedition up the Chesapeake to the Capital of the US' was published in the Bermuda Gazette in full. 'Our army has beaten that of the enemy double their number, captured their cannon and entered the City of Washington in triumph. The capital, the palace of the President, the military arsenal, the naval yard, . . . the Treasury, the War Offices and all the Public Buildings have all been destroyed.' Vice-Admiral Cochrane also referred to waiting in the Chesapeake for the arrival of Rear-Admiral Malcolm with the expedition from Bermuda.

A heart-warming reminder of the War of 1812 lies in the memorial service held in May of each year in the old graveyard of St Peter's Church, St George's. Here, Bermudians and Americans alike gather to honour the memory of Richard Sutherland Dale, U S N. It all happened over 150 years ago in the little town that had just ceased to be the capital, he was only a boy, just out of his teens, he was an enemy alien, yet we honour him to-day just as St Georgians mourned him those many years ago. His grave lies just north of the choir door at ancient St Peter's Church. The inscription on the old tomb runs:

In memory of
Richard Sutherland Dale
eldest son of Commodore Richard Dale of Philadelphia in the US of America, a midshipman in the US Navy.
He departed this life at St George's, Bermuda, on the 22nd day of February, AD, 1815, aged 20 years, 1 month and 17 days. He lost his right leg in an engagement between the US Frigate President and a squadron of His Britannic Majesty's ships of war on 15th January AD, 1815.
His confinement caused a severe complaint in his back which in a short time terminated his life. This stone records the tribute of his parents' gratitude to those inhabitants of St George's whose generous and tender sympathy prompted the kindest attentions to their son while living and honoured him when dead.

The *President* had been sailed into St George's Harbour by a prize crew and the wounded brought ashore to be tended – young Dale to Stennett's Hotel on King's Square (where the Bank of Bermuda now stands) and his shattered leg amputated. 'The Bermuda Gazette and Weekly Advertiser' of Saturday 25 February 1815 noted that he had 'fallen a victim to this un-natural war.'

Another, more controversial incident, is remembered concerning this same frigate under Commodore Stephen Decatur's command. The American vessel was taken, as we have seen, after a running battle of 6 or 7 hours off Long Island by Captain Hope of HMS *Endymion*. Decatur, with some of his officers and men, was transferred to *Emdymion* and 90 British officers and men were put on board *President* with orders to take her into Bermuda. How many Americans were left in *President* could not at once be determined since all ship's books and papers had been jettisoned. The ships ran into a gale which separated them during the passage south and it was only by a fortunate accident that 68 Americans who had been concealed on board *President* with the hope of retaking her by surprise, were discovered.

Edmund Ward, editor of *The Royal Gazette* and Government Printer at Bermuda from 1809 mentioned this attempt as a 'treacherous surprise' in the next issue of his paper. He was at once directed by the Governor, Sir James Cockburn, to contradict the story on his assurance that it was false. After doing so, Ward discovered that he had been misled into making his retraction and thereupon repeated his original assertions. Although the Hon. Lieut. Perceval, who had been on board the captured *President*, supported the editor's statement, the Governor again required retraction and, when it was not forthcoming, deprived Ward of his commission as King's Printer.

The Vice-Admiralty Court was busy over these critical years and the position of King's Advocate, as well as that of Attorney-General of Bermuda, was filled by a brilliant young man still in his twenties: this was Francis Forbes, the son of Dr Francis Forbes and grandson of Dr George Forbes both of whom had rendered conspicuous service during the terrible small-pox epidemics of the eighteenth century. It had been a fortunate day for Bermuda when this outstanding Scottish family settled in the islands; and now, this youngest scion was to carry on the tradition. After the War of 1812 he became Chief Justice of Newfoundland, then of New South Wales, Australia, and was knighted for his services. Since he had been born, brought up and schooled in St George's, he is remembered with pride as one of Bermuda's most outstanding sons.

7

Great Social and Economic Changes

When the War of 1812 was over, Bermuda was plunged into a century not only of great development but of unprecedented social and economic change. The war had helped to underline the island's strategic importance, and the Imperial Government now pressed ahead with Dockyard construction on Ireland Island which, as we have seen, had been acquired in 1809 with the idea of establishing a naval depot. Construction was to continue till at least 1874, affecting the whole development of the islands and gradually turning them into the Gibraltar of the West. Local slave labour soon proved too sluggish for such arduous tasks. Soon Bermudians became accustomed to the sight of prison hulks moored off the coasts housing the new convict labour; the first to arrive, *The Antelope*, was established in the Government Dockyard in 1824. Three others soon joined her, the *Dromedary*, *Coromandel*, and *Weymouth*, lodging altogether an average of 1,200–1,400 convicts. Many famous British ships ended their days in this sombre fashion as prison hulks in different parts of the world. Chaplains from England accompanied the prisoners and a detachment of Royal Marines, 393 strong with twenty officers, were sent out to Bermuda to act as guards and wardens.

Eventually, three of the four islands that compose Sandys Parish, Watford, Boaz and Ireland Island, all became naval property, as did some of the islands in the Great Sound. This expansion started in 1848 when the overcrowding in the hulks became intolerable.

Very varying accounts have been written as to the conditions under which the convicts laboured. A warden, Stephen Norton, stated that they had beef four times a week, pork three, grog, a school, and church services every morning. They were paid threepence a day for their work and were well treated. Perhaps it was inevitable that, writing from the viewpoint of the twentieth century, Paymaster Lieut. W. E. Brockman, RN, in his *Bermuda, the Growth of a Naval Base*, should have painted the scene in very different colours:

'Living conditions in the hulks must have been incredible'. And we know that the mid-nineteenth century governor, Captain Charles Elliott, bombarded the Colonial Office with requests to ameliorate conditions of servitude.

In addition to the one prisoner, William Facey, released in Bermuda as already mentioned, the most famous occupant of the Bermuda hulks was John Mitchell, the Irishman who had been convicted of 'treason-felony' for his articles in the *United Irishman* and sentenced to fourteen years transportation. His *Jail Journal* describes the men on the hulks — English and Irish — who lay so far away from central authority; it was first published in the New York newspaper *The Citizen* from 14 January to 19 August 1854 . . . The whole system of Penal Exile was abolished in 1863.

Money was poured into all the new projects (which would provide Bermudians with employment right into the twentieth century) and solid buildings like Casemates were well and truly built to last, since the money all came from English taxpayers' pockets — a condition which could not be expected to last for ever, as was warned by Colonel F. Whittingham in his *Bermuda, a fortress, a colony and a prison* written anonymously after an eighteen months tour of duty in Bermuda 1855–6. Most of the money was necessarily spent but there was at least one case of monstrous absurdity — in 1823 the commissioner then in charge of the Dockyard spent some £56,000 on building Commissioner's House on Ireland Island. It was used for its purpose for ten years only and still stands as a monument to folly, and has had a chequered career. A great ugly two-storey building it contained imported marble fireplaces, mahogany panelling, marble baths, an eleven-stalled stable and two coach-houses — all this 'on an island only a mile long and unapproachable save by boat' as Lord Dundonald vehemently protested.

Bermuda was headquarters of the America and West Indies Squadron but at first no permanent residences were set aside as Admiralty House. However, in 1816, a typical old Bermuda homestead in NW Pembroke, overlooking the dockyard to the westward, was set aside at Clarence Hill for the Naval Commander-in-Chief and served as Admiralty House till 1956. At that time, Her Majesty's Government withdrew the Commander-in-Chief of the America and West Indies Station from Bermuda which then became headquarters of the West Indies Station under a Commodore.

But to return to great local changes early in the

1800s — nothing affected parochial feelings more than the transfer of the capital from the old town, St George's, to the new central town, Hamilton, in January 1815. It had been inevitable for some time with the spread of people westward, and with so many ships slipping in and evading customs, that the little town on Hamilton Harbour which had been incorporated on 29 June 1793, (with a seal showing a sailing-ship next a wharf, a warehouse nearby and the motto *Sparsa Collegit*) would, by its very position make a more convenient capital. Its motto denoted its purpose as a trading depot and it had been named for the governor at the time of incorporation, Henry Hamilton.

Naturally, St Georgians and their members in the House of Assembly strenuously opposed this move from the ancient town where all Bermuda's early history had been enacted. What better Sessions House, they must have asked, could there be in the new town of Hamilton to compare with the solid State House in St George's, home of the legislature for nearly 200 years? What more suitable site for a Government House than that behind its imposing pillars built north of the old town in 1722 — the culmination of a series of less pretentious houses? And what church could be used as suitable for State Services as St Peter's where the first parliament had met in 1620?

Those pillars still stand though the meagre remains of that Government House to-day form St George's Rectory; the State House still dominates its little hillock to the east of the town and is ceremoniously rented for a peppercorn a year by the Freemasons; the Church, the early forts around the coasts, the old houses behind their high walls — all are so redolent of the past that one would hardly be surprised if, in those narrow unchanged alleyways, the sedan chair of Governor Popple suddenly materialized.

But despite the protests of the four members of the House from the former capital, (Messrs Hayward, John Musson, William Tucker and H. Todd,) by 23rd January 1815, Parliament, the Courts, and all public offices had been moved by sea to Hamilton, and Government House to a country manor north of the town designated Mount Langton by the governor, Sir James Cockburn, after his Berwickshire estate. The present stately Government House, built slightly to the east of this original modest home, was not finished till 1892. In the meantime, every succeeding governor contributed ornamental plantings, such as bougainvillea, to the grounds.

Not that the Sessions House, so conspicuous now on the highest eminence within the boundaries of Hamilton was ready for the transfer. The original building was a simple two-storey edifice. The sum of ten thousand pounds had been granted in 1814 to provide accommodation for the public bodies of the islands including a Sessions House for the Assembly. As the Journals of the House of Assembly show, this was not ready by the early 1820s; so the members had been meeting, first in the Town Hall (on the corner of Front and Court Streets) from 23rd January 1815, and later, circa 1817 in a ground floor room at the Court House shared with the Supreme Court — above which they would eventually have their Chamber.

The Town Hall was a simple rectangular building erected in 1791 as the Customs House Warehouse. It became the City Hall in 1897 when Hamilton attained that status and so remained until the present City Hall was built. The Department of Tourism now uses it as its headquarters.

The present consequential appearance of the Sessions House has been gradually attained. The Italianesque style and terra cotta facings and the Clock Tower were additions to commemorate Queen Victoria's Jubilee in 1887 and the Diamond Jubilee ten years later. The Supreme Court meets in the large room on the ground floor while the Chamber in which the House of Assembly meets is upstairs, has galleries

---

(*above*) Fort Hamilton. As the main settlements of the islands were extending westward and the threat came from the neighbouring continent, the Defence Act of 1865 led to the expropriation of land throughout the colony for defence purposes. A large slice of Devonshire was taken to form Prospect Camp and its three forts: Fort Prospect, Fort Langton and Fort Hamilton. Later Fort Hamilton was used as headquarters of the Bermuda Volunteer Rifle Corps but has now been turned into a worthwhile tourist attraction with views across Hamilton Harbour, White's Island and the shores of Paget and Warwick.

(*below*) The Unfinished Church, St George's. On 21st January 1874, the foundation stone of this new church in St George's was laid by Bishop Feild. It had been started by a set of parishioners who considered the old church beyond repair, but fortunately St Peter's was eventually saved and it was the new church that was allowed to decay into this picturesque ruin. (*Bermuda News Bureau photos*)

for visitors, and follows the arrangement of the House of Commons. The Speaker's Chair and the Members' seats and desks are constructed in English oak. On the wall behind the Speaker's Chair hangs the Royal coat of arms above the Bermuda coat of arms. On either side of these are contemporary portraits of King George III and Queen Charlotte. On the side walls of the Chamber are portraits of Speakers of the House.

Another change that commenced early in the nineteenth century was the recognition (after the War of 1812-15 was over) that the United States of America should have an accredited agent in Bermuda. So it was that in August 1818 William R. Higinbothom of Maryland, already a resident of St George's for the previous ten years, received his appointment from President James Monroe and the US Secretary of State, John Quincy Adams, to become the First Consular Officer of the United States in Bermuda. His credentials were presented to the governor, Sir James Cockburn, with the concurrence of the British Minister in Washington, Sir Charles Bagot. Although he did the work of a consul till his death in 1832, he was merely regarded locally as Commercial Agent for the USA. It remained for his successor to be officially commissioned as Consul in 1838. However, the State Department, Washington, regards the date of establishment of Bermuda Consulate as 1818, the Consular Office being in St George's

---

(*left*) Gibbs' Hill Lighthouse, Southampton. Bermuda's first lighthouse stands some 362 feet above sea level on a hill 246 feet high. The many shipwrecks around Bermuda's coasts had long made its necessity evident and its light was first displayed 1st May 1846. Mr (later Sir) George Grove was the English Civil Engineer who, at the age of 26, erected the first two cast-iron lighthouses in the world, of which this was one, the cast iron being sent out from London in plates. While in Bermuda he also designed two churches; Trinity Church on whose site the Cathedral now stands, and the newer church in Devonshire Parish. In May 1965 the light was converted to electrical power.

(*right*) Somerset Bridge spans the narrow channel between the Main Island of the group and Somerset Island where there has been a bridge from the earliest times. The middle planks have to be raised to allow passage of the tip of a sail-boat mast — so little Somerset Bridge is described as the world's smallest drawbridge, and is certainly one of the most picturesque. (*Bermuda News Bureau photos*)

till May 1872 and in Hamilton since that date. Since 1951, the position has been that of Consul-General. The appointment is of great moment in Bermuda where there is much mingling of American residents and tourists with English and Bermudians at every level, social and official.

Another substantial building that was soon to improve the appearance of Front Street, Hamilton, is the dignified two-storey structure of native limestone, standing in well-kept grounds and to-day known as the Secretariat, though originally designated The Public Buildings. Its cornerstone was laid in 1833 and it was completed three years later. Here His Excellency prorogues and convenes the sessions of Parliament in colourful ceremonies. (Holding pride of place among the fascinating relics of the past is an ancient chair used by Captain Josias Forster, three times governor of Bermuda between 1642 and 1658. Crudely carved across the top section are the words: 'Cap Josias Forstore Govornor of the Sumer Islands Anno 1642.')

It was in a small room in this building that the Bermuda Library (since 1916 housed at Par-la-Ville on Queen St) was started in 1839 by a splendid and exceptional governor, Sir William Reid. Shocked at finding the couple of ploughs long ago imported by Gov. George James Bruere were still the only ones in use, he imported all kinds of agricultural implements; he was a Fellow of the Royal Society for his publication *The Law of Storms*, part of the fruit of his meteorological labours in Barbados where he had been sent to rehabilitate the Barbadians after the catastrophic hurricane of 1831; he continued his studies of tropical storms in Bermuda and aided every form of scientific inquiry and education; he was instrumental in getting Bermuda's first – and long overdue – lighthouse erected on Gibbs Hill by forwarding to HM Government a map of thirty-nine recent wrecks around the coast drawn up by the Pilot Commissioner, Daniel Robert Tucker. Gibbs' Hill Lighthouse first showed its beacon 1st May 1846. (St David's Lighthouse was erected in 1879.) Reid was indefatigable in his scientific studies and agricultural pursuits for Bermuda; in the library at Yale University are three volumes of unpublished correspondence between Governor Reid and Mr William C. Redfield, mainly devoted to discussions of the laws that govern storms – subjects in which both writers were experts. Little wonder that the grounds of the Secretariat contain an obelisk to the memory of this 'good governor'.

But the greatest water-shed of social change and one that has left an impress on the world for all time was the Abolition of Slavery Law passed in England on 29th August 1833, making the holding of slaves in any British possession illegal — this at a cost to the Imperial Government of twenty million pounds sterling. Immediately following the official receipt of this news, the Bermuda House of Assembly, as its first motion of 1834, passed its concurring Emancipation Act setting 1st August 1834 as the day on which all slaves in Bermuda should be unconditionally freed. An accompanying Act conferred on the coloured race the rights and privileges, together with the legal pains and penalties, of the white man.

The great Day of Freedom which fell on a Friday, was marked by services in all the Churches, marches, enthusiasm, joy.

The late Archdeacon John Stow, speaking of that great day in St Peter's Church says: 'A service was held in the church, crowded to the doors, in which the remaining slaves — freed that day by the order and at the vast expense of the British Parliament in one of the most altruistic acts of justice ever performed by any nation in history — gathered to give thanks to Almighty God, and to hear a sermon from the Rector explaining their new responsibilities and duties as free and equal citizens.'

The local newspapers of the period reflect the decorum with which the occasion was met by the four thousand bondsmen in the islands. It was to be another thirty years before slavery was abolished in the neighbouring United States of America.

Most great changes in the life of a community take place so gradually they are only realized in retrospect; but this was a great watershed in history. In Bermuda, where the total population in 1833 was 9,195 of whom 4,297 were white and approximately a thousand were free coloured — the sudden emancipation of 4,026 in the following year affected every section of society.

The MS. Registry of Baptisms in St Peter's Church, St George's, shows an eloquent page commencing 24th July 1834 with lists of those baptized, their condition, parents, whether slave or free, and the signature of the Rector, John Lough. After twenty entries for that date a line is drawn right across the page. The next baptism is on 3rd August — and no longer is the standing of the person given — all are free.

(Few visiting old St Peter's to-day are aware of the small

slaves' burial ground to the west of the main churchyard. Some of the graves there are marked, many with merely a first name, others are hardly visible having been flattened by time and the elements.)

The yellow fever epidemic of 1853 would lead to the passage of an act forbidding any more burials in St Peter's churchyard and the Crown vested two acres of the western extremity of the Government park in the rector of St George's, subject to the same conditions as if the ground were a part of the yard of St Peter's. Exactly a hundred and twenty years later it was re-opened for the burial of the assassinated Sir Richard Sharples and his ADC. The fear of yellow fever had long passed.

No such transition as emancipation, however right and inevitable, is easy. As Chief Justice the Hon James Christie Esten remarked in his *Plan for the Instruction of the Emancipated People of Colour of the Bermudas* (pub. in London 1837) 'Happy had it been for these favoured isles — favoured in climate and most attractive in beauty — if the desolating foot of slavery had never stalked the land. As mercy is said to be twice blessed, so slavery is twice cursed — a curse to the master and a curse to the slave.' And he outlined the problem that faced the white artisan class now that the employment of a large number of paid workers became of immediate concern; and foresaw that many white mechanics would have to emigrate leaving a surplus of spinster women in the islands. Indeed, as early as 1674 a law had been passed prohibiting further importation of slaves since employment could not be found for those already here; they increased far more rapidly than the whites who often found it difficult to clothe and feed them.

Archdeacon Aubrey Spencer saw the necessity of their education. He surrendered his glebe rents, and worked tirelessly in the cause of building and equipping school-houses, employing teachers, and getting support from the Society for the Propagation of the Gospel, the Society for the Education of Negroes, and the Society for Promoting Christian Knowledge. In fact, by 1844 there were sixteen schools supported both by colonial grants and by contributions from these societies, in addition to twenty private schools maintained entirely by parents of the pupils.

For many years, Freedom Marches were staged throughout the islands culminating in a Centennial of Emancipation celebrations held on 1st August 1934 from St David's to Sandys.

Canadian visitors to Bermuda frequently enquire as to the Canadian exiles who spent thirteen weeks in the island in 1838. Wolfred Nelson, Bonaventure Viger, Henri Alphonse Gavin, Rodolphe des Rivieres, Robert Shore Milnes Bouchette, Simeon Marchessault, Toussaint Goddu, and Luc Hyacinthe Masson were the leaders of a treasonable revolt in lower Canada which was suppressed by the Canadians themselves. There was no question but that they deserved punishment; where they were lucky was in the fact that Lord Durham, the High Commissioner of Canada, in ordering their banishment to Bermuda, exceeded his authority since only the Imperial Government could say that Bermuda should receive them. The governor, Sir R. S. Chapman, and the Council, therefore allowed them to land when HMS *Vestal* put in on 24th July from Quebec but would not unduly restrict their liberty as long as they remained on parole in the Main Island. A small picture of Exile Cottage, (long since demolished, which stood immediately east of the site to-day occupied by the Bermuda Cathedral,) and of the eight men who were hospitably entertained here, now hangs in the Museum of the Bermuda Historical Society. It was indeed a 'moderate punishment for their high offence' as the local newspaper commented at the time.

Of course it was during this century that the great transition from sail to steam took place. From the October of 1833 when the first steamship, *Marco Bozzaris*, appeared off the coast striking terror and amazement into the observers' hearts through the notable date 1st March 1842 when the first steamer of the Royal Mail Line, the SS *Thames*, arrived en route from Nassau to England, down to the development of steamship communication from 1847 onwards with regular monthly calls from the West Indies Mail SS from Southampton, a new period of prosperity would gradually open up. However, its first effect on the islanders was a resurgence of pride in their own shipbuilding. Spurred by competition from the developing steamship services Bermudians, between 1853 and 1864 built five of their fastest and most beautiful clipper ships: the barque *Sir George F. Seymour*, launched in 1853, the *Koh-I-Nor* and the *Pearl* (252 tons) in 1855, *Cedric* in 1862 and the *Lady Milne* two years later. The barque *Eliza Barss* proudly beat the SS *Canima* in the New York – Bermuda run, Captain Henry Hollis making the trip in three and a half days. The Bermuda names associated with these famous and elegant barques are still household words: Nathaniel T. Butterfield, Nathaniel A. Butterfield, James Henry Trimingham, Henry Mills Stowe, John Joseph Outerbridge, Captain Henry Joseph Watlington, William John Cox, Foster M. Cooper, Joseph Dill, William Smith Hutchings, Captain Henry Hollis, Captain Nathaniel A. Vesey, Captain Edmund G. Young, and Captain Elliott Cooper. As owners, as builders, as masters and captains – or as young sea-farers gaining their first experience – it would be possible to list nearly every Bermuda surname.

All philatelists are interested in the famous – and rare – Perot stamps. The gracious old building still standing behind a huge Rubber Tree on Queen Street was named Par-la-Ville by the family of French Huguenot extraction, Perot, who bought four acres on the fringe of the new town of Hamilton and built this house between 1807 and 1814. William Bennett Perot, son of the original owner, became Postmaster of Hamilton in January 1819. By 1842 an alternate-day penny post was officially started for mails between Hamilton and St George's, the contract to carry them being awarded to the ex-convict from the hulks, William Facey by name, whose career we have already noted. When it appeared that the pennies deposited in the ground-floor box seldom tallied with the number of letters to be cancelled, William Bennett Perot, with advice from his friend the apothecary James Bell Heyl, in 1848 started using his cancellation stamp with the words 'Hamilton, Bermuda,' to make whole sheets of stamps on which he inserted 'one penny,' and his signature, W. B. Perot. These hand-made stamps 1848-56 are now worth thousands of pounds apiece. The small Perot Post Office in the grounds of Par-la-Ville was built later than the main house and has reverted to its former use though for many years it was a souvenir shop.

The famous Rubber Tree was planted by William Bennett Perot in 1847. The main house now contains the museum of the Bermuda Historical Society; the Bermuda Library (founded by Governor Reid in 1839 at the Secretariat), with a large Bermudiana section with local newspapers 1784 to to-day; and the Bermuda Archives. The grounds, famous for citrus in Perot's time, are still extremely beautiful.

Oleanders – introduced from South Carolina in 1790 – hibiscus, Royal Poincianas and many other imported plants and trees lend brilliance and colour to Bermuda. But none seems of more local significance than the chance introduction of what is now known as the Bermuda Easter

Lily whose production was to become an important export industry each spring. A botanical water-colour drawing of a specimen sketched here bears the date 12th April 1856. The first bulbs were brought by a missionary from Japan whose ship, en route to England, put into St George's in distress. The lily industry has gone through many vicissitudes but it remains one of the island's most beautiful products and large shipments of buds and bulbs are supplied to the USA, and Canada. The fields of flowers at Easter-tide are a joy to behold, and the churches are heavy with their scent.

8
The American Civil War and Aftermath

If you open the *Royal Gazette* extra of 3rd July 1861, you will come across Queen Victoria's Proclamation of Neutrality. Date-lined 13th May, 1861, one month after the outbreak of the American Civil War – or War of the Secession – it absolutely prohibited 'all British subjects from taking part, or participating in any way whatsoever, either by land or sea, in the existing hostilities between the United States and the Confederate States.' Despite this wise royal edict, the impact of the four-year war changed the whole pattern of life in Bermuda, bringing violence, excitement and a great wave of false prosperity that nearly engulfed her.

At first it seemed simply a case of the Southern States wanting to leave the Union (whose oppresive rule appeared to them to spell ruination for their way of life,) and the Northerners' determination to compel them to remain within it. Eventually, as a result of the war, slavery was abolished in the United States; but to Bermudians, who had seen slavery abolished throughout the British Empire many years before and her own slaves freed, this was not at first the point at issue.

Their sympathies being with the Southern States because of long connection, friendship and tradition, commerce and blood ties, Bermudians threw all their energies into helping the Confederate cause by running the Federal blockade. In addition this was big business.

Till the Southern States seceded, the little colony had only been known as a British military outpost, with a limited trade, rather poverty-stricken inhabitants and scant communication with the outside world.

The mighty political contest in the United States that was to place Abraham Lincoln in the White House, must have appeared a far cry from Bermudian concerns.

But now, the foundation of the Confederacy was laid; Sumter fell; on 19th April 1861, the President proclaimed a blockade of the Southern States from South Carolina to Texas – soon extended to include Virginia and North

Carolina. By September, the United States government became aware that the Bermuda Islands were horribly well-situated as a base for blockade-runners.

Soon they were supplying the South with food and munitions and bringing back bales of cotton for trans-shipment to England. That sleepy little town, St George's — hardly more than a village, and accustomed for the last forty-six years to being of secondary importance and no longer the centre of island affairs — suddenly found its harbour crowded with blockade runners and its narrow alleyways almost impossible to negotiate. Spies, adventurers, secessionists, captains and crews from the ports of many countries shouldered each other in the packed narrow streets. Money flowed like water and the grog shops did a roaring trade since for each trip on which they successfully eluded the Federal cruisers a captain received $5,000.00, the pilot $3,750.00, and others on board compensation in proportion. Hamilton Harbour, though alive with vessels, could not compare with St George's Harbour where twenty or thirty steamers would be moored at a time since it was closer to the open sea, wharves were crowded with cotton bales, merchandise bulged from the warehouses.

A hundred Federal cruisers patrolled about 3,000 miles of the American Coast to pounce on the speedy little craft which, by dodging through with supplies, prolonged the war for months, if not years. Many blockade-runners were seized, sunk, run aground or burned by the US Navy, but some ran the blockade constantly without mishap. The names of Bermuda vessels were on every tongue: *Penguin, Devonshire, Excelsior, Peerless, Bigelow, Princess Royal*, and many another including the famous *Robert E. Lee* which made twenty-six successful runs. Although the Virginia port of Norfolk was almost always in Union hands, President Jefferson Davis must have been delighted with the Bermuda-based runners that managed to slip through the Union cordon to reach Charleston and Wilmington.

One of the oddest episodes of the war as far as Bermuda was concerned was the blockade of St George's for a week in the autumn of 1862. Rear-Admiral Charles Wilkes, USN, flying his flag in the USS *Wachusett* and commanding a small squadron, entered this neutral port, leaving one of his gunboats, the USS *Sonoma* (Capt. Stevens) outside to intercept any blockade-runners. Governor H. St George Ord sent a naval lieutenant to direct Stevens either to come into port or put to sea. Capt. Stevens curtly replied that he only took orders from his superior officers, whereupon some very sharp communications passed between the Governor and Admiral Wilkes, already noted for his outrageous behaviour in what came to be known as 'the Trent Affair'. (This had been the occasion t en months earlier when, as captain of the *San Jacinto*, Wilkes had taken Mason and Slidell from the *Trent*, nearly precipitating war between Great Britain and the United States.) Now Wilkes even went so far as to fire a shot across the bow of the Royal Mail steamer *Merlin* as she was approaching the harbour. 'Thereupon,' as Col. Roger Willock remarks in his invaluable *Bulwark of Empire*, 'the governor lodged an official protest and at once took steps to prevent Federal warships from communicating with Bermuda's shores, thus denying them coal and forcing their return to United States ports. His determination in this instance was particularly commendable, for had he displayed any visible signs of weakness or indecision, the inevitable results might well have proved disastrous to the already strained relations existing between the British and American governments.'

In Dolly's Bay, on the north coast of St David's Island, there lay for a century a mouldering piece of a relic of that war fought over a hundred years ago: the remnant of a Civil War torpedo-raft built in New York and intended to be used, with two others, in the assaults on Charleston. Towed south by the steamer *Ericsson* in 1862, this one broke away during a gale and cost the life of a boy who tried to save it. In 1868, after six years of drifting on the broad Atlantic, currents brought it to Bermuda. It was not until 1872 that another strange chance brought the Captain to Bermuda who had commanded the *Ericsson* on that wild night ten years earlier – and he instantly recognized in this odd derelict his 'shipmate' of long ago – by then a mere skeleton of rusty spikes and rotting wood but still showing a decipherable government number.

The various colourful personalities in Bermuda involved in aiding the cataclysmic struggle on one side or the other have never been forgotten. Diplomatically, the Bermuda Government recognized the Federal Government of the United States and was careful to have no breach of protocol; on the other hand, sympathies definitely lay with the south as evidenced by the enthusiasm shown for the blockade-runners, who legally, were prohibited from carrying arms for defence and had to depend on speed and skill.

John Tory Bourne, a prominent Bermuda merchant whose mother was a descendant of the first Samuel Trott of Walsingham, lived at Rose Hill, St George's (the site on which the St George Hotel was later built.) This was the house once occupied by Marshal-of-the-Court William Tucker and his wife, Hester Louise, soon after Tom Moore's Bermuda sojourn. Now it became the commercial headquarters for the Confederate States as Bourne was appointed Commercial Agent: tales are still recounted of the vast stacks of gold laid out on the dining-room table to pay, in advance, the captains and crews of the blockade-runners.

Major Norman S. Walker, a former captain in the Confederate Army, was made Political Agent for the Confederacy in November 1862. As his office, he rented the building opposite St Peter's Church, now known as the Confederate Museum which had been built as Government House by Governor Day in 1700. Major Walker's wife, Georgiana Gholson Walker, of a prominent Virginia family and a renowned Southern belle, was at this time in her late twenties, and so desolated at separation from her husband that with their three small children she ran the blockade to join him despite Mrs Jefferson Davis, in tears, trying to dissuade her from so dangerous a journey.

On 18th March 1863, the little family embarked in the SS *Cornubia* at Wilmington. Mrs Walker kept a detailed diary (edited by Dwight Franklin Henderson and published by the Confederate Publishing Co. Inc. in 1963). She describes the Hotel of St George's where they first stayed on the Town Square as 'a quiet boarding-house kept by a widow and three maiden sisters.' On 20th May they moved into 'a snug cosy little cottage, embowered with trees and flowers which bloom throughout the year' – and here, on 15th June 1863 was born their fourth child – Randolph St George Walker. This factual diary thus definitely disposes of the local legend that Randolph St George was born at the present Confederate Museum – with the colourful but probably apocryphal detail usually added that he was born under the Confederate flag stretched over the bed as a tester! The diary simply records that 'another little rebel appeared in these scenes,' after they had moved to the cottage. In later years, one of Randolph Walker's more successful dinner-time stories – he lived till 1949 – was that he could boast of being the only person ever accepted at a Government House party in the nude! According to his mother's written account, it was at *tableaux vivants* given at her cottage, enlivened by the Band of the 39th Regt., that 'my baby Randolph (6½ months old) appeared (naked) as "Moses in the Bulrushes" and I will venture to assert that the original Moses was not a more magnificent boy. Col. Hamley's daughter made a beautiful princess,' – Colonel Hamley being the newly-arrived Colonel of Engineers. Governor and Mrs Ord also were quite converted to the Southern cause by the very persuasive Mrs Norman Walker.

By far the most famous of the blockade-running officers was Captain Roberts of the *Don.* Like many semi-retired R.N. officers he assumed a *nom de guerre* while running the blockade; he was in reality the Hon. Augustus Charles Hobart-Hampden, son of the 6th Earl of Buckingham. After his Bermuda adventures, about which he wrote *Never Caught in Blockade-running*, and where his 400-ton vessel was a familiar sight, he eventually became an Admiral in the Turkish navy under the title of Hobart Pasha.

Although the town of Hamilton was the capital of the islands, the American Consulate was still in St George's where it had been for more than forty years. One cannot but feel deeply sorry for the fourteenth man to hold the office of American Consul, to which he had been appointed by the Federal Government. To-day his file in Washington reads as follows:–

'Charles Maxwell Allen of New York. Commissioned Consul August 7, 1861 (recess of the Senate); assumed charge November 15, 1861; recommissioned April 14, 1862; died at his post December 24, 1888. Funeral from his home, Wistowe, Flatts, Bermuda, to Smith's Parish Church attended by His Excellency the Governor, Lieut-General Edward Newdigate-Newdegate, and representatives of the Royal Navy, the Army and the Civil Service.'

He could hardly have foreseen at the terrible commencement of his duties that he would eventually wish to remain for twenty-seven years and be held in such honour. During the war he had the greatest difficulty to obtain living quarters, merchants were reluctant to serve him, ladies fussily drew their dresses away from the contamination of his presence in the streets, twice he was knocked down in public, and on the eve of 4th July his Flagpole was cut down so that he could not display the Stars and Stripes. His letters home to his wife make pitiful reading while his Consular Reports over the Civil War period (published by the Bermuda

Historical Quarterly 1962) are enthralling, especially as he was prominent in detecting that the celebrated Dr Luke Blackburn, so far from coming to Bermuda to aid sufferers from yellow fever, was, as an agent of the South, endeavouring to cause epidemics of the disease by collecting clothing and blankets from dead yellow fever victims to send to New York and other northern cities. Consul Allen unmasked the plot but Blackburn escaped, though his confederates were punished by the Bermuda courts. Ironically enough, Blackburn was to die in such an odour of sanctity as governor of Kentucky that historians have cast doubts on the existence of so diabolical a plot, but his widow later confessed that such had been the case.

And when the 'beautiful little steamer,' the blockade-runner, *Mary Celestia*, sank off Gibbs' Hill Lighthouse 6th September 1864, Charles Maxwell Allen entered in his records the rumours that accused him of having bribed the pilot.

Such, with the majority of Bermudians, was the violence of feeling on behalf of the South. It says much for the character and disposition of Consul Allen that after the war he became contented in the islands and won so many friends.

A happier memory of the war is recalled by the career of Joseph Hayne Rainey, a freed slave from South Carolina, who managed to reach Bermuda by serving as a steward on a blockade-runner and set up as a barber on Water Street, St George's, next to the Tucker House. His wife, a very accomplished dress-maker, who operated under the name Madame Elise, was soon making 'elaborate and very beautiful toilettes' for Georgiana Walker and other ladies dining at Government House with the Ords. Joseph Rainey himself found many of the St Georgians, who visited his barber's shop, anxious to help him with his self-education. How this couple regarded Bermudians is clearly shown in the columns of the local newspaper when they took their leave, thanking many local patrons, immediately after the war. It was intriguing later to hear that Rainey was elected to the United States House of Representatives being the first Negro to be a member of that body and was much respected in Washington for his eloquence and integrity.

Silk Alley, the side lane off Water Street where their shop stood, was re-named Barber's Alley in his honour.

But through it all, the town of St George's was, admittedly, in a filthy state, having no drains or sewers, cess-pits abounding and the streets filled with abominable odours, rendered worse by the mass of shipping in the harbour and the large numbers of 'reckless, roaring, devil-may-care fellows' who were generally to be seen on shore, more or less intoxicated and always in a perpetual state of debauch. The newspapers were full of such descriptions especially in 1864 when a terrible wave of yellow fever again swept the islands. Of the total civil population of 11,450 (of whom 6,826 were coloured) no less than 3,148 were attacked and 237 died. The second battalion of the 2nd regiment lost 120 out of 148, and 206 soldiers died out of the total garrison of 1460. This was the epidemic during which the sinister figure of Dr Luke Blackburn put in an appearance. It was not until experiments during the Spanish-American War (1898) that the rôle of the mosquito as a carrier was determined since when, with improved sanitation and hygienic advances in science, and strict control of the mosquito, Bermuda has had no further yellow fever visitations. But though the bad epidemic of 1864 is often quoted as Bermuda's final bout, as a matter of fact there were two minor outbreaks later, one in 1867 and the last in 1879.

A Sunday in 1864, 31st August, was set aside as a Day of Humiliation and Prayer because of the devastation of 'Yellow Jack' as it was called. But, through it all, the local newspapers – and 'the man in the street' – reflected such a positive assurance of the South's eventual triumph that the news of the fall of Wilmington was a stupefying blow to Bermudians. Their belief that the Confederacy must win had never been shaken, so that when, in April 1865, the 'fond hopeless dream' faded with General Lee and the Confederate Army's surrender to General Grant, and the poignant tragedy of the destruction of the South, Bermudians were stunned. In fact, they soon realized financial demolition stared them in the face. St George's was suddenly a deserted town. Debts that had been blithely incurred, would take years to liquidate. Bermuda's short period of false prosperity had ended.

But work was still proceeding at the Dockyard, and now it became obvious that the west end would need as heavy fortifications as had early been built to defend St George's. For the next twenty-five years from the close of the Civil War in America, building and strengthening of forts went steadily forward. Strong lana forces from England supplemented them, and the largest floating dock in the world was towed across the Atlantic to see service at the Dockyard. She was considered one of the mechanical marvels of her era, and until the experiment of long distance tow had been used in her case it had been customary for floating docks to be despatched in sections and set up at their destination. Of 8,300 tons displacement, she was capable of lifting a 10,000-ton vessel and was towed across by men-o'-war in thirty-six days arriving without incident at Grassy Bay, Bermuda, on 28th July 1869. Henceforth, the Dockyard became an active yard in fact as well as in name. By 1904 she had been displaced by a larger dock, was to be towed away to a ship-breaker's yard when she broke away from her tug in high winds and stranded on Spanish Point – where her rusting ribs may still be seen.

Ireland Island was divided into three sections by two 'cuts'. Two handsome clock towers were built on the waterfront, one of which gave the time of high tide. Grey's Bridge, opened in 1850, which connects Ireland Island with Boaz, was named for the then Home Secretary, Sir George Grey. (It is often mis-spelled 'Gray's' on Bermuda maps.) However communication between Watford Island and Somerset was inconveniently maintained by a jerry barge until as late as September 1902 when Watford Bridge was opened.

From 1871-1877 Bermuda had as governor a man who left a permanent mark for all time – Sir John Henry Lefroy. This truly great man saved from oblivion the tattered and neglected early colonial records, had them bound in thirteen great volumes and from them in his 'spare time' published his *Memorials of the Discovery and Early Settlement of the Bermudas or Somers Islands 1515-1687 compiled from the Colonial Records and Other Original Sources*, which still form the basis of our knowledge of Bermuda history. He also collected, and wrote about, the unique Bermuda coinage – Hog money – botany, and horticultural experiments, and edited the Sloane MS. in the British Museum of the ancient *Historye of the Bermudas*, erroneously attributed to Captain John Smith, but now to Governor Nathaniel Butler. Many of the plants he introduced were genera new to the island and extremely rare.

All the MSS. he saved from oblivion are carefully guarded in the Bermuda Archives at Par-la-Ville in Hamilton.

Perhaps the most publicly triumphant happening of his administration was the gala opening of the Causeway – that two-mile long series of bridges that connects St George's with the Main Island. Until that September morning in 1871 when 6000 people (half the population) witnessed the joyful event, the only link between the two islands had been supplied by the old ferry at Coney Island. (No one could have believed that this solid causeway, costing £32,000, would only last twenty-eight years; yet it was to be swept away in the terrible hurricane, already mentioned, of September 1899.)

But what remains to-day to remind us of a past era includes, not only the wonderful Colonial Records preserved by Sir John Henry Lefroy, but water-colours of Bermuda executed by Thomas Driver who arrived in 1814 and served the town of Hamilton with paintings and decorations at the time of the transference of the capital, and from 1819 onwards advertising portrait painting, and making aquatint etchings of both towns; excellent draughtmanship by that gifted but pathetic character 'Edward James', who was reputed to be a sort of remittance man here under an assumed name but whose Civil War drawings (he advertised water-colour drawings of most of the blockade-runners at prices ranging from 10s 6d up to £3-3) of ships and launchings are of inestimable value; and a series of panoramic wash drawings by the adjutant of the 20th Regiment, Lieut. E. G. Hallewell, stationed in Bermuda 1841-1847. All these are among Bermuda's heritage and highly prized by collectors – as are those of Sir John G. LeMarchant.

Earlier pictorial records that still look down on us from the walls of such museums as Camden, Verdmont, the Tucker House, the St George's Historical Society, the Bermuda Historical Society, and many private collections, are the portraits of a score or so leading men and women painted by Joseph Blackburn who arrived from England in 1752 to work for a year before proceeding to America where also his work is cherished; and portraits of fifteen years later, painted by

---

Government House, Pembroke, the present official residence of His Excellency the Governor, north of the City of Hamilton. In 1882, the Legislature authorized the erection of this building (which was completed in 1892) immediately east of the simple two-storey house, Mount Langton, which had served as Government House from 1815 when the seat of government was transferred from St George's. Mount Langton's 75-acre property was so named by Sir James Cockburn, after his Scottish estate. (*Bermuda News Bureau photo*)

John Green who came from Philadelphia in the sixties, fell in love with Polly, the daughter of Collector Smith, and settled at Verdmont, Smith's, which they inherited from Polly's step-mother. Later John Green became a councillor and a judge of the Admiralty Court, but his portraits still remain for the delectation of posterity.

As for written records by visiting authors, it would require a tome in itself to record all who have left their impressions. But two very contradictory nineteenth-century accounts by world-famous writers may be mentioned: Anthony Trollope and Mark Twain. The former, as an Inspector for the General Post Office in London, came for a couple of weeks, May and June 1859, by the then once-monthly steamer, *Delta*, from St Thomas. In his *West Indies and the Spanish Main* he extols the fertility of the soil and the beauty of the rampaging oleanders but dislikes the climate ('muggy, damp, disagreeable . . . I was always anxious to be supine'), the islanders ('stronger traces of the breed of Caliban than that of Ariel'), their laziness and poverty ('Bermuda is very poor . . . contented with her poverty . . . the people both black and white only half awake') and above all, their neglect of the fertile soil.

But Mark Twain, who came for the first time aboard SS *Quaker City* in 1867 at the end of the memorable European journey which was to form the basis of his *Innocents Abroad*, fell in love with the islands and was to return again and again, until shortly before his death in 1910, making many permanent friends, giving humorous lectures, and uttering pungent sayings, long remembered.

He describes Bermuda as a Paradise – but 'you have to go through Purgatory to get there'. The sleepiness that Trollope hated, Mark Twain considered made the island 'the right country for a jaded man to loaf in . . . the deep peace and quiet . . . sink into one's body and bones.' And he wrote of the shimmering brightness of local houses as 'exactly the white of the icing on a cake.' He also thought it 'the tidiest place in the world'.

Bermuda was still in many ways a somnolent peaceful

Bermuda Railway, October 1931-1947. Carriages, bicycles and train on Front Street, Hamilton to meet the Furness ships before the days of automobiles. Notice how busy the 'cop' is, directing traffic at foot of Burnaby Hill! (*Photo by Walter Rutherford*)

backwater – whether that condition was to your taste or not.

As for the spoken word – Du Bose Heyward, the South Carolinian novelist and dramatist (born in Charleston 1885) felt quite at home when he visited Bermuda in the 1920s. The author of *Porgy* was a southern aristocrat with a sympathy and understanding of the southern Negro quite alien to the feeling of the poor Whites who regarded them as an economic threat. Heyward's family had been impoverished by the Civil War; his books and plays brilliantly presented the Negroes of South Carolina. His popular lecture given in Hamilton, Bermuda, commenced with the words: 'In Charleston, we have never forgotten that, during the Civil War, our best friends were here in Bermuda.' . . . Perhaps he was remembering that the only international salute ever tendered the Confederate flag was fired in St George's when Capt. Maffitt of the Confederate frigate *Florida* exchanged a 21-gun salute with the military commandant, the Confederate flag flying from the signal station at Fort George.

9

Agriculture and the Beginnings of Tourism

So it was that towards the closing decades of the nineteenth century, Bermudians at last – willy-nilly – turned towards the products of the soil. No longer 'marooning' among the West Indian Islands, or salt-raking at Turks whose jurisdiction they had lost in 1801, nor able since emancipation to rely on a large supply of Negroes to man their ships, faced with the stiff competition of steamship lines, and remembering the bitter nemesis following the fallacious affluence of blockade-running years – what else could they do?

They were not yet interested in their own history or they might have realized the ironical twist fate was giving to the determined efforts of past governors to push them exactly in this direction. As early as 1764, we have noted George James Bruere who planted land and imported agricultural implements. The good governor, Reid, coming in 1839 had been staggered to find only two dilapidated ploughs left in the islands, all cultivation being done shallowly with the hoe; he increased the number of ploughs to fifty-four, held exciting ploughing matches and Agricultural Exhibitions to disprove the residents' assertion that the contours of the land were unsuitable for ploughing, and was personally beloved enough to make an impression – that faded alas! on his retirement when Agricultural Exhibitions died out for forty years. Before leaving Bermuda, Reid strongly advocated 'bringing in new agricultural settlers ... to reimplant here those arts in agriculture which have been gradually lost from the time the people of these islands betook themselves exclusively to sea-faring habits'. (Journals of the House of Assembly 1845.) The (1871) historian-governor, Lefroy, already noticed mainly in that connection, also imported gardeners, agricultural implements, plants, and, backed by the Colonial Office this 'scholar, gardener, gentleman' improved agricultural methods so that the land itself gradually became more significant.

The fact was, Bermudians had inherited their attitude from the earliest settlers who had always been so engrossed in following the sea that farming was looked upon as an unworthy occupation; even among the slaves only the oldest and least competent Negroes and aged women tilled the land. The more active men had been trained by their masters to be sailors and mechanics.

So all through the 1870s and 1880s, now that the islanders had perforce taken seriously to agriculture, Bermuda families were struggling to establish it on a paying basis. Every member of the family joined in the preparation and wrapping of field and garden produce for the New York market and to catch the twice-monthly steamers. There gradually developed a specialized production of vegetables – onions, celery, potatoes, tomatoes – in addition to the excellent already-famed arrowroot, fifty acres of which were grown as early as 1820. And so world-famous did Bermuda onions become, that the island group was widely referred to as 'The Onion Patch'. Then, too, the Easter Lily, introduced so fortuitously in mid-nineteenth century became extensively cultivated for exportation of bulbs reaped in July and August, and buds cut by the cartload and mailed to the U.K., U.S.A. and Canada in time to bloom at Easter.

From early days, mariners had imported citrus and many other fruit trees, but these had been left uncultivated and became the prey of blights and fruit-fly. It has remained for the twentieth century to combat these pests successfully. The Agricultural Station was set up in 1896 and their beautiful Botanical gardens, eastward of the City of Hamilton are well worth a visit. The present Department of Agriculture and Fisheries does yeoman service promoting agricultural exhibitions and keeping the islands beautiful and productive.

This great occupational change had a further big effect – the arrival of Portuguese farm workers from Madeira and the Azores. This immigration was, in fact, exactly what Governor Reid had suggested. The earliest, a small but steady drift, began coming before the Civil War, but later official immigration was undertaken which gathered momentum in the latter part of the nineteenth century and continued till to-day when there are thousands of Portuguese settlers in Bermuda. They became noted for their thrift, agricultural skill, exemplary conduct and an unequalled tempo of hard work. By the present century, a group of them has emerged, interested in public affairs and the professions, though the majority retain the European peasant's knowledge of the soil, and continue to engage in rural occupations.

With all this hard work, the economy seemed at last to be settling on firmer foundations, reinforced by the Imperial Government's decision to station units of the Regular Army at White's Hill (or Prospect) in Devonshire close to the town of Hamilton, in addition to those stationed in St George's. By this time the Army estimates for Bermuda totalled £1000 per day. And fortifications were continually being built, or reinforced towards the centre and west of the islands – in addition to the original St George's defences – now in order to protect both Hamilton and the Dockyard.

The improvement in SS services made a second lighthouse advisable and a sturdy stone structure, half the height of the iron shaft at Gibbs' Hill, was built on St David's Island in 1879. The view eastward from its balcony is superbly beautiful.

Perhaps the final irony of all is that the reluctantly-assumed agricultural occupation brought in a totally unexpected bonus with a thousand-fold interest. The steamers that began arriving regularly to transport early vegetables to the New York market, laid the tentative basis for Bermuda's huge present industry – tourism. At first a mere trickle of winter-weary New Yorkers escaped from the rigours of the north by spending the season in Bermuda. Hotels sprang up which only remained open from Christmas to Easter. Such visitors as arrived were wealthy winter residents; the islands reverted to somnolence in the summers.

The Hamilton Hotel (on the site where the City Hall now stands) had actually been commenced before the Civil War but conditions then halted its construction. (Greatly daring, it had projected facilities for as many as thirty bedrooms.) But it was this later regular and easy access to the U.S.A. by small steamers that saw its development and enlargement and the building of another winter-season hotel in 1883 – the Princess. This still-popular hotel on Hamilton Harbour was named for H.R.H. Princess Louise, Duchess of Argyll, who took Inglewood, Paget – a Trimingham residence – for herself and suite in the winter of 1883 when her husband, Lord Lorne, was stationed in Ottawa as Governor-General of Canada. Soon other hotels sprang up in quick succession and expansion became rapid.

In 1887, Bermuda took a great step forward with the adoption of the telephone system. 'Central' became the unseen friend who would advise you whether the in-coming ship had yet entered Two-Rock Passage, whether your friends were likely to be giving a party, and even sometimes received requests to ring back when the three-minutes for boiling an egg had elapsed! In 1890, the Halifax-Bermuda cable was laid, and in 1904, the Electric Light Co was incorporated.

How rapid change had become was evident on considering that whale-oil lamps had only been discarded in the 1860s with the introduction of Kerosene, (and, for many families, kerosene lamps continued to be used into the 1920s.)

Another big change in the Hamilton skyline was the erection of the present Bermuda Cathedral, a Gothic edifice which, on its small hillock north-west of the Sessions House, is Hamilton's central and dominating feature. It stands on the site of Holy Trinity Church destroyed in an incendiary fire in January 1884. As we have seen, since the earliest days of the colony's history, each parish had built its own simple church. With the development of the town of Hamilton in Pembroke, it was decided to build a church within the township in addition to the old parish church, St John's. The beautiful little church, Holy Trinity, had taken a quarter of a century to reach completion when this disaster struck it. The Building Committee recommenced its work on 6th January 1885 by pulling down the ruins and planning for the erection of the present structure with a seating capacity of 1200. The building stone was imported from England, Indiana, and Nova Scotia to blend with the native limestone. In November 1890 a gale delayed completion for several years and made the architects decide to abandon the spire which was to have risen above the 144-foot-high tower, the cap-stone of which was formally laid in 1905. By an Act of the Bermuda Legislature the building had been constituted the Bermuda Cathedral in 1894. Many impressive State Services and Naval and Military occasions have been held here. The pulpit and lectern are copies of the ones in St Giles, Edinburgh and there are fine examples of church sculpture.

It was not until 1826 that the colony received its first Episcopal Visitation – before this time none of the churches had ever been consecrated. Bishop John Inglis therefore consecrated all the parish churches and churchyards. The Mother Church of the Colony in St George's, till then simply The Church, now became St Peter's. No visitor interested in the past neglects to enter this church with its Communion Chalice dated 1625-6, and other plate presented by King William III, its red-cedar altar traditionally made under the direction of Richard Moore, Governor in 1612, the seventeenth-century three-decker pulpit and the historic wall-tablets. But, strange to say, there is a second church, just north of St George's town behind the pillars that once led to Government House – or rather, what appears to be the ruin of an ancient abbey, still standing in picturesque decay. But, oddly enough, this apparently historic relic, which stirs the curiosity of every tourist, is in reality a New Church, planned but never finished. Throughout the second half of the nineteenth century all records keep repeating that 'the venerable structure (St Peter's) is falling into decay and scarcely anything can be done to avert it.' At first it was decided to demolish the old church and rebuild on that site. A few voices were raised passionately in its defence. Whereupon the site of the old Government House north of the town and part of the building that remained there were granted for the New Church and the Rectory. By the end of the century the roof of the new church was almost complete – yet there were still many who wished to retain the old church. During the present century the whole colony united to see that our ancient St Peter's was thoroughly restored. The unfinished church was left to decay.

One of the oldest Presbyterian Churches in the Commonwealth overseas, is Christ Church, Warwick, where the pulpit used by George Whitefield in 1748, is carefully preserved. Near the Bermuda Cathedral, churches were built by Methodists, Presbyterians, Roman Catholics, and African Methodist Episcopalians, all of whom also have churches throughout the parishes. While to-day the Roman Catholics have an impressive Cathedral, St Theresa's, on Cedar Avenue and a Bishop in residence in Bermuda. The islands are in fact loaded down with many sects and churches of every denomination.

If the Jubilee of Queen Victoria's accession to the throne had been celebrated with enthusiasm in 1887, it was nothing compared to the sixtieth, or Diamond, anniversary observed in 1897 – as history relates – 'in every portion of her dominions'; and the town of Hamilton that year legally took upon itself the status of a city.

When the Boer War broke out in 1899 to Bermudians the struggle seemed at first like the echo of a distant drum and it was with astonishment that they learned that 5000 Boer War prisoners were to be interned on islands in the Great Sound.

And it was in June of that same year that the prisoner-of-war ships began arriving. Soon bell tents were being raised on

Tucker's, Morgan's, Darrell's, Burt's, Hawkins' and Ports' Islands. Each island also had its own church, library, school, dining and wash-tents and ran its own affairs. Numbers of newspaper correspondents from New York sought admission to the camps, and, on being refused permission, wrote stories of oppression and bad treatment. However, in 1901, Francis Horace Vizetelly of *The Independent* (N.Y.) came to Bermuda to investigate conditions in the camps and through the courtesy of Sir G. Digby Barker, the governor, was the first civilian given free access to the camps. In concluding his article he says: 'The prisoners . . . gen₂rally looked a healthy set of men. So far as general care is concerned, there are without doubt many persons, especially in our big cities, who would gladly exchange their present surroundings and opportunities to share the life of the burgher prisoners-of-war in the Boer laagers of beautiful Bermuda'. Naturally, they went through mental stress and suffering; there were some attempts to escape. On Darrell's Island alone there were 1,100 prisoners with a tennis court, croquet ground, and a gymnastic club. The stone buildings on Ports Island were utilized as headquarters of the Camp Commandant and as a hospital. Long Island, which had been used for a burial ground before, now had a special plot set aside for those of the prisoners who should die before the war was over. Enteric and dysentry were the worst enemies, but the men had adequate diet, frequent sea bathing and good medical care. When the war ended in May 1902 most of those in Bermuda took the oath of allegiance to Great Britain and were repatriated. However, there was a group of 'irreconcilables' who would not take the oath and remained, popular long-bearded figures in khaki hats, who ran wood-carving shops, and at the end of the war, they raised an obelisk on Long Island, dedicated in 1903 by the bishop of Newfoundland and Bermuda, with the forty names of those whose bones were left behind on this foreign shore.

The Horse-drawn Age: Parking space on Front Street, Hamilton before the advent of motorcars in 1946. (*Bermuda News Bureau photo*)

(*overleaf*) Part of the City of Hamilton from the air. The town of Hamilton became the capital in 1815 and was made a city in 1897 by an Act of Legislature. A line of motor-cars can be seen, driven along Front Street at a leisurely pace: speed limit 15mph in built-up sections and 20mph outside municipal areas! (*Bermuda News Bureau photo*)

10
Sport in Bermuda and Other Changes

With Bermudians attaining in a quiet way some sense of security with the development of agriculture and a sprinkling of winter tourists, more time was available to them for sports and social activities. Such was the peace and quiet of the little colony that most journeying was done on 'shank's mare', in small boats around the coast, by lumbering horse-drawn bus, and, for the wealthier citizens, by horse and buggy. The pedal cycle began increasingly to be imported from 1897 when it was becoming modernized from the original 'Penny-farthing' with their enormous front wheel and tiny rear. In the early twentieth century pedal cycles – or push bikes as they were termed – became a joyous sport to tourists and a necessity to every Bermudian. (In 1931, with a population of 27,789 persons, more than 12,000 bicycles were being registered per annum. Only Holland could compare in the universality of their use.)

Outdoor sports have a particular appeal in Bermuda since they can be played in every month of the year. Croquet was

---

(*overleaf*)

The Cathedral of the Most Holy Trinity, Church Street, Hamilton, is a commanding object on the skyline and is well worth a visit. The carved pulpit is a reproduction of the famed one at St Giles' Cathedral, Edinburgh. This Church of England cathedral occupies the site of Trinity Church (destroyed by fire 27th January 1884) and was consecrated by the Bishop of Newfoundland and Bermuda on 11th May 1911. (*Bermuda News Bureau photo*)

The City Hall, Hamilton. In 1959, Bermuda celebrated its 350th birthday, and a noteworthy permanent addition to the City of Hamilton was that of the fine new City Hall on Church Street, with its Art Gallery. Theatre, Exhibition Room, and offices of the Mayor and Corporation. This beautiful building, a worthy memorial of Bermuda's noted architect, the late Wilfred Onions, was formally opened in February 1960. A Time Capsule was buried in the hall, to be disinterred at Bermuda's 500th anniversary in the year 2109. (*Bermuda News Bureau photo*)

enthusiastically adopted in the 1860s – an early date considering that in the British Isles the All England Croquet Club was formed in 1868, by which time croquet was well entrenched in Bermuda. Its tempo suited the modes and manners of the time; it could be played with dignity and decorum in wasp-waisted dresses, whose hems gracefully swept the grass.

But it was tennis that became Bermuda's royal game; the story of its local genesis is an amusing one. Dignified Mr Thomas Middleton saw it played in England in 1873 where it was just regaining popularity, and he brought the first tennis set into Bermuda in September of that same year, intending to build a tennis court where he, his wife and friends, might take a little gentle exercise. On landing, he had second thoughts. Surely it was a shade inelegant and unrefined for ladies – and perhaps a trifle strenuous for his own advancing years. So he promptly disposed of the whole paraphernalia to the Gray family at Clermont in Paget where Sir Brownlow Gray, suffering from no such misgivings, promptly laid out a tennis court. Shortly, a second court appeared at Dudley, home of the Chief Justice, Mr Thomas L. Wood, whose daughters later lived at Woodhaven, Harbour Road, Paget, and built another court there.

Meantime, Mr Wood enthusiastically made 'bats' for his young daughters and their friends the Grays. All became first-class players – in fact, each generation of the Gray family has contributed largely to the advancement of tennis in Bermuda. In 1877, the first Tennis Tournament to be held in the Western Hemisphere took place in the grounds of Admiralty House, Pembroke. Vice Admiral Sir A. Cooper Key staged this event in which the enthusiastic Sir Brownlow Gray and Miss Mary Gray – first Bermuda Champion – proved outstanding players. The photographs extant of the event show the delightfully decorous skirts of the period in which to-day's players would declare active participation impossible.

Not only does Bermuda hold this record for the Western Hemisphere, but it was actually from these islands that the game was introduced into the United States in 1874. In that year Miss Mary Outerbridge went to New York with her brother (afterwards Sir Joseph Outerbridge) taking with her a tennis racquet, all equipment for the game, balls and a book of rules. Through the agency of her brother, A. Emilius Outerbridge, she obtained permission for a court in the grounds of the Staten Island Cricket Club. The Customs officer who inspected Mary Outerbridge's baggage on her arrival in N.Y. long remembered his puzzlement in assessing duty on this outlandish equipment being brought into the country. History is silent as to Mr Middleton's reaction to all these unexpected developments.

The Americans took up the game with professional zeal and soon were visiting their Bermuda cousins and defeating them regularly in the big international championships that soon became a feature of each Bermuda season.

Another outstanding sport is cricket, as befits a British colony. Played by regiments stationed here, it quickly gained many local adherents; in the late 1890s the Hamilton Cricket Club organized a Cricket Week each season when Australian and American teams visited to play the local teams on what is now the Bermuda Athletic Association field, then known as the Richmond Cricket Club. It was at this time that cricket became the most popular sport as anyone will believe who is here on the Thursday and Friday immediately preceding the first Monday in August when the two-day Annual Somerset-St George's Cup Match is played between these two Coloured clubs for the supremacy of the island. This event is a great Bermuda festival which began modestly enough in 1902 and is now attended by His Excellency the Governor, thousands of tourists and residents, and everyone who enjoys an excellent and sporting spectacle, with bands playing and flags waving.

But, inevitably, the indigenous sports are those connected with the sea — swimming, game-fishing, yachting, and, above all, dinghy-racing. Bermudians take to boating as soon as they can walk. And no water sport is more exciting than a race between dinghies — little open boats no more than 14 feet 1 inch over all with no limitation on sail-spread, sloop-rigged, with leg-o'-mutton mainsail, 35-foot spar, 16-foot bowsprit and 21-foot boom — and, roughly 550 feet of canvas. A tricky boat to manoeuvre, easily capsized — dinghy-racing is a sensational sport. It was in 1882 that the first organized dinghy-racing took place, arranged by the boys of Mr Charles E. Clay's school in Hamilton. To-day there is a very active Royal Hamilton Amateur Dinghy Club situated on the south-east bank of Hamilton Harbour, a St George's dinghy and Sports Club, a Sandy's Boat Club as well as several smaller clubs, all indulging in dinghy racing.

The Royal Bermuda Yacht Club on the opposite coast of

the harbour, was organized on 1st November 1844 by a group of enthusiastic yachtsmen who met under Tom Moore's famed calabash tree at Walsingham. The Prince Consort was the first Patron, hence permission from Queen Victoria for use of the word 'Royal.' It would have been difficult to foresee in the modest beginnings of an Ocean Yacht Race in 1906, with three starters, and a cup offered by Sir Thomas Lipton at the suggestion of the editor of *The Rudder*, the really great International event this bi-ennial 650-mile race from Newport, R.I. to Bermuda would become, famed in the annals of yachting, with six or seven countries represented, well over 150 boats competing, and the whole island agog for their safe arrival. (The 1972 great race in this, the world's blue-water classic, took place in June of that year with 180 yachts in six classes competing, eight of these being Bermuda boats. The 1974 was equally successful.)

Despite a pleasant drift of winter visitors, the islands were still struggling to live mainly by agriculture at the opening of the twentieth century. As late as 1910, Walter Hayward of the editorial staff of *The New York Times* and author of *Bermuda Past and Present*, could write: 'Bermuda's sole industry is agriculture, the development of which began in earnest after the fictitiously prosperous years of blockade-running. American and Canadian tourists contribute a large sum annually to the colony's wealth, and the expenditure of the naval and military establishments still represents a valuable asset. The bulk of the produce goes to New York, the colony's natural market, but prices fluctuate to such an extent that the farmers are no longer assured of a profit. About 2600 acres are under cultivation; several thousand more might be utilized if adequate capital were available.' Mr Hayward's conclusion was: 'It is doubtful, however, in view of the increasing population, whether the people could live by the proceeds of the tourist trade, and even if this were possible it would not be sound economic policy to do so. The colony should be prepared to take advantage of its agricultural resources [in case] through an epidemic of disease or other unlooked-for causes the tourist trade should suddenly fail.' The 'increasing population' now numbered 18,994 souls.

However, shortly the colonists' feet would be set on that road down which there is no returning – almost complete reliance on the Tourist Trade. The 'unlooked for causes' of its interruption would include two World Wars. Perhaps forebodingly, in July of that same year (1910) 'a strange cigar-shaped sinister-looking craft' glided quietly and unexpectedly into Hamilton Harbour one Sunday morning. This was the United States' submarine *Salmon* – hailed as the first 'submersible' ever to visit Bermuda. She was of 340 tons and 135 feet long. Her armament consisted of four 17-feet Whitehead torpedoes having a range of 4000 yards. The mysterious stranger had come through many hundreds of miles of ocean trials prior to being handed over and becoming an integral part of Uncle Sam's navy, having been built by the Electric Boat Co. at Quincy, Mass. Many sightseers gathered along the wharves of Hamilton that bright Sunday morning to gaze speculatively at the strange craft. The public was rigidly excluded from going aboard.

The local newspaper bemoaned the fact that such a 'terrible engine of warfare' could hardly be adequately tested in these modern times of peace. Unhappily, that obstacle to complete trials would, all too soon, be completely removed.

In considering the balance between agriculture and the slowly rising tide of tourism as to which should be the main, if not sole, island industry, it is significant that by 1913 an Act was passed by the local Legislature to develop and control the bourgeoning tourist business.

At the same time, it must be remembered that Bermuda's area is but a scant 12,000 acres. People accustomed to larger countries may not immediately realize the implications in the use of each yard of land in such a circumscribed plot. Actually, the acreage under tillage at different periods is most significant.

As we have seen, Bermuda's maritime period closed with emancipation. At the time (1834) only 584 acres were under cultivation. In 1861, 1962 acres; 1871, 2223 acres; 1891, 2422 acres; 1901, 2636; 1911, 2761; 1921, 3012. This last figure was the absolute peak of the agricultural economy. World War I had pricked the balloon of the swelling tourist industry. Improved methods of agriculture and an increasing population enforced the best use of the soil; and the discovery of the lucrative New York market for a specialized production of winter vegetables completed the picture. The Board of Agriculture which had been berating the population for reliance on outside sources of revenue – with Imperial money spent on army, navy and dockyard – undertook scientific experiment, suggestion, and help with marketing to further 'our one industry'. On steamer days, Front Street, Hamilton, was a mass of wagons taking produce to the ships for the New York market at a season when for them such fruits and vegetables were unobtainable elsewhere.

The cessation of the Tourist Trade caused by war conditions, had thus stimulated the agricultural economy to its swan-song.

Not that market-gardening, dairying and poultry-feeding are ever likely to die out – the local demand is too great for this to happen. But, as we shall see, there inevitably came a steady decrease in available land with the construction of more houses and hotels. And in USA tariff walls were raised against such imports, while Texas produced 'Bermuda potatoes' and 'Bermuda onions' for the N.Y. market by the simple expedient of naming an area after the islands.

But the necessity for hard application to the soil is reflected in the Debates of the House of Assembly of the period. For when in 1909 the suggestion was put forward that, since 28th July of that year marked the three-hundredth anniversary of the landing of Sir George Somers and the beginning of Bermuda's story as an inhabited place the occasion should be marked in a modest but permanent manner, some of the Honourable Members of the House derided the idea as a waste of time and money. What really did history matter? And if Admiral Sir George Somers had been 'passed along' for 300 years – why, he could be ignored for a further period while sensible men earned their livings!

Eventually – but not till February 1911, a Ter centenary Committee headed by the Chief Justice having induced the Colonial Legislature to grant some funds – a Memorial Column in honour of the Father of this colony was unveiled by His Excellency the Governor, General Sir F. Walter Kitchener, K.C.B., (brother of Lord Kitchener) at the entrance to the Somers Gardens, St George's, at that time merely called The Public Gardens. Well worth a visit today.

Eighteen years later, the St George's and the Bermuda Historical Societies succeeded in establishing Somers Day as our National Celebration and by 1931 the date 28th July was officially recognized by Proclamation and made a holiday. Ironically, the popular two-day Cup Match has rather affected this date by their fixture and the official Somers Day has latterly been observed as a 'moveable feast' on some convenient near-by date – to the confusion of historians.

A more permanent mark of this tercentenary was the Royal Warrant of 4th October 1910 that the Bermuda coat of arms should revert to the armorial ensigns borne by the Royal Charter of the Somers Island Company in 1615 and which had appeared on their Book of Laws in 1622 and on Richard Norwood's map published 1626. The official description: Argent, on a Mount Vert a Lion Sejant Affronté, Gules, supporting between the fore-paws an Antique Shield, Azure, thereupon a representation of the wreck of the *Sea Venture* (A.D. 1609) all proper, together with this Motto *"Quo Fata Ferunt."*

The design is, of course, highly symbolical. That is to say, although the *Sea Venture* was wrecked on a sunken reef, it is here shown dashed against a high cliff; obviously a submerged rock would not be effective in the picture. In any case, the heraldic designer had never set eyes on Sea Venture Flat as it is called to-day.

The Bermuda flag is of special interest since it is the Red Ensign with the above Arms of Bermuda, without any background, placed on the 'fly.' Other colonies and dependencies use the Blue Ensign in this way — in fact, Bermuda is the only British territory to use the Red Ensign defaced with its Arms. It appears that no official reason is known for this anomaly except the local slogan 'Bermuda is different'.

And at Government House, while His Excellency is in residence, the Union Jack, with, at the centre, the Bermuda Arms on a white disc encircled by a green garland, is flown. This is the Governor's flag.

Large schools destined to serve the central part of the islands indefinitely had been established towards the close of the nineteenth century. Saltus Grammar School was founded in 1888 specifically for white boys with funds left by Samuel Saltus who died in 1880.

In March 1890 the Mt St Agnes Academy was opened by the Sisters of Charity from Mt St Vincent, Halifax, and this has run most successfully on co-educational lines.

A school for girls, The Bermuda High School, took over on Reid St from Miss Eliza Williams' school of 1890, and later moved to the Serpentine Road.

The Berkeley Educational Society opened a school on Court St in September 1897. In 1903 the Berkeley Institute removed to a handsome building on the road leading westward from St John's Church, Pembroke. The name perpetuates the memory of eighteenth century Bishop George Berkeley and his fantastical scheme to attract Red Indians to Bermuda for conversion, and education at a college to be called St Paul's, before returning them to America as missionaries. A hundred or so years later two attempts were made at running a school in Devonshire – one, St Paul's, the other, Devonshire College – both eventually failed. However, the proceeds from the sale of the land was divided between White and Coloured educational schemes: The Berkeley Educational Society was founded, and Samuel Saltus' will was augmented.

Further out of town are two other large schools: the Whitney Institute in Smith's Parish which was opened in 1883 and named for the benefactors of the school who lived at Villa Mont Clare in charming Flatt's village. And in Warwick East we come upon the oldest school in Bermuda – if not in the Western Hemisphere – Warwick Academy, one of the schools established by the Bermuda Company in 1662; the present handsome buildings were added to the original edifice in 1922.

Mention of the Bermuda Company is a reminder that from the earliest days of the colony, that Company, together with other interested persons, had put aside lands in each parish as 'school lands', while in the eighteenth century several private schools had been maintained by clergy resident in the colony. However, by the nineteenth century, much of the privately donated land had reverted to the descendants of the original grantees. So that the late nineteenth century developments were a great necessity.

Bermuda had some brilliant outstanding citizens in the first quarter of the twentieth century. That many of them were educated in small local schools and then made their mark here or in the wider outside world, reminds us of that seventeenth-century genius, Richard Norwood, whose formal education stopped in his early teens.

But great changes in Bermuda's educational system took place mid-twentieth century.

One of Bermuda's early attractions – the Natural Arches at Tucker's Town. This is an example of a cave roof-collapse at some earlier age, leaving one part holding firm and forming a spectacular sea-worn natural archway. A view taken at sunrise. (*Bermuda News Bureau photo*)

11
Two World Wars and the Rise of Tourism

With the outbreak of World War I the whole Empire rallied to resist the aggressive policy of Germany. The Bermuda Volunteer Rifle Corps (White) was mobilized to assist the Lincolnshire Regiment by manning outposts and guarding vital points, while the Bermuda Militia Artillery (Coloured) was trained as a coastal defence corps, and soon both units were to play their parts in France. HM Dockyard, Bermuda, was so well protected with powerful coastal batteries that these islands were never invaded, and the Dockyard carried out its important work of repairing and servicing large numbers of destroyers, submarines, submarine-chasers, without interruption. Inevitably, the regular steamship service with the United States was dislocated; towards the end of the war, Bermuda was relying on an antiquated cruiser, HMS *Charybdis*, to carry her supplies.

In 1914, the Bermuda dockyard welcomed Rear-Admiral Sir Christopher Cradock's training squadron. Then, one by one, HMS *Suffolk, Berwick, Donegal, Monmouth* and *Cumberland* slipped silently away to protect the Atlantic sea-lanes from German raiders. Alas! part of the news that filtered back was of the loss of the *Monmouth* and the squadron's Commander at the naval battle of Coronel off the Chilean Coast.

With the entry of the United States into the war in April 1917, the Bermuda Dockyard became even more strategically important both as a repair depôt and a refuelling station. Not only was it used by Royal Naval ships but was placed at the disposal of the Commanding Officer of the American Naval Base at Bermuda. For in March 1918 permission was granted to the Isle of White Co.,. Ltd. to sub-lease tiny White's Island

Two views of the lovely wide South Shore beaches and sun-trapped rock-enclosed coves where turquoise and purple seas roll to pink sands. Spikes of Spanish Bayonet bloom in the foreground. (*Bermuda News Bureau photo*)

in Hamilton Harbour to the United States Government to be used as an operating base for American U-boat chasers. A 10-year lease was signed to this effect which lapsed when the war ended that same year.

Naturally, close links between the USA and Bermuda were forged at this time. Not only was the American fleet using Bermuda for a base, their ships were also helping to provision the island. By mutual consent of both governments, Bermuda was placed under the American Food Controller through whom most supplies came.

Such patriotic organizations as the Imperial Order of the Daughters of the Empire, whose Bermuda branch had been founded in 1911, worked tirelessly to provide recreation and refreshment for sailors ashore. And it was no uncommon sight to see the Revd Canon Arthur Tucker rowing out in a small boat to meet incoming vessels, British and American, to minister to sailors' needs. (Later, in 1927, his son would found The Sailors' Home, to-day known as the Mariners' Club.)

Meanwhile, General Sir James Willcocks had arrived in Bermuda as governor on 1st June 1917. Despite his war wounds, he made desperate attempts to return to France in any capacity. He wrote of that time: 'I felt utterly depressed. The war was going on and I was no longer there . . . The United States Navy was very much *en évidence* in Bermuda during the latter end of 1917 and 1918. All newly built small war vessels, either for themselves or the French and Italians, called at the Islands before crossing the Atlantic, and we saw hundreds of their officers and men.' On 4th July 1918, the governor took advantage of a large number of allied warships in harbour to invite 1,400 officers and men to an afternoon of sports and entertainment at Government House. In fact, he acted as an excellent liaison officer throughout. Early on the morning of 11th November 1918, the booming guns from Government House carried the glorious news of the cessation of hostilities. At noon, His Excellency gave a stirring address at the Public Buildings, (now known as the Secretariat) where the three cheers for the King was followed by cheers for the Allies with the East Yorkshire Regiment playing each National Anthem in turn . . . Soon the Bermuda lads would begin straggling home to their islands from service on land and sea in distant Europe – and from the graves of their fallen comrades. The Cenotaph on Front Street (a small replica of the larger one in London,) whose foundation stone was first used in an Armistice Day ceremony on 11th November, 1920, is their memorial. Each year a service of remembrance is held here with full military honours, attended by His Excellency the Governor, who lays a wreath on the monument, and the Lord Bishop of Bermuda who conducts the service.

Even during war-time, one big step had been taken in the facilities for the islanders intellectual development. The little Library which the good governor, Sir William Reid, had founded in 1839 in one room of the Public Buildings (Secretariat) on Front Street, still served the public seventy-seven years later. Now, in 1916, the beautiful Perot property, Par-la-Ville, further west on Queen Street, housed behind William Bennett Perot's huge rubber tree, was rented as a library from the Corporation of Hamilton. The first five Librarians had been men – the last of these, Florentius Frith was a colourful unforgettable character, who refused to be disturbed, if he were playing chess, by a client seeking a book during the two or three short hours per day the Library remained open! Miss Kate Seon was in office when the Library was transferred and its growth was rapid. By 1957 a new wing had had to be added to the old house which to-day includes the Bermuda Historical Society's Museum, the Archives, and the Library itself of some hundred thousand volumes with, on the ground floor, a Reference Room containing a special Bermuda section. A file of local morning newspapers from 1784 to date, and all available books and pamphlets on Bermuda subjects, render this room a spot no visitor can afford to miss who is seriously interested in any topic relating to the islands. There is also, of course, an excellent Circulating Department and there are branch libraries in Sandys and St George's.

During the whole twenty years of uneasy truce between the two World Wars, all that had been envisaged of the friendship and alliances to spring from the British-American naval comradeship in Bermuda during 1917 and 1918 bore fruit. Some of the most widely-heard voices in America began analyzing Bermuda's attraction for such as themselves. The famous editor of Harper's Magazine, the late Frederick Lewis Allen, a regular seasonal visitor, noted approvingly: 'Although Bermuda lives by its American tourist traffic, it makes little attempt to offer travellers what they appear to want in the most frequented American resorts. The Bermudians have had the incredible good sense to realize that they

do better business in the long run – and also enjoy themselves more – by offering people what is native to Bermuda.
In its way of life, as well as in its outward appearance, the
place is individual.' And in his magazine he features articles
stressing the peace, the potent charm, the lazy pace and
restfulness of this tiny colony, whose British 'image' made
Americans feel they had adventured abroad.

With the improvement in sea-transport in the 1920s, the
tourist industry moved into first place. Agriculture was
retained but on a limited scale as it became evident that what
the islands should take advantage of was not so much their
slight natural resources for export, as the charm and beauty
of their mid-Atlantic position and climate now that modern
transportation made them so accessible. They began to enjoy
a post-war boom when Furness Withy & Co. built a
succession of luxury liners for the N.Y.-Bermuda run, and
further developed the budding tourist trade by building in
1920 a six-storey Bermudiana Hotel immediately west of the
City of Hamilton, and the Castle Harbour Hotel (ten years
later) on the lovely coast of Castle Harbour. In Tucker's
Town, famed from the earliest days yet still undeveloped, the
Company was permitted to buy a large area, and to build the
splendid Mid-Ocean Golf Course. This more sophisticated
sport was very popular with Bermuda's visitors and many
other golf links were laid out . . . No motor-cars, no railways,
few aeroplanes – to residents from noisier lands, Bermuda
was paradise indeed. It became entirely a winter-season resort
for those who could afford to flee the rigours of northern
winters.

With a larger population and an influx of visitors, the
question of water-supply became acute. All householders are
accustomed to catching their own supply on roof-tops, piped
to a tank underneath the house or in the garden. Sinking a
vertical well simply meant drawing on brackish water since
the rock is so porous. Fortunately, the late Sir Harry
Watlington, scion of one of Bermuda's oldest families, and a
most public-spirited citizen, instituted at this stage a remarkable system of water-works tapping the reservoir of fresh
water floating on the heavier sea-water at water-table level, in
a series of horizontal wells. His impressive system, officially
opened by the governor in February 1932, supplies Hamilton
and adjacent areas with what is known as 'Watlington Water.'
Additionally, in the 1960s, the government set up a
Distillation Plant on North Shore capable of producing over

25 million gallons of water annually, thus cutting down on the occasional but expensive importation of fresh water from USA. But the main individual supply is still the private roof-top-to-tank system, required by law, the roof being whitewashed regularly to ensure the purity of the water.

The first sucessful air-plane flight between N.Y.-Bermuda had been made on 2nd April 1930 when a Stimson cabin monoplane, powered by a 300-horsepower Wright engine, swooped down and settled its pontoons in Hamilton Harbour thus bridging more than 600 miles of ocean. Twice forced down on the water near the islands, it managed a successful take-off on each occasion.

Occasional calls by other aircraft and the rapid development of aerial transportation in other parts of the world, led the Bermuda legislature to decide on an airport for Bermuda. In May 1934, Darrell's Island in the Great Sound, quarter of a mile from the Warwick shore, was decided upon as the site of a marine airport with a huge rectilineal hangar for the great new seaplanes. In 1937, a million-dollar terminal building was erected there and Bermuda became widely known as the mid-Atlantic seaplane airport. The first passenger flights were in 1937. But when airlines switched to landplanes, and long runways were a necessity, Darrell's Island became an anachronism.

By this time, six steamship lines were also serving Bermuda: Furness-Bermuda Line, Eastern SS Co., Canadian National Steamships, Royal Mail, Pacific Steam Navigation, and Elders & Fyffes. People no longer shunned the sun, visitors arrived in every month of the year instead of merely a winter 'season.' The problem of inland transportation became acute in a determinedly motorless island. So it was that in October 1931 the Bermuda Railway ran its first trains, and relieved the over-worked horses and carriages, the countless pedal bicycles of the main road. Its 25-mile track from Somerset to St George's through the City of Hamilton, skirted the coast so closely over much of its route that the views were breathtaking, particularly as it crossed open sea in nine places. A single-track system, it became a part of the landscape, and the cost of travel was minimal. First class from Hamilton to St George's was, by certain trains, a mere two shillings. The inflated price of land had meant that it cost more per mile to build than any other railway known – yet its brief life was only to be sixteen years, when, mistakenly as many thought, it was scrapped after the advent of the motor-car. There has been agitation recently for its (expensive!) restoration.

In the 1930s, the *Crown Colonist* published a world map, labelling each British possession with its chief industry. The little speck in the western Atlantic that represented Bermuda was entirely blocked out by the words 'Tourist Traffic,' a fact which elicited howls of anguish from some writers – in particular E. G. Whitbread in *The Bermudian* – who protested that the agricultural indusry was still vital to Bermuda, that the Department of Agriculture, energetic and up-to-date, worked might and main to attain a Canadian market when high tariff walls almost closed the N.Y. market to Bermuda produce. And owned that the agricultural industry was 'but a ghost of what it was in the old days when she was N.Y.'s vegetable garden.' But now an equally dedicated Trade Development Board (to-day the Dept. of Tourism) was leading her in a destined and different direction.

And then, in September 1939, with the outbreak of World War II it became immediately apparent that, economically speaking, the day of reckoning had come. The island's one life-line, the tourist trade, inevitably went into a tail-spin. Near-panic was felt for a few days by the authorities as passenger ships alongside were rapidly painted camouflage grey and silently slipped away on more pressing duties. The streets were empty of visitors. The public was warned that the necessities of life, including food, were to be severely rationed. Mail would be frequently cut off and even local mail strictly censored. Unemployment stared many people in the face. The feeling of isolation was like a reversion to early days, but now with a far heavier population to support.

The local government set up a Service Corps and instituted various civic projects to provide employment – the laying out of Bernard Park was one. In October 1940 a Conscription Act was passed to ensure replacements for men gone overseas. Only two unexpected happenings saved the economy – the second at what appeared to be a bitter price.

The first event was the stationing here by Britain of fifteen hundred censors to intercept Atlantic mail. They were housed in the abandoned Princess and Bermudiana Hotels and were the most important and largest Censorship Station within the British Empire, the first detachment arriving August 1940. The second was the sacrifice of one-tenth of Bermuda's whole area, given up for defence bases to the

United States of America. 20th August 1940, the day on which the Prime Minister, Winston Churchill, announced to the House of Commons, and thus to the world, that the Imperial Government had agreed to grant facilities to the United States for Military Bases in Newfoundland, the West Indies and Bermuda, marked a profound change in Bermuda's whole way of life. As Frederick Lewis Allen questioned at the time: 'What happens to a British colony when it becomes the site of American bases?' And he added that to many it would be a terrible sacrifice that tiny Bermuda, with her burgeoning population, should turn two sites over to the United States 'freely and without consideration' as military and naval bases – and that, since the United States was not even in the war at the time, the sacrifice must be a little hard to swallow. The agreement was signed 27th March, 1941, despite memorials of loyalty to King George VI, delegations to London, misgivings on many sides – and actual tears from the St David's Islanders who were asked to give up their modest homes in their isolated and beloved island that had not even been physically attached to the remainder of the group till the opening of the Severn Bridge only seven years earlier.

The exact position in respect of the lands acquired in Bermuda for the defence of the coasts of the United States was as follows: 694.33 acres were given over for a 99-year lease to the United States. Bermuda did *not* come into the agreement affecting the British possessions in the Caribbean, whereby bases were granted in exchange for certain naval units. In Bermuda, local consent was given unconditionally on no exchange whatever. Of the area mentioned 34.87 acres were Crown Lands, in respect of which no charge was made – the balance of land was bought outright from private owners for the purpose of the leases, the payments being met by the British Treasury as required by the Lands Acquisition Act. It was announced in Washington that the British Government would bear the whole of the expenditure in connection with the purchase of lands for the Military and Naval bases in Bermuda and that no charges whatever for rental would be made against the United States on the 99-year lease.

Construction workers for the bases soon flooded the islands, housed, oddly enough, in an old Hudson river steamboat, the *Berkshire*, moored near St George's. Others slept four to a room in some of the abandoned hotels. The

peace of the islands was shattered completely by too many
men with too much money and too many frustrations. It was
a difficult time for all concerned. But the construction of the
bases went ahead. On 1st March 1941 the Stars and Stripes
was officially unfurled over what had been Morgan's and
Tucker's Islands in the Great Sound, now converted to US
Naval Operations Base . . . though still nostalgic to many of
us with memories of moonlight sailing picnics. At the other
end of Bermuda, Kindley Field was so designated in US War
Department Orders on 25th June 1941 (deriving its name
from Capt. F. E. Kindley, an American Flight Commander of
World War I,) the last runway not being completed till 11th
August 1943: Cooper's Island, the greater part of St David's
Island, and Longbird Island between St George's and Castle
Harbours form the nucleus of this area which also absorbed
into its construction such islets as Grasbury's, Long Rock,
Grace's, Round, Little Round, Jones, Sandy, Cave, Goat,
Pear, Long, and Long Cay.

Approximately 18 square miles was all that remained as
living space for the entire civil population of over 30,000
souls.

Then came 7th December 1941 with its surprise attack on
Pearl Harbour. Immediately, the whole picture changed. The
USA was in the war – and we were all brothers in arms. In
Bermuda, the officers of the Royal Navy not only gracefully
yielded responsibility and pride of place to the Americans,
but gladly taught them the local mores. The American
Rear-Admiral took top rank while the British Admiral simply
became Senior Naval British Officer. It was all done with
exemplary smoothness and courtesy on both sides and the
relief at realizing that Bermuda was still a British colony
enabled the islanders to reconcile themselves to the loss of
land and to show the greatest hospitality to the Naval
personnel. The Sailors' Home, the Imperial Order of the
Daughters of the Empire, the United Services Organizations,
the Ladies' Hospitality Organization, all rallied round to
entertain sailors whenever some of the hundreds of ships,
seeking safe anchorage, lay alongside.

At the close of the war, Bermudians realized that the
sacrifice of land was not all loss. To the acreage given them,
the Americans had added a large area – 491 acres – dredged
from the bottom of the sea. So that in the year 2040, when
the Bases are restored to Bermuda, the colony's total area
will be 20.59 square miles instead of the original approximate
19.34.

As an immediate result, Bermudians have a civil airport they could never have afforded without help, a source of constant employment, a large group of resident American service men and families who form a welcome part of the Bermuda scene, and whose spendings help the local economy. The wheel had come full circle – fear was expressed locally at the possibility that American Bases might be cut back by the US Government. For, as always immediately after a war, there was a slight let down of military and naval activity. The Naval Station at N.O.B. went on a 'care and maintenance' basis, and later reverted to 'reduced operating status.' But world tension did not relax so that by August 1951 the Naval Station in Southampton was once again on full strength with 60 officers and 750 men. Captain Franklin Karns, then Commanding Officer, stated: 'Bermuda will always be important to the defence of the United States.'

As for the base then still called Kindley – at the eastern end of the island – Vice-Admiral Booth, Commander of the US Naval Air Forces in the Atlantic, visited it too in 1965 and expressed himself as delighted with the cordial relationship between the Bermudians and the American Services. The only airfield in Bermuda is this at the USAF Base which, completed in 1943 as Kindley Field for military purposes, has a sub-leased area at the western end open to civil aircraft since 1948 under an agreement between the government of USA and that of the United Kingdom. Both military and civil aircraft use the same runways and technical facilities; thus Bermuda benefits from an Airfield she could not easily have afforded single-handed. On 1st July 1970, a Transfer of Command Ceremony was held at Kindley Air Force Base at which the control passed from the Department of the US Air Force to the Department of the US Navy. It is now, therefore, the United States Naval Air Station. But so far as Bermuda operations are concerned, the Department of Civil Aviation is responsible to the Member of Executive Council for Marine and Air Services for carrying out civil aviation policy. And the Director of Civil Aviation is responsible to the Governor on matters concerning the Colonial Air Navigation Order.

To revert to Bermuda's more direct share in World War II: in 1939, the young men of these islands again, as in World War I, played their part by willingly volunteering to go overseas. Battalions of the (White) Bermuda Volunteer Rifle Corps (later to become the Bermuda Rifles) and the

(Coloured) Bermuda Militia Artillery, went to the Front in Europe and Africa to serve on land, sea and air. Those who remained guarded the islands' coasts and manned two coastal defence batteries. As we have seen, food and other necessities were strictly rationed; also travel out of the island was forbidden, restrictions were imposed on currency exchange, at night the streets were in total darkness.

Both of these local military units had originally been raised in 1895 and up to 1946 were subsidized by the British Treasury. At the latter date they were demobilized, retaining only a small nucleus. In 1951, both were re-organized, and in September 1965 were amalgamated into the present local defence force – the Bermuda Regiment. This was a step forward in the integration of the races; colours were presented to this amalgamated regiment on 24th November 1965 by HRH Princess Margaret, Countess of Snowdon.

Two indirect results – at least in part – of the war were the passing of the Woman's Suffrage Bill in 1944, and the general use of motor cars in 1946. That at last women were no longer classed with children and lunatics, were allowed to vote in parliamentary elections, was the climax to years of struggle (since 1898) intensified in 1918 when the women of England won enfranchisement. In Bermuda, women have always undertaken a large share of public responsibilities, a share that was increased tremendously by war-time conditions – a fact that doubtless led to the final assent to the Woman's Suffrage Bill. That the commemorative cedar planted in celebration in the Sessions House grounds fell victim to the terrible blight that destroyed Bermuda's cedars, merely emphasises an island-wide tragedy.

For in 1943-4, the one prolific and beloved Bermuda tree, Juniperus Bermudiana, known as the Bermuda cedar and a species peculiar to the islands, incredibly began to show signs of decay. And until at least 1952, a scale insect (carulaspis minima) waged a spreading war-fare throughout the land, gradually leaving a skeleton forest in its wake, over 99 per cent of the once-abundant and famed trees being virtually destroyed. Every effort was made by the Department of Agriculture and several imported specialists to combat this devastating attack, but all in vain. Local legend ascribed the onslaught to its accidental introduction on imported plants, but some visiting scientists considered that the scale insect was no new arrival but that the balance of nature had been upset by the extraordinary amount of spraying undertaken

— mainly because there was so much 'fresh blood' in the islands — to combat the mosquito which had spread dengue fever (or 'break-bone' as this acute tropical epidemic was locally dubbed.) Even a hurricane, with its deluging of salt spray, might have acted as Nature's pruning fork in the halting of the rapid advance of the scale insect ravaging the cedars, but, as it happened, a cycle of years, 1939-1947, passed with no direct hit. The Department of Agriculture and Fisheries (as now designated) worked for many years on the removal of dead trees and the mammoth task of reafforestation, chiefly with casuarinas, a genus of Australian origin.

Another indirect result of the war was the introduction of motor-cars in 1946.

When the news of the Bases agreement was divulged to the House of Assembly in March 1941, one of the questions most anxiously asked was: 'Will the Americans be allowed to operate motor-cars over the Colony's roads?' For not only had Bermudians jealously guarded the peace and unhurried quiet of the islands, but a very large number of influential American visitors had signed petitions to request that the law against motorization be retained. The reply in the Legislature was: 'The answer is "No".' However, the sting was in the qualifying tail: 'When the United States is engaged in war or in time of other emergency, they may operate motor-cars outside the leased areas.' To Bermudians toiling along their highways on foot, on pedal-bicycles, in buggies — often to the same destination as their American friends — it often appeared that the word 'emergency' was an elastic one. And, at the end of the war, the Americans declined to re-surface the badly traffic-scarred roads between their two Bases unless they could continue to operate motor-vehicles on them. At any rate the result was a foregone conclusion — one of the oddest indirect effects of the war after it was over was therefore the introduction of motor-cars for general use in August 1946. It is a change that has profoundly affected the pace, the restfulness of life, and has brought further problems in its train. The Motor Car Act was hotly debated by colonial parliamentarians for many months and only passed by the narrow margin of 15 votes to 14. The most comforting (and delusive!) assurance was that offered by the proponents of private cars: 'There will never be more than 500 of them on the roads — they're far too expensive.'

Cars were rigidly restricted to one per household, with a 2000 cc engine capacity and maximum width and length restricted to 64 and 166 inches respectively. ('An animated sardine-tin!' as one Honourable Member of the House of Assembly termed it,) while speed-limits were set at 20 mph, with 15 mph in built-up areas.

Twenty years later the total number of motor vehicles was in excess of 20,000. More than 12,000 of these were auto-cycles, scooters or auxiliary bicycles and there were 7,447 private cars in addition to some 500 taxis. Buses also covered all the main routes.

Several experts were called in by the government to solve this congestion problem on Bermuda's meagre network of roads – a mere 120 miles of public highway excluding the two municipalities of Hamilton and St George's – but their drastic advice was seldom followed. To abolish all private cars by 1965 as urged by the Tressider Report was unacceptable to the majority and H. Thornley Dyer's 1963 detailed report emphatically stated that to widen and straighten roads would be a palliative only and it would be fatal to Bermuda's charm to convert the lanes to major highways . . . Now, ten years on, there are approximately 36,000 registered vehicles including over ten thousand private cars and twice that number of two-wheeled motorised vehicles. The government realizes that positive action is necessary but any solution has considerable drawbacks since the use of private cars has at least resulted in a better spread of population.

Directly World War II was over it became apparent that the tourist trade was the one income-earner. The government, through the Department of Tourism, co-operated with steamship lines, travel agencies and hotels to develop it still further. Hotels and guest houses were being built in every part of the islands – even the destruction by fire of the old Hamilton Hotel in December 1955 and the Bermudiana in 1958 only meant that building and re-building went urgently on.

It was as well that Bermuda was now standing on her own feet for at last two Imperial sources of income ceased: in March 1951 the Admiralty closed the Bermuda dockyard, a source of employment for many years; and the British Garrison, after 174 years' occupation, was withdrawn in April 1953. A tentative return in 1954 was followed by a final withdrawal three years later. The Bermuda Crown Lands Corporation was formed to administer the dismantled land and buildings and in 1956 a Free Port was established on Ireland Island to encourage light industry.

Since there are no minerals or other material resources, Bermuda has to depend entirely on her lovely climate, beautiful scenery, and kindly genial inhabitants for her attractiveness to outsiders. In realizing this, she has moved into an era of prosperity, and become an affluent society with a high standard of living.

12

The Present Era : Politics and Problems

With all this surge of attention from the outside world intensified by the thousands of visitors who regarded the history of the little group of islands as unique — and, often, as shedding an oblique light on the early development of their own countries and their own ancestors — the proverbial man in the street began to take an enthralled interest in the colony's earlier days. The two, still-active, historical societies (the Bermuda Historical Society in Hamilton and the St George's Historical Society); the devoted body of men and women who, as the Bermuda Historical Monuments Trust, laboured for thirty years to preserve all old buildings and ancient relics; and the Bermuda National Trust which has taken over from this last have all stimulated the concern and carried forward the torch lighted by such nineteenth century historians as Sir John Henry Lefroy and William Frith Williams. The reverse of the coin — that some careless pseudo-history is compiled as tourist-bait — is probably inevitable in a resort and is easily rectified by studying early records or such standard scholarly works as those written by Dr Henry Wilkinson and published by the Oxford University Press from the 1930's onward. In fact, for those who will take time and trouble, Bermuda history is heavily documented.

And not only historians, but botanists, zoologists, bibliographers, meteorologists, seismologists: students of every form of scientific data began in the early twentieth century to make the islands a happy hunting ground. To give but one instance: Dr William Beebe, the famous oceanographer, and Director of Tropical Research for the New York Zoological Society, set up an experimental station in the late 1920s and early 1930s on that high and pleasant 14½-acre island on the fringe of Castle Harbour known as Nonsuch. From here he conducted his sub-marine experiments in the bathysphere, attaining a record depth of 3028 feet, and wrote his books on oceanography and the natural wild life of the island. In 1962, the government conservation officer, warden of the Castle

Harbour Islands as a bird sanctuary, took up residence on this island and attempted to preserve it as a nature reserve for strictly endemic flora and fauna. In particular, the breeding habits of the cahow were carefully studied since this rare bird, so named by the early castaways and long considered extinct, had been re-discovered in 1951. And amazing finds of sub-marine treasure around the coasts from the sixteenth century wrecks were made by such treasure-divers as Teddy Tucker with his partner, Bob Canton, also by Harry Cox.

With all the outside interest in Bermuda's uniqueness, it was inevitable that local celebrations of all kinds began to assume considerable éclat. It was true that, back in 1920, the 300th anniversary of Bermuda's parliament had occasioned considerably more stir than had the rather tepid commemoration in 1909 of the islands' historical commencement, but both of these were totally eclipsed by the 350th anniversary of the latter in 1959 when ten successive nights of pageants were enacted before thousands of spectators on the very foreshores where Sir George Somers had originally landed. And a more permanent memorial was the erection of the fine new City Hall on Church Street (on the site of the fire-destroyed Hamilton Hotel) with Art Gallery, Theatre and other public rooms in addition to the offices of the Mayor and Corporation – the whole a fitting memorial to Bermuda's noted architect, the late Will Onions. The building was formally opened in February 1960 by the new governor, Major-General Sir Julian Alvery Gascoigne, substantial funds having been left towards the project by Catherine Browne Tucker in memory of her father, the Hon. George Somers Tucker. A Time Capsule, with recorded talks by mid-twentieth century Bermudians was buried in the hall to commemorate Bermuda's 350th anniversary, with directions for its disinterment at the 500th anniversary in the year 2109.

By this time – 1959 – population figures had climbed to 42,000, an increase of 140 per cent during the first half of the century, Bermuda was having the biggest building boom on record, the tourist figures soared as the new Bermudiana Hotel was opened in April of that year on the ashes of the old one (destroyed by fire in 1958) to be followed by the Sonesta Beach being built in 1961 (under the name Carlton Beach) and subsequent plans for others. The islands had indeed ceased to be a simple agricultural community, were entirely committed to tourism and its accompanying high standard of living.

Not that the British heritage was forgotten. Six years before these commemorative celebrations, the ties of loyalty for the Mother Country had been re-inforced by the first visit of a British reigning monarch: in November 1953, five months after her coronation, Her Majesty Queen Elizabeth II, accompanied by Prince Philip, was enthusiastically welcomed for a twenty-four-hour stay. There had been previous royal visits, the very first of all being that of Prince Alfred, second son of Queen Victoria who arrived 6th May 1861 when serving as a midshipman in HMS *St George* – followed in April 1880 by two sons of the then Prince of Wales serving as midshipmen in HMS *Bacchante*; the younger of these, Prince George, Duke of York, returned in 1890 in command of HMS *Thrush* and, twenty years later became King George V. Meanwhile, Queen Victoria's third daughter, HRH Princess Louise had resided at Inglewood, Paget, for the winter season 1882-83 when her husband, then Marquess of Lorne, was Governor-General of Canada. But the list of royalties is too long to detail – although two more future kings should be recorded in the visits of Prince Albert – afterwards King George VI at the abdication of his elder brother, King Edward VIII – who came here as a naval cadet in 1913 in HMS *Cumberland*. And, perhaps the best remembered, that of the late Duke of Windsor (d. May 1972) who spent three days in the islands in 1920 as the acclaimed Prince of Wales, returned briefly with his brother, Prince George in 1931 – and last, in September 1940, four years after his abdication, passed through with his Duchess en route to the Bahamas. Absurdly enough, the most oft-reiterated Royal Visit, that of King William IV as Duke of Clarence and Sailor Prince, during the reign of George III, is an entire fabrication – the

---

(*above*) New York-Bermuda Biennial Ocean Yacht Race. Craft assembling off Brenton's Reef near Newport, R.I. for the start of this gruelling race over 700 miles of ocean. Two Bermuda entries, KB 5 and KB 7, are in this picture of the start of one of the classes.

(*below*) The truly indigenous sport of Bermuda dinghy racing is recognized as the most acrobatic and hazardous of aquatic sports. The boats (14 foot 1 inch 'wood ends to wood ends') may carry as much spread of sail as 1000 square feet. The *Venture*, built, owned and sailed by the Worshipful Mayor of St George's, the Hon. Norman R. Roberts, is a frequent sight during races in St George's Harbour. (*Photos by Bernard Brown*)

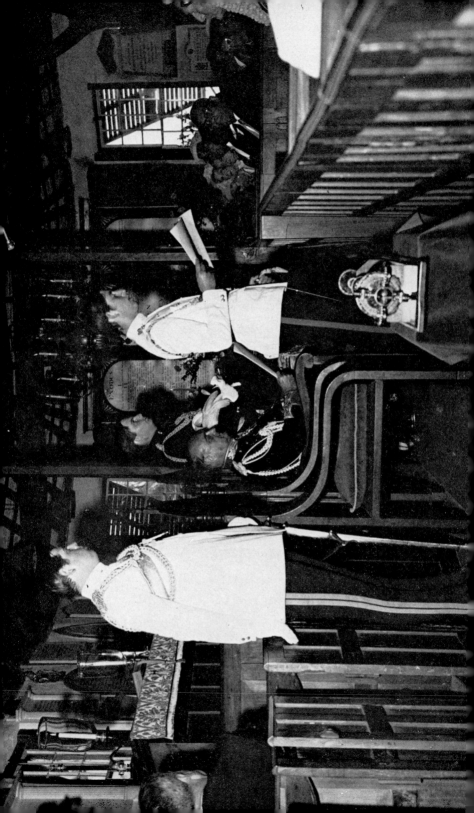

archives in the Round Tower at Windsor Castle, the logs of each ship on which His Royal Highness, was 'borne,' and the National Maritime Museum Records at Greenwich all disprove that most persistent and long-lived legend. Actually he was never within fifty miles of Bermuda.

But none of these was of a reigning monarch, consequently that of Queen Elizabeth II in 1953 was truly memorable. In her speech in the House of Assembly she said (in part): 'Nor is it British parliamentary institutions alone which have grown and flourished in Bermuda: for our British outlook and customs have taken firm root and in the old country they may be proud of this plant which has sprung from British seed. I am sensible that the loyalty which you have expressed to me in words has in the past found expression in deeds. This colony has played a long part in the struggles which have built up the British Commonwealth overseas, and in recent years in two world wars Bermudians have proudly stepped into the position they inherit as the oldest unit of the British Commonwealth overseas and have fought side by side with their fellows for its preservation.'

This great occasion naturally overshadowed in popularity even the arrival in December of that same year of Winston Churchill to take part in the Three-Power Talks with the President of the USA (Eisenhower) and the Premier of France (Laniel.) But Churchill was regarded with pride and affection since his previous surprise visit to Bermuda in January 1942, necessarily shrouded in secrecy at that dark period of the war, had brought re-assurance to the islanders when he had addressed a joint meeting of the Legislature in which he gave thanks for their 'important contribution to a better world' in sacrificing precious land . . . So it was with sincerity that Bermuda, as Britain's oldest colony, shared the

---

The 350th Anniversary of Bermuda's Parliament in 1970 was marked by a visit from His Royal Highness, Prince Charles, Prince of Wales, to participate in the celebrations. On 21st October, Parliament was convened in St Peter's Church, St George's, site of the first meeting of Bermuda's Parliament on 1st August 1620 when convened by Governor Nathaniel Butler. His Royal Highness read the Throne Speech presented to him by the Government Leader, Sir Henry Tucker. His Excellency the Governor, Lord Martonmere, listened from a chair beside him. This marks the fact that the Bermuda Parliament is the oldest of all the parliaments of British Commonwealth countries overseas. (*Bermuda News Bureau photo*)

grief of the Commonwealth at Winston Churchill's death in January 1965. The Hon. Sir John Cox, then Speaker of the House of Assembly, flew to England to attend the funeral.

But to return to 1959 – the great 350th anniversary year of the island's history as an inhabited place – it was a year that saw Bermuda at its best and its worst. Amid the almost continuous celebrations, there had also been the first labour troubles of any note: tension, strikes, boycotts, and an unprecedented wave of violent crime.

That same year saw the voluntary end to segregation for dining and dancing in the islands' major hotels: Bermuda was swiftly moving towards the biggest social, economic and political changes in her entire history, most of which have taken place since 1963 when the first General Election was held under Universal Franchise.

It was in the 1960s also that Trade Unionism was generally accepted as a fact of life; a new Trade Union Bill became law in July 1965. This was recognition legislation, and by the close of the following year new picketing rules had to be enforced. By the 1970s there were eight or nine Trade Unions with thousands of members, among them the very powerful Bermuda Industrial Union. The Amalgamated Bermuda Union of Teachers, the Dockworkers Union, Bermuda Federation of Variety Artists, the Electric Supply Trade Union, the Union of Government Industrial Employees and several others proliferated.

But although to many Bermudians this seemed a recent phenomenon, actually the movement evolved from the activities of Dr Edgar Fitzgerald Gordon, a Trinidadian of Coloured and Portuguese parents who came to Bermuda in 1924 in his thirtieth year. In 1946 he won a seat in the House of Assembly as a member for St George's and was a leader of the labour movement, having founded the Bermuda Workers' Association in 1944. As President of that Association in 1946 he took a petition to London praying for the appointment of a Royal Commission to report on social, economic, and political conditions in the Colony. As a result, the Colonial Office produced a White Paper for the attention of the Bermuda Legislature which resulted in a joint Parliamentary Committee formulating certain recommendations. In addition to being President of the Bermuda Workers' Association he was President-general of the Bermuda Industrial Union, and President of the Bermuda Progressive League. He called a post-war Dock Strike as protest against low wages and the high cost of living. In 1947 he renounced the name of Gordon and took that of Mazumbo.

He died in Bermuda 20th April 1955 and three thousand people attended his funeral.

The emergence of political parties in England in the seventeenth and eighteenth centuries was not echoed in Bermuda until the middle of the twentieth century with the emergence of the – mainly Black – Progressive Labour Party, six of whom won seats at that time in the then 36-member House of Assembly. Another political group, the United Bermuda Party, developed in the following year eschewing racial lines. It did not, in fact, take long for the advent of universal franchise to bring in its wake various political groupings – as many, at one time, as eight sporadic parties – but later they mainly boiled down to the Progressive Labour Party, the United Bermuda Party, the Independents, and the Bermuda Democratic Party.

The Bill of 1961-62 which reformed the Parliamentary Franchise had stirred considerable controversy. Up to 1963, when the new Act was implemented, the franchise had been restricted to owners (Black or White) of real estate to a modest stated value who would therefore have a stake in the colony's well being. Bermuda was then a paternalistic oligarchy – perhaps closer to the famous Athenian democracy than we admit to-day! The new Act made provision for universal adult suffrage from the age of 25 years to all British subjects who had resided in the Colony for at least three years and the constituencies consisted of 18 electoral districts, two for each of the nine parishes, each to return two members to the House of Assembly – 36 M.C.P.s in all. A last minute amendment, a concession to the land-owners who had formerly been the only voters, allowed them a 'plus vote' in addition. This plus vote was abolished before the next general election (of 1968) by the Parliamentary Election Act of 1966 which also lowered the voting age to 21, and appointed a Boundaries Commission to revise constituencies before 1968. By this revision, heavily populated Pembroke Parish was divided into four constituencies, the other eight parishes continued with two each, thereby increasing the number of seats in the House of Assembly from 36 to its present 40 . . . The Parliamentary Election Act had exactly quadrupled the potential electorate.

The General Election of May 1968 was therefore the first to appoint 40 members, the first conducted on political party lines, and with the voting age reduced to 21 years. It was a milestone in Bermuda political history. The result was a bi-racial vote of confidence in the United Bermuda Party which won 30 out of the 40 seats, the remaining 10 going to the Progressive Labour Party. The Bermuda Democratic Party and the Independents failed to win seats. The Governor, Lord Martonmere, invited Sir Henry Tucker, C.B.E., J.P., to be Bermuda's first Government Leader: and Mrs L. M. Browne-Evans was appointed Opposition Leader.

In the next General Election of June 1972 only two of the parties ran for seats; there were 23091 registered voters with a potential 46,182 votes. Again the U.B.P. attained 30 seats in the House of Assembly, the P.L.P., ten. Sir Edward Richards, Bermuda's first Black Knight, became Government Leader in place of Sir Henry Tucker (who retired from politics after thirty years in the House), and Progressive Labour Party Leader, Mr Walter Robinson, became Leader of the Opposition.

With the emergence of and struggle between political parties it had become obvious before 1968 that Bermuda's Constitution itself, which had remained unwritten and virtually unchanged, needed considerable overhauling. In the earliest days, as we have seen, the governor had represented the Company, and from 1684 he was the representative of the Crown. The members of the Governor's Council, which performed functions akin to these of the present day Legislative Council but in essence was the fore-runner of the Executive Council whose advisory role remained virtually unchanged until 1968, together with the members of the House of Assembly, were representative of the people of Bermuda. Until 1968 therefore government was representative rather than responsible — by personalities and not by political parties or policies.

The new Constitution which came into force 8 June 1968 made sweeping and fundamental changes while preserving the ancient designations of Governor, Executive Council, Legislative Council and House of Assembly. It brought responsible government to Bermuda. The 63-page Bermuda Constitutional Order, 1968, was agreed upon at a Conference held in London November 1966. Under its provisions, Bermuda's administrative head is the governor, who is appointed by the crown. He has special responsibility for external affairs and matters of security. There is a bicameral legislature, which consists of an upper house, (the Legislative Council) of 11 members appointed by the governor, some with the advice of the government and opposition leaders; and a lower house (the House of Assembly) of 40 members elected in 2-member constituencies by universal franchise. They meet in the Sessions House, Hamilton.

The Governor is assisted by an executive council consisting of The Government Leader and at least six other members of the legislature. The Governor must take the advice of the Council in all matters except those that are reserved to him.

The Legislative Council meets in the Legislative Council Chambers of the Cabinet (Public Building), Hamilton. The Executive Council now meets in the General Post Office Building.

The main effect of the new Constitution is to make the relationship between the law-making Assembly and the Executive which carries those laws out, more workable.

From the earliest days of the Colony, there had been Secretaries, but it was in the eighteenth century that the term Colonial Secretary in the modern sense was used. With the new Constitution of Bermuda, the office of Colonial Secretary as such has been abolished, and a Chief Secretary has been appointed who deputizes for the Governor in the event of his absence or illness.

The bi-racial government of the United Bermuda Party settled down to make the 1968 Constitution work, especially in such fields as housing, education and social services. The Opposition, Progressive Labour Party, whose platform calls for independence from Britain and for direct taxation, voted against all measures to implement the new constitution.

Perhaps inevitably, the political campaigns preceding the May 1968 general election had generated tension and some racial antagonisms particularly among the growing segment of youth, that resulted in an outbreak of civil disorder in the last week of April. Rioting and arson on three successive days led to His Excellency, Lord Martonmere, declaring a state of emergency, imposing a curfew, and calling for assistance from Her Majesty's government. HMS *Leopard* arrived on 27th April and the following day a Detachment of the Royal Innis-Killing Fusiliers flew in from England. The state of emergency was lifted by 8th May, and a commission of inquiry was appointed under the Chief Justice of Trinidad and Tobago. Vast changes have since been implemented in youth services, integration in education, housing, social services.

In fact, Lord Martonmere under whose twice-extended term of duty as governor many of these adjustments had taken place, was warmly thanked and congratulated by all segments of society at his departure in August 1972.

To bring completely up to date the sweeping changes in Bermuda's Constitution, it must be noted that further developments took place in April 1973 when the title of Government Leader was changed to that of Premier; thus Bermuda's first Black Knight, Sir Edward Richards, became the colony's first Premier. At the same time, former government Members were now designated Cabinet Ministers, and the office of Chief Secretary (which had taken the place of Colonial Secretary in June 1968) was now abolished. While members of Colonial Parliament are now Members of Parliament — M.P's —. All these advances were significant proofs of the power wielded by the elected representatives of the people.

High hopes had been entertained for the next several years of the new governor's tenure of office. Sir Richard Christopher Sharples, who arrived in the islands on 12th October 1972, had served with distinction in World War II as assistant to Field Marshal Viscount Montgomery, had a parliamentary career at Westminster which included his appointment as Minister of State for Home Affairs, and, to Bermudians, it mattered even more that he was an experienced agriculturalist and a keen yachtsman. He and Lady Sharples reached out in friendship and sympathy to every segment of the population, making an indelible impression full of hope and promise, since Sir Richard's ambition was to be 'The People's Governor.' But alas! 10th March 1973 was a black day in Bermuda's 364-years of history for it was then, after a brief five months of governorship, that he and his young A.D.C., Capt. Hugh Sayers, were riddled by an unknown assassin's bullets while walking in the grounds of Government House. All Bermuda was shocked and outraged by the senseless crime. On her return to England in May 1973, Lady Sharples, who had shown great magnanimity throughout, was created a Life Peeress.

In the meantime, the Hon. Ian A. C. Kinnear had again taken up the reins as Acting Governor till the arrival in July 1973 of the new appointee, Sir Edwin H. C. Leather, who, born in Hamilton, Ontario, had held a seat at Westminster and been Chairman of the Tory Party Conference in 1970.

To revert to the welter of problems faced over recent

years, that of currency must be mentioned. Up until the first few weeks of 1970, the local currency consisted of Bermuda Government notes in denominations of £10, £5, £1, 10s and 5s in addition to the metal coinage of Great Britain. On 6th February 1970, the currency was decimalized; the Bermuda Monetary Authority issued new notes of $50., $20., $10., $5., and $1., and coinage of 50¢, 25¢, 10¢, 5¢, and 1¢. BD $2.40 was established as equal to £1 sterling.

However, in June 1972, the colony received an unexpected jolt in the decision made by Britain to float the pound and disband the sterling area. This ejection of Bermuda from the sterling area was a traumatic experience which resulted in an immediate – fruitless – financial delegation to London, and then the set-up on 30th June 1970 of Bermuda as the world's smallest independent monetary area – this in an effort to stave off the threat to the island's economy. The local economic set-up is complicated by Bermuda's reliance on tourism (founded on the dollar) and on the, partly sterling, off-shore company business known as exempted companies, scores of which are established at the Freeport at Ireland Island where they are relieved from property taxes and customs duties but pay licence fees to the Bermuda government.

Bermuda currency is now pegged to the US dollar, but there is some discussion as to a change in the designation of the local currency unit. Unfortunately this experience may weaken the colony's ancient links with the Mother Country.

Such ties have been emphasized, of course, by such recent happy events as the two-day visit in October 1970 of His Royal Highness the Prince of Wales, to take part in the 350th Anniversary of Bermuda's Parliament. At the convening of Parliament in historic St Peter's Church in St George's, Prince Charles – at the express wish of Her Majesty the Queen – read the speech from the Throne to a deeply-stirred congregation (consisting of Members of the Legislature and invited guests) which listened while some of the idealistic phrases used on 1st August 1620 in 'the Church in St George's' by Governor Nathaniel Butler reminded them of what a government should stand for – and then continued with a programme of present and future aims. The then Governor, Lord Martonmere, listened from a chair beside him.

Following a tour of the island in an open car when all school children were ranged alongside the roads to greet this smiling young prince, he attended the Speaker's Dinner where the then Speaker of the House, Lt Col J. C. Astwood (now Sir Jeffrey) was host for the evening, and Prince Charles made the principal speech — both grave and gay.

There had been outbreaks of vandalism, violence and arson during the year, but the Royal Visit passed off happily and peacefully. The Opposition Progressive Labour Party abstained from events arranged for the visit but theirs is not a policy of violence. To show that law and order form one of the few barriers left between civilized life and barbarism has become a world problem — on the whole, Bermuda is relaxed and easy-going due both to her climate and her intimate size.

These are indeed the fortunate islands. From being shunned, unwanted, isolated, impoverished, they have emerged as a prosperous and affluent society that still combines with its natural loveliness and mild climate the facilities of modern life; so far from being isolated, to-day its geographical position renders it a cross-roads for air-lines and steamship services. Still further, it has managed to preserve enough of its traditional and historical background to retain character — its appeal is therefore unique. And though residents sometimes bewail that the noise and bustle of the outside world is intruding on the ancient peace, visitors are always quick to comment on the relaxed atmosphere, the slower pace and the freedom of friendliness that rightly belongs with a small and intimate community.

Almost 11,000 families own private cars (restricted to one per household); in addition there are more than 24,000 auxiliary and motor-cycles. Bermuda boasts 50.84 telephones per 100 of the population. Nearly every household has a television set and certainly a radio; in fact, the number of radio receivers in use averages one for every two persons, one of the highest figures in the world. There are no slums or shanty towns. Jobs are guarded for local residents since no non-Bermudian may take employment without specific per-

---

The ancient capital, St. George's, has, in the 1970s, been busy restoring its historic buildings. Among them is the State House, whose history has already been given (picture p. 82), now occupied by the Freemasons, as seen opposite.

(*overleaf*) The Tall Ships with their nostalgic reminders of early days in Bermuda's history.

mission from the Board of Immigration. Even the lower paid workers make about $100 a week. Education is compulsory and free between the ages of 5-16 (fees only being charged in the three private schools,) and integration is accelerating on a new government 'amalgamation' scheme. Although there is no university, extra-mural courses are available from two North American Universities. Rhodes scholarships to Oxford have been held by Bermudians since 1904, while firms, private agencies and the Bermuda Government provide opportunities for some 40 persons each year to be trained abroad at university level. In fact, there are numerous scholarships and bursaries in addition to interest-free government loans.

Income tax is not levied but there is a land tax. And Customs Tariff is approximately 57 per cent of the total revenue, its object being to raise revenue not to exclude imports.

And against this social background, approximately 388,000 tourists a year pour some $73,000,000 into the island's economy, enabling the residents to enjoy an enviably high standard of living, while the visitors themselves are enraptured by brilliant seas, golden sunshine, burgeoning flowers — above all, a relaxed and peaceful atmosphere.

But even a boom economy may suffer economic indigestion. Even Paradise produces its problems.

PROBLEMS

First — the problem of sheer living space.

We may recall that in 1940, 1.08 miles of the colony were leased for Bases to USA out of the 19.34 square miles which composed the group, thus leaving 18.26 square miles available to the local population. The Americans sensibly dredged a further 1.25 square miles, so now occupy 2.33 square

---

Since it opened in early 1975, the Bermuda Maritime Museum has attracted tens of thousands of visitors who have been able to take a close look at the island's historic love affair with the sea. Housing a vast collection of nautical artifacts and memorabilia, the Museum is situated at the extreme western end of Bermuda in the Keepyard of the former Royal Navy Dockyard. The building housing the main section of the museum served at one time as an ammunition magazine.

miles making the total land area due to be returned to the
Bermuda government in A.D. 2040 an enlarged 20.59 square
miles. In the meantime, the total space available to the local
population is, of course, still 18.26 square miles.

And the population for that area? The last Census, that
of 1970 states that there are 53,000 residents plus 3000
members of the UK, US and Canadian armed forces with their
dependents, i.e. approx. 56,000 persons − more than 3000
per square mile − if one includes military personnel. And the
Colonial Report estimate for 1969 gives two-thirds of the
population Coloured to one third White.

Britain is one of the more densely populated countries of
the world with 580 people per square mile − nine times as
many as in the United States. India, considered grossly
over-populated, has only one-fifth the population pressure of
Bermuda, even if we omit our military personnel and
tourists . . . It is obvious then that unless we wish to face a
future of complete social breakdown, sooner or later com-
pulsory legislation will have to compel zero population
growth − unless, that is, voluntary birth control becomes
more effective. The Bermuda government has sponsored birth
control clinics for over thirty-five years but this has not
halted population increase sufficiently. Of course the whole
world is facing population explosion but in restricted areas
like Bermuda it is soonest noticeable. In 1972 there were
some 14,000 children in Bermuda schools. Eventually, jobs
will have to be found for all of them. And living space.

Dredging 2000 acres from the sea is one of the suggested
future necessary projects − but a palliative only at best.

Not that the undulating countryside gives an impression of
over-crowding. On the contrary − except for Hamilton and
St George's − it resembles a continuous village, each little
snow-white roof its own water-catch nestling among hibiscus
and oleander. But land is inevitably at a premium, therefore
rents are stiff, and the government is forced to underwrite
middle and lower-price housing projects. In fact, Nicholas
Colchester (*The Financial Times* 29th June 1971) sums up
Bermuda's problems as stemming partly from the paradox
that 'now . . . Bermuda finds itself too much loved.' A far cry
from the sixteenth century shunned Island of Devils!

To support this burgeoning population, a steady expansion
of the tourist industry is a necessity. The extremely active
Department of Tourism steers continually between Scylla
and Charybdis: a drop in the tourist trade would be a
disaster, hence their advertising campaigns, lecture tours,

insistence on no neon signs, no billboards, no litter, and on the other hand, limits on hotel construction (no more to be built through 1975-6 except those already approved) and a definite ruling on Cruise Ships which are now limited to two berthed in Hamilton and one at St George's simultaneously – in fact, Bermuda has turned away 134 proposed cruise ships for 1973, and accommodates about 170 a year. This is to ensure that there are sufficient facilities for everyone – taxis, room in buses, tables in restaurants, service in shops . . . Even so, by 1975 the colony had 10,400 beds for tourists compared with 7800 in 1972.

Bermuda's roadage is a mere 120 miles (exclusive of the two municipalities), evolved in picturesque curves from early unpaved cart-tracks. Great efforts are made to keep the number of mechanised vehicles down to the 35,000 now using them. And to avoid construction of a straight motor highway from one end of the island to the other. Here, again, it would be a palliative at best soon overtaken by the expanding number of vehicles. The only answer is to keep their number down.

As for arable land – 550 acres of farming land is all that remains, and even that is disappearing at the rate of 25 acres a year despite the protests of the Agriculture and Fisheries Department which points out that, at this rate, in twenty years not an open field will be left . . . Sewage, garbage disposal, pollution – all the problems of dense population are being faced with courage and determination.

Inflation is of course one of the specific problems. The cost of living rises inexorably. The Government set up a Rents Commissioner in 1972 to help combat it. The 1972/3 Budget was $48.4 million. But though the visible balance of trade continues adverse, invisible items provide fully compensating revenue – among others the tourist business, services supplied the US Bases, and the continued establishment of exempted international companies. Bermuda's economy continues in a sound condition. Her social welfare and Social Security services have taken giant steps forward in the last few years, with the Budget for 1978 at $89 million.

Nevertheless, as we have seen, tragic events of March 1973 rendered that a deeply shadowed year. Concern was also felt at the increase in crime, in the pressures of motor traffic, and at local inflation caused by the world energy crisis. But even these must be seen against the day-by-day living of a tiny community where the smallest happenings become part of the warp and woof of destiny, and where the large majority of citizens are concerned to retain not only law and order but neighbourliness. To recall typical events, great and small, of these years, is to visualize something of the local scene.

In 1973, the Mayors of both Hamilton and St George's were returned to office and have so remained since: the Wor. Graham Gibbons as mayor of the capital, Hamilton, and the Wor. Norman Roberts in the old town, St George's. . . . In April, the Bishop of Bermuda, the Rt Revd Eric J. Trapp, announced that he wished to disestablish the Church of England in Bermuda, in order to bring it in line with modern times; it is now the Anglican Church, one of very many religious sects in the Islands.

Both the Bermuda National Trust and the Biological Station continued their devoted services to conservation and to scientific research — as did also the Conservation Officer, David Wingate. Also, by early 1974, the Housing Corporation began actively assisting residents towards home ownership. But there were still spectres of inflation, and, in some disputes, strikes were called by the Bermuda Industrial Union. The world-wide energy crisis was felt in Bermuda households; land-tax rates were approximately doubled in July 1974.

In April of that year, the *Queen Elizabeth II* limped into local waters under her own power, after lying helplessly at sea 250 miles off Bermuda due to engine failure; her 1600 passengers had to be rescued and evacuated by a ship on the Bermuda run. The event was a godsend to some journalists who were thus enabled to write on occult forces at work within the so-called Bermuda Triangle. (This hocus-pocus backfired later with a rival resort having to retract an advertisement that led travellers to believe the whole Bermuda area too hazardous to approach with impunity!).

Happily, this was a year for the bi-ennial Newport-Bermuda Yacht Race, and by July over three thousand yachtsmen, relations and friends were here, enjoying the nautical atmosphere so natural to Bermudians — and adding an estimated $4 million to local coffers. . . . Also, adding to the aquatic attractions was the happy idea, formulated by Lieut.-Col. Michael Darling and the late Forster Cooper, of turning the old Keepyard, at what had been H.M. Dockyard, into a Maritime Museum. This had been the Royal Navy's base in the Western Atlantic for almost 150 years, and its massive buildings and vaulted ceilings are a wonderful setting for exhibits dealing with Bermuda maritime history. The scene is dominated by the figure-head of Neptune, originally borne by H.M.S. *Irresistible.* Fortunately, the whole exhibit was ready by February 1975, when the Queen and the Duke of Edinburgh were here on a visit and Her Majesty formally opened what has become a valuable attraction. This successful royal visit was not affected by a strike called during that month by the Bermuda Industrial Union which resulted in a complete halt to bus and ferry services.

On the eve of 1976, the Hon. Sir Edward Richards resigned from the Premiership, his position being taken by the Hon. Jack (later Sir John) Sharpe. In February, the new Anglican Bishop, the Right Revd Robert Stopford, arrived by air and was warmly received. Sadly enough, he died six months later. His successor, the Right Revd Anselm Genders, appointed from a Community of Anglican monks, was enthroned in a ceremony at the Bermuda Cathedral in November 1977. May 1975 had seen the arrival of the new Roman Catholic Bishop, the Most Revd Hennessy, who was warmly welcomed.

The story of American colonization and that of Bermuda is so intertwined that it was natural for the islanders to take an interest in the Bicentennial celebrations being held in the United States. The Queen and Prince Philip had already — in July 1976 — passed through Bermuda, arriving by air and departing in the royal yacht, *Britannia,* to honour the ceremonies in America, and now in November 1976 Bermuda herself presented a salutation by holding a week's historical conference, stressing the importance to world peace of the alliance of the English-speaking peoples. Dr William E. Tucker chaired this very successful conference which included professional speakers from universities in several countries, as well as our local historians, and was under the patronage of His Excellency Sir Edwin Leather.

But if all of these were events of special dates and occasions, of even greater general significance are the loved annual celebrations in which the people as a whole take part from year to year, regarding them as the highlights of their existence. We have already commented on the origins and early days of two of the most popular — the three-day Agricultural Exhibition (which includes everything possible in addition to the fruits of the earth!) and the two-day Cup Match, — cricket and all that goes with it. Bermuda's fortieth Annual Agricultural Exhibition was celebrated in May of 1976 with over 22,000 people attending and a record fifteen hundred exhibitors. The two succeeding ones to date have proved equally popular. The Department of Agriculture and Fisheries does yeoman service in these islands.

The seventy-fifth Annual Cup Match, played in August of that same year before a crowd of 12,000 spectators, resulted in a draw between the Somerset and St George's teams – as did those of the two succeeding years. This is the great sporting event of Bermuda's cricketing world.

No more majestic a sight can be imagined than that provided by the graceful fully-rigged tall ships which visited us in June 1976 on the third leg of their race to Newport. This Tall Ships Race is always a dream of beauty when, sails fully set, they disappear over the horizon before the enraptured gaze of hundreds of people who climb the hills of St David's Island to watch, almost nostalgically, this reminder of the "Sea Venture" and the beginnings of their history.

In April of 1977 Sir Edwin and Lady Leather left for a holiday in England at the close of his governorship and were given an affectionate send-off by many sections of Bermuda into whose concerns Sir Edwin had entered so heartily. He and Lady Leather returned to live here as private citizens, and Sir Edwin then published his first novel.

In May of that year Sir Peter Ramsbotham, the British Ambassador to Washington, was named as governor. He was not entirely unknown to Bermudians as he had attended the previous year's Bicentennial Salutation and banquet. As an accomplished diplomat, he is a great addition to the list of Bermuda's outstanding governors. Until his arrival, with Lady Ramsbotham, in September 1977, the Hon. Peter Lloyd, CMG, took up the reins as Acting Governor.

As the Queen's Silver Jubilee Year, 1977 took on an added significance with its series of celebrations in June, commencing with an Interdenominational Service at the National Stadium. A military tattoo, a 'sail-past', and brilliant firework displays in the night sky above Hamilton Harbour, were all part of the rejoicings.

Another notable event of that year was the extension of Bermuda's territorial waters from twelve to two hundred miles, as enacted in June by the House of Assembly and approved originally by a Law of the Sea Conference held in April 1976. This should be beneficial to the local fishing industry.

The Bermuda Regiment also came under scrutiny after some criticisms made regarding its activities in Barbados while in training camp. Major-General Glyn Gilbert was selected to head a probe into allegations, and to make suggestions regarding the Regiment's future.

These continuing and yet gradually changing scenes in sports, amusements, celebrations, briefly outlined here, are part of the warp and woof of this little closely-knit community that is Bermuda: a mere 18¼ square miles of civilian living-space, heavily populated by two races, which meet, mingle, greet, every day at every level of society. And beneath this surface, public opinions, tastes, habits, prejudices, customs, also change, and yet continue endlessly. Perhaps this is nowhere more true than in the area of politics.

We have seen the emergence of political parties (at one time as many as eight!) in the 1960s, and the results in the General Elections of 1968 and 1972. The assertion is sometimes made that the adoption of party politics heightens tensions. Nevertheless, the system is popularly accepted and, for the most part, with merely two parties. In the 1976 General Election held in May, the (bi-racial) United Bermuda Party was again returned to power, but with a narrower majority in the forty-seat House of Assembly, with the Hon. Jack Sharpe as Premier and Sir Dudley Spurling as Speaker. The (mainly Black) Progessive Labour Party, under its new Leader, Mrs Lois Browne-Evans, picked up an extra four seats and considerably enhanced its position.

By August of 1977, dissension within the United Bermuda Party ranks resulted in the resignation of the Premier, Sir John Sharpe, and the appointment of the Hon. David Gibbons as his successor, with the Hon. C.V. Woolridge as Deputy Premier, and the swearing-in of a new Cabinet, emphasizing a united Bermuda of all persons and both races.

Unhappily, the first three days of the December of that year saw a repetition of the riots of 1968. This time the distrubances were sparked off by politically-motivated inflammatory speeches relating to the legal execution of two murderers, convicted in Bermuda courts by a Bermudian jury. A State of Emergency was declared, a curfew imposed, and the Royal Regiment of Fusiliers was called in as a standby, if needed, for the exhausted local forces of law and order: the Bermuda Regiment and the Bermuda Police. As it happened, the active services of the Fusiliers were not required; but it was reassuring to realize they had been on their way within one hour of the island's request to England for assistance. And, as Frank Manning remarks in his *Bermudian Politics in Transition* (published 1978): "Law and discipline issues provide a common ground, and a very conservative one, on which all Bermudians stand."

The Governor called in the Premier and the Leader of the Opposition for a riot enquiry. This resulted in a Royal Commission under Lord Pitt holding lengthy public hearings of anyone and everyone's idea of their grievances – sessions which lasted from 5th April to 23rd May 1978. The resulting "Report of the Royal Commission into the 1977 Disturbances in Bermuda" was produced by 14th July 1978 in which it was urged that a conference be held before the close of 1978 to decide all the recommendations made therein, particularly that relating to the question of independence.

The majority of Bermudians, when confronted with this option, are apt to reply in astonishment: "Independence? Independence *from what?*" For as things stand at present, the island seems to enjoy what foreign newspapers dubbed "the best of both worlds" – i.e. entire freedom to run her own internal affairs through her own parliament, yet with the protective wing of Great Britain ready to be called upon only in moments of calamity or emergency. . . . To choose either the United States or Canada to take over this protective role, seems of dubious benefit, since we would not only be cutting ourselves off from an historic past of great interest both to our tourists and to ourselves, but – in the case of the United States – would be throwing away the huge income we derive from their exempted companies. Though England leaves it entirely to the islanders to make their own final decision, it would indeed be a final step from which there is no returning. And to what end?

By June of 1978, the economy generally, and the tourist trade in particular, were reported by the Banks to be thoroughly recovering from the devastating effects of the six-months-earlier disturbances. The rally was due to tremendous efforts to restore the tourist trade made by the government, the hotels, and all others involved in the welfare of Bermuda as a whole. And, fortunately, international business had ignored these unfortunate events. Bermuda, indeed, is back to normal.

To-day we realize that in an area so small as that of Bermuda there is absolutely no room for racial conflict; perhaps our most emotional problem lay in that complex inheritance from the days of slavery that pinpoint our entire history, although the old Bermuda laws recognized not only Negro but Indian and White bondsmen. To-day we are aware that only racial tensions can blight our present and our future. Consequently giant strides have been made in Race Relation laws, Race Relation Councils, and Advisory Committees, Integration of Schools, and a political stability which ensures freedom and justice for all.

The overwhelming majority of our visitors come from North America. To them, part of Bermuda's charm is being in a 'foreign' country where all the stage properties are very British — and yet very individually Bermudian with its own flag and its own folk-lore — not to mention such dramatic ceremonies as the Convening of Parliament or Beating the Retreat. That traffic may not exceed 20mph, that the long stretches of beaches are lapped by the most brilliant waters in the world, that Bermudians — White or Black — are apt to salute the passer-by as a friend — all this spells not only welcome, but peace. Little wonder that every visitor longs to return . . . 'Too much loved'? Surely not, when it is this passionately-held affection which assures the islands' future.

And it was towards the close of the 1970s — in the spring of 1979 to be exact — that this universal pride was expressed in the inauguration of a Bermuda Heritage Week to be held annually over the period of Commonwealth Day, 24th May, in which all of the four ethnic groups who, as we have seen, compose today's Bermudians, could express their pride in their inheritance. Now, in the 1980s, under the co-ordination of Mr Reginald Ming, the period has extended to a month's celebration of our historical past and of that Unity in Diversity which is the hope of the future — from the earliest settlers of the United Kingdom, the swiftly-following Negro and American–Indian groups, to the Portuguese who have added so much to our agricultural skills in particular. This Unity in Diversity gives today's Bermudians an extreme individuality implicit in the four-fold heritage and a way of life balanced between the traditional and the ultra-modern — founded originally on British laws, institutions, sports.

And the Americans at the United States Naval Air Station, as well as the many who make their homes here, take a pride in helping to preserve our history, provide all auxiliary services for Bermuda's civil aviation, and supply us with our weather-forecasting and other practical help. In 1980, the United States Government voluntarily returned to the Bermuda Government 25 acres of precious land at the Southampton Annex Base — part of the land originally ceded to them in 1941 for a period of 99 years. . . . It may well be said that the 3000 U.S. Navy personnel and their descendants living in Bermuda have the warmest possible relationship with local residents.

As we moved into the 1980s, many sociological changes became significant. Women Recruits now train at Warwick Camp with the Bermuda Regiment (an innovation that started in 1979) – and the Women Police fill a very special need. In April of that same year, a local woman, Gina Swainson, won the World Beauty Contest, being so recorded on Bermuda's postage stamps.

The Census, the official enumeration of the inhabitants with statistics relating to them, was taken on 12th May 1980 and a lengthy analysis published in 1981. Including armed forces with their dependents, and more than ten thousand visitors, a total of over 67,000 persons had spent the previous night in the islands. Of these 54,050 are considered the resident civilian population. (See p. 186.) And, on a different note, in August of 1980, six Vietnamese refugees ("boat people") were taken in as residents of Bermuda.

A keenly-contested Parliamentary General Election was held in December 1980 for the convening of Parliament in January 1981. Of the forty seats in the Lower House, 22 were won by the United Bermuda Party (which therefore continues in office) and 18 by the opposition, the Progressive Labour Party; the latter had made great strides under the leadership of Mrs Lois Browne-Evans. The Hon. J. David Gibbons continued as Premier and Minister of Finance, and the Hon. F. John Barritt was elected as Speaker of the House of Assembly. In 1982, the Hon. John Swan became Premier (see p. 181).

Thus, the Executive Authority of Bermuda is vested in Her Majesty the Queen, represented by the Governor & Commander-in-Chief. A Deputy Governor takes over in the event of the Governor's illness or absence and assists His Excellency. The Upper House of Parliament, previously designated Legislative Council, now has become the Senate (this took practical effect at the convening of Parliament in January 1981.) And the 40-member House of Assembly, whose members are designated M.P.'s., and who are elected under universal adult franchise from the twenty local constituencies; these Members of Parliament elect a Speaker and a Deputy Speaker. The Opposition Leader is the Leader of the largest minority group in the House of Assembly.

On 30th December 1980, His Excellency the Governor, the Hon. Sir Peter Ramsbotham, had retired to England, bidding a ceremonial farewell to the people in the Cabinet Office grounds – for many an emotional event since both Sir Peter and Lady Ramsbotham had endeared themselves by their whole-hearted support of many worthy causes. The Deputy Governor, G. Peter Lloyd, Esq., C.M.G., J.P., again took up the reins as Acting Governor till the arrival of the new appointee, His Excellency, Sir Richard Posnett, K.B.E., C.M.G., who arrived 24th February 1981, to take up the position of Governor & Commander-in-Chief. Sir Richard, a Colonial Constitutional-affairs expert, resigned 15th March 1983 following discussions with the Foreign and Common-wealth Office for which he had been recalled to England.

Life in the islands has improved materially during the last decade, and the 1980s sees an almost doubled tourist trade – the one industry that affects the life of every man, woman and child in Bermuda – over this period, due largely to the devoted efforts of the Minister of Tourism, the Hon. C. V. Woolridge; the Department of Tourism Director, D. Colin Selley, Esq; and the untiring work of such officials as the Secretary to the Cabinet, W. James Williams, Esq., C.V.O., O.B.E., J.P. An hotel-training college, the Stonington, was opened in Paget in 1980 to great acclaim.

But the resident population-pressures – high for such a limited area – augmented by the necessary surge in tourism (over six hundred thousand visitors in 1980) – are also reflected in motorized traffic congestion despite all efforts to control this at the lowest possible level, and to retain a nostalgic reminder of our past with the retention of some twelve hundred horses on our roads. Inevitably, all this is reflected in an inflated cost of living (rents, for instance, have more than doubled) and an increase in crime. On the other hand, there are many dedicated groups of citizens who support the Bermuda National Trust, the Keep Bermuda Beautiful group, and the more than one hundred and fifty registered local charities in their fight to retain the best of our inheritance for everyone.

The last few years have seen the emergence of various new religions and cults; in fact now, in the 1980s, some forty different religious groups exist. However, the Anglican Church remains the denomination with the largest number of adherents, while the African Methodist Episcopal, as well as the Presbyterian, the Methodists, and the Roman Catholic Church have large followings, and work hard for the good of their people. In the Anglican Church (as the Church of England is now called) one of the many concerns of the Lord Bishop, the Rt, Revd. Anselm Genders, since his arrival on 6th November 1977 until his resignation in August 1982 due to ill health, has been to stamp out the exhibition of pornographic material in the shops. The Salvation Army does its habitual courageous work for re-habilitation.

Unhappily, the most damaging labour crisis in Bermuda's history commenced in April 1981, among members of the various Unions. For the first week of the strikes, those who took part were some 1,150 Government industrial workers and non-medical staff at the two hospitals, demanding approximately a 20% increase in pay. The Government warned that such increases might result in loss of jobs and the cutting back in services. Official arbitration was rejected and demands were made for all Government blue-collar workers. Soon sympathy strikes spread throughout even the best-paid industries until most island functions had come to an almost complete stand-still. Affected were — the ferry services (discontinued), the bus service, the General Post Office, mail delivery, tenders for cruise ships, garbage disposal, hospital facilities, and the island's schools since some members of the Amalgamated Bermuda Union of Teachers joined the strikers. Cruise ship passengers were marooned in the Great Sound, airline service was cut back — Bermuda was losing $1m per day. Hotel staffs had walked off their jobs in wild-cat sympathy strikes so that hotels, guest-houses and cottage-colonies had no choice but to close down en masse, cancel all further bookings and eject their guests. Meanwhile, pickets paraded the streets flourishing banners and almost five thousand took part in a demonstration.

On Thursday, 7th May 1981, the almost 4-week labour crisis was partially resolved with approximate 20% pay award to many Government blue-collar workers. This result was described as a victory for the Bermuda Industrial Union — but factually and economically everyone had lost. Costs and prices have risen drastically, the Department of Tourism valiantly put on an expensive 'blitz' in New York for 600 travel agents in order to get our one industry re-started — the hotels began re-opening on 13th of May but with extremely few guests. Some of the foot-loose staff would have to remain foot-loose. It would take months of intensive hard work at the top to regain the pre-strike level.

Yes, strikes are a perfectly legitimate weapon — but that

they should escalate to unrelated work-areas in order to bring the community to a complete stand-still is an example of the modern form of total disruption by a controlled minority of the population that is a threat to the very roots of democracy itself. The silent majority, and voluntary workers, helped the authorities to bring the island up the staggering road to normalcy: hundreds of members of the hospitals' Women's Auxiliary (the 'Pink Ladies') and the St. John Ambulance Brigade, gave their time round-the-clock to enable the hospitals to continue functioning. And people in every walk of life offered their free services there and elsewhere.

For these islands have retained the magnetic charm that compels visitors to return year after year – a fascination compounded of a moderate climate, plentiful sunshine, an ideal geographic position, a wide diversity of heritage, seas of unrivalled beauty, and the friendliness that small island communities often attain. Thus Bermuda remains Britain's oldest self-governing colony, with historical ties and facilities for intercourse that go back to her beginnings – but with complete freedom as to self-determination: – the best of both worlds.

In January 1982, further political changes took place within the United Bermuda Party when the Hon. David Gibbons resigned from the Premiership while retaining the office of Minister of Finance. The Hon. John Swan was thereupon elected as Premier; this appointment is clearly a practical and popular one since the Hon. John Swan has not only carved out his own career but evinces a deep concern for the well-being of all his fellow countrymen. One of his earliest duties as Premier was to accompany His Excellency the Acting Governor and His Worship the Mayor of St. Georges, in conducting the Prince and Princess of Wales around the old capital in a whirlwind visit of a few hours on 16th February 1982 when the honey-mooning couple were en route to Eleuthera by 'plane.

That these islands are increasingly aware of their fascinatingly unique past is also evidenced by the fact that plans are afoot for a statue by Desmond Hale Fountain to be erected in memory of Admiral Sir George Somers and that unforgettable moment on 28th July 1609 when he sighted 'land!'.

Postlude

The author may perhaps be privileged to express two insubstantial desires: that her spirit may, like that of Old Morgan, hover over the islands in the year 2040 when the Bases are being restored, and again in 2109 as the Time Capsule is being disinterred and her descendants of the fifth generation are listening to her disembodied voice, among other voices of the by-gone twentieth century!

Population Facts and Figures

from 28th July 1609 when Bermuda's story as an inhabited place begins. At that date the English came to an uninhabited Bermuda. (Previous to this, those thrown on her shores either perished or escaped as soon as possible.)

1609   28th July 150 castaways from *Sea Venture*.

1610   10th May 2 men left on Island till Somers' return that year.

1610-12 3 men left to hold the Island while *Patience* takes Somers' body to England.

1612   11th July The *Plough* arrives with 60 settlers under Gov Moore.

1622   About 1500 people, according to Governor Butler.

1629   estimation of between 2000 and 3000.

1639   'overpopulated in proportion to existing resources'; emigration to W.I.

1657/8 200 or more emigrants sail for Jamaica, New Providence, & Va.

1674   Law passed prohibiting importation of slaves, as there was insufficient employment, they increased more rapidly than Whites who found difficulty in feeding and clothing them.

1679   Pop. estimated at 8000 in Company's official statement to Imperial Government.

1684   Pop. decreased (as did area of cultivated land) after dissolution of Bermuda Co.

1699   Pop. given as 5889 – 4152 White, 1737 of Negro descent.

1727   Pop. given as 8270 – 4770 White, 3500 Coloured acc. to Gov. John Hope.

1749   Pop. given as 9270 – 5290 White, 3980 Coloured acc. to Gov. Alured Popple.

1774   Official report of Gov. George James Bruere gave 10655 – 5632 White, 5023 Black.

1833   Pop. given as 9195 – being 4297 White; 3612 slaves + 1286 free Coloured.

1834   (However, number of slaves reported for Emancipation was 4026.)

1835   Official total pop. 8810 – being 4259 White; 4459 Coloured some having emigrated.

1842   Pop. 8624 – being 4058 Whites; 4566 Coloured.

1844   Pop. 10126 4337 Whites; 5789 Coloured.

1853   Population 11,092.

1870	Population 12,121	4725 White	7396 Coloured
1880	Population 13,948	5384 White	8564 Coloured
1890	Population 15,013	5960 White	9323 Coloured
1900	Population 17,535	6383 White	11,152 Coloured
1910	Population 18,994	6691 White	12,303 Coloured
1920	Population 20,127	7006 White	13,121 Coloured
1930	Population 27,789	11353 White	16,436 Coloured
1940	Population 30,814	11481 White	19,333 Coloured
1950	Population 37,403	14724 White	22,679 Coloured
1960	Population 42,640	15892 White	26,748 Coloured

1970   Population 53,000   (including City of Hamilton approx. 1600
Town of St George's approx. 2100)

1980   Population 54,050   20892 White   33,158 Black
and over 600,000 visitors in 1980.

FIGURES ARE EXCLUSIVE OF NAVAL AND MILITARY ESTABLISHMENTS

Since 1940, the area for the civil population is only 18.26 square miles, with the American Bases occupying the remaining 2.33 square miles.

Since 1980, only 870 acres of arable land (or open spaces) remain. The Government Green Paper on Transport, November 1982, reported intolerable traffic levels in Hamilton, there being almost 15,500 cars on the islands, and a total of 53,000 motorized vehicles on our 120 miles of roadway.

MAPS AND SURVEYS (Twentieth century.)

All references in text to Bermuda maps and surveys are indexed chronologically under that subject title. Nothing exemplifies the spread of population better than the maps published in the twentieth century:—

1) At the end of the nineteenth century, it was realized there had been no complete survey since Norwood's second survey of 1663. So Lieut. A. J. Savage, R.E., was sent from England with two assistants. The excellent result is the six sheet contoured map published in 1901 by the Ordnance Survey Office, scale six inches to one statute mile (on Survey made 1899).

2) In July 1962, Hunting Surveys Ltd made the first complete Aerial Survey with co-operation from the Public Works Dept, Bermuda. The Directorate of Overseas Surveys constructed the multi-sheet map in 1966-67 on a scale of 25.344 inches to 1 mile.

Governors of Bermuda

28th July 1609, is the date from which Bermuda's story as an inhabited place begins – with the wreck of the Sea Venture *(en route from England to Virginia) on these uninhabited shores. Since that date the islands have been continuously occupied and held, though at one time by only two, and later merely three, men. However, with the arrival of* The Plough *from England in 1612, deliberate colonization commenced, and a Governor was despatched. The following list, then, covers Governors (and some Acting Governors) from 1612 to 1978*

1612	(July) Richard Moore
1615	Charles Caldicot, Captain John Mansfield, Captain Miles Kendall, Christopher Carter, Thomas Knight and Edward Waters. The last two sailed with Caldicot for the West Indies, after the first month in office.
1616	Captain Daniel Tucker
1618/19	Captain Miles Kendall
1619	Captain Nathaniel Butler
1622	Captain John Bernard
1622/3	Captain John Harrison
1623	Captain Henry Woodhouse
1626/7	Captain Philip Bell
1629	(Dec.) Captain Roger Wood
1637	(Mar.) Captain Thomas Chaddock
1640	(Nov.) Captain William Sayle
1642	(Mar.) Captain Josiah Forster
1643	(July) Captain William Sayle
1645	(Feb.) Captain Josiah Forster with Stephen Paynter and William Wilkinson
1646	(Apr.) Captain Thomas Turner
1649	(Sept.) John Trimingham
1650	Captain Josiah Forster
1658	(June) Captain William Sayle
1662/3	Captain Florentius Seymour
1668	Captain Samuel Whalley
1669	Sir John Heydon
1681	Captain Florentius Seymour
1682	Captain Henry Durham
1683	Colonel Richard Coney

Sir Robert Robinson, Gov from 12th April 1687 to 20th June 1690
Isaac Richier, Lt.-Governor from 1691 to 1693

John Goddard, Governor from 1693 to 1698

Samuel Day, Lt-Governor from 20th October 1698 to 18th December 1700.

Benjamin Bennett, Governor from 2nd May 1701 to 1713.

Henry Pulleine, Lt-Governor from 1713 to 1718.

Benjamin Bennett, Governor from 1718 to 1722.

John Hope, Governor from 1722 to 1727.

John Trimingham, President from November 1727 to August 1728.

John Pitt, Governor from 1728 to 1737.

Andrew Auchinleck, President from December 1737 to May 1738.

Alured Popple, Governor from 2nd August 1738 to 9th November 1744.

Francis Jones, President from 20th November 1744 to 19th June 1747.

William Popple, Governor from 1st July 1747 to November 1751.

Francis Jones, President from November 1751 to November 1755.

William Popple, Governor from November 1755 to December 1763.

Francis Jones, President from 2nd December 1763 to August 1764.

George James Bruere, Governor from August 1764 to August 1780.

Thomas Jones, President from September to October 1780.

George Bruere, Lt-Governor from October 1780 to December 1781.

William Browne, Governor from 4th January 1782 to 15th October 1788.

Henry Hamilton, Lt-Governor from 28th October 1788 to 30th October 1794.

James Crauford, Governor from 8th November 1794 to 28th October 1796.

Henry Tucker, President from 27th October to 22nd November 1796.

William Campbell, Governor from 22nd November to 1st December 1796.

Henry Tucker, President from 1st December 1796 to 20th February 1798.

George Beckwith, Governor from 14th February 1798 to 12th March 1803.

Henry Tucker, President from 15th April 1805 to 29th April 1805.

Francis Gore, Lt-Governor from 8th May 1805 to 7th June 1806.

Henry Tucker, President from 13th June to 30th July 1806.

John Hodgson, Governor from 31st July 1806 to 20th June 1810.

Samuel Trott, President from 20th June 1810 to 31st August 1811.

Sir J. Cockburn, Governor from 31st August 1811 to 4th July 1812.

William Smith, President from 4th July to 14th September 1812.

George Horsford, Lt-Governor from 11th September 1812 to 24th July 1816.

Sir J. Cockburn, Governor from 24th July 1814 to 18th July 1816.

William Smith, President from 18th July 1816 to 11th November 1817.

Sir J. Cockburn, Governor from 11th November 1817 to 13th April 1819.

William Smith, President from 15th April to 25th November 1819.

Sir W. Lumley, Governor from 26th November 1819 to 23rd May 1822.

Wm. Smith, President from 23rd May 1822 to 16th October 1823.

Sir Wm. Lumley, Governor from 16th October 1823 to June 1825.

William Smith, President from June 1825 to 14th February 1826.

Sir H. Turner, Governor from 14th February 1826 to 7th July 1829.

Robert Kennedy, Acting Governor from 7th July to 2nd November 1829.

Sir H. Turner, Governor from 2nd November 1829 to 30th July 1830.

Robert Kennedy, Acting Governor from 30th July to 1st November 1830.

Sir H. Turner, Governor from 1st November 1830 to 10th January 1832.

Sir R. S. Chapman, Governor from 16th January 1832 to 23rd April 1835.

Henry G. Hunt, Acting Governor from 23rd April to 17th September 1835.

Robert Kennedy, Acting Governor from 17th September 1835 to 22nd January 1836.

Sir R. S. Chapman, Governor from 22nd January 1836 to 12th April 1839.

William Reid, Governor from 12th April 1839 to 30th November 1846.

W. N. Hutchinson, Governor from 30th November to 26th December 1846.

Charles Elliott, Governor from 25th December 1846 to 26th August 1852.

W. H. Eden, Acting Governor from 26th August 1852 to 12th May 1853.

George Philpots, Acting Governor from 12th May to 18th September 1853.

Thomas C, Robe, Acting Governor from 18th September to 24th September 1853.

Soulden Oakley, Acting Governor from 24th September to 11th October 1853.

Arthur W. Byles, Acting Governor from 11th October to 12th November 1853.

Soulden Oakley, Acting Governor from 12th November to 20th November 1853.

Charles Elliott, Governor from 20th November 1853 to 13th February 1854.

Montgomery Williams, Acting Governor from 13th February to 3rd October 1854.

Freeman Murray, Governor from 3rd October 1854 to 18th June 1859.

A. T. Hemphill, Acting Governor from 18th June to 17th October 1859.

William Munroe, Acting Governor from 17th October 1859 to 16th February 1860.

Freeman Murray, Governor from 16th February 1860 to 14th March 1861.

H. St George Ord, Governor from 14th March 1861 to 15th June 1864.

William Munroe, Lt-Governor from 15th June to 27th July 1864.

W. G. Hamley, Lt-Governor from 27th July 1864 to 18th October 1865.

H. St George Ord, Governor from 18th October 1865 to 24th November 1866.

W. G. Hamley, Lt-Governor from 24th November 1866 to 13th April 1867.

Arnold Thompson, Acting Governor from 13th April to 30th April 1867.

Sir F. E. Chapman, Governor from 30th April 1867 to 29th May 1870.

W. F. Brett, Lt-Governor from 29th May to 13th September 1870.

T. G. Brown, Administrator from 13th September 1870 to 12th April, 1871.

A. A. C. Fisher, Acting Governor from 22nd April to 9th May 1871.

Sir J. H. Lefroy, Governor from 9th May 1871 to 28th May 1874.

Fitzroy Somerset, Acting Governor from 28th May to 30th May 1874.

J. H. Lefroy, Governor from 30th May to 2nd June 1874.

Fitzroy Somerset, Acting Governor from 2nd June to 5th November 1874.

Sir J. H. Lefroy, Governor from 5th November 1874 to 10th May 1877.

W. L. Morrison, Acting Governor from 10th May to 10th August 1877.

Sir R. M. Laffan, Governor from 10th August 1877 to 10th June 1880.

E. C. A. Gordon, Acting Governor from 10th June to 14th September 1880.

Sir R. M. Laffan, Governor from 14th September 1880 to 1st August 1881.

E. C. A. Gordon, Acting Governor from 1st August to 6th November 1881.

Sir R. M. Laffan, Governor from 6th November 1881 to 22nd March 1882.

E. C. A. Gordon, Acting Governor from 22nd March to 3rd July 1882.

T. L. J. Gallwey, Governor from 3rd July 1882 to 17th June 1885.

F. E. Cox, Administrator from 17th June to 13rd August 1885.

R. M. F. Sandford, Acting Governor 13th August 1885 to 13th February 1886.

T. L. J. Gallwey, Governor from 13th February 1887 to 23rd August 1888.

R. M. F. Sandford, Acting Governor from 23rd August to 29th October 1888.

E. N. Newdegate, Governor from 29th October 1888 to 2nd October 1890.

Herbert F. Eaton, Administrator from 2nd October to 7th December 1890.

E. N. Newdegate, Governor from 7th December 1890 to 6th August 1891.

Samuel Pym, Administrator from 6th August to 11th October 1891.

E. N. Newdegate, Governor from 11th October to 7th December 1891.

Samuel Pym, Deputy Governor from 7th December 1891 to 8th January 1892.

E. N. Newdegate, Governor from 8th January to 23rd June 1892.

Samuel Pym, Administrator from 23rd June to 18th July 1892.

Thomas C. Lyons, Governor from 18th July 1892 to 27th July 1893.

Samuel Pym, Administrator from 27th July to 4th September 1893.

Thomas C. Lyons, Governor from 4th September 1893 to 26th June 1894.

Samuel Pym, Administrator from 26th June to 30th August 1894.

Thomas C. Lyons, Governor from 30th August 1894 to 1st August 1895.

E. C. S. Moore, Administrator from 1st August to 7th October 1895.

Thomas C. Lyons, Governor from 7th October 1895 to 28th May 1896.

E. C. S. Moore, Administrator from 28th May to 6th July 1896.

G. Digby Barker, Governor from 6th July 1896 to 2nd September 1897.

E. C. S. Moore, Administrator from 2nd September to 10th October 1897.

G. Digby Barker, Governor from 10th October, 1897 to 1st September 1898.

W. A Yule, Administrator from 1st September to 18th October 1898.

G. Digby Barker, Governor from 18th October 1898 to 22nd August 1900.

J. W. A. Marshall, Adminstrator from 22nd August to 14th October 1900.

G. Digby Barker, Governor from 14th October 1900 to 30th January 1902.

Arden L. Bayley, Administrator from 30th January to 3rd February 1902.

Henry LeGuay Geary, Governor 3rd February 1902 to 28th April 1904.

A. N. Roberts, Administrator from 28th April to 2nd May 1904.

R. M. Stewart, Governor from 2nd May 1904 to 12th July 1905.

A. N. Roberts, Administrator from 10th July to 29th October 1905.

R. M. Stewart, Governor from 29th October 1905 to 22nd August 1906.

S. Frewen, Administrator from 22nd August to 14th October 1906.

R. M. Stewart, Governor from 14th October 1906 to 26th June 1907.

Josceline H. Wodehouse, Governor from 26th June 1907 to 2nd September 1908.

F. H. Chapman, Administrator from 2nd September to 9th November 1908.

Frederick Walter Kitchener, Governor to 6th March 1912.

Lieut-Col W. F. Brook-Smith, RGA, Administrator to 25th June 1912.

Lieut-Gen Sir Geo. M. Bullock, KCB, Governor to 2nd August 1913.

Lieut-Col N. C. Coles, Administrator to 12th September 1913.

Lieut-Gen Sir Geo. M. Bullock, KCB, Governor to 25th July 1914.

Lieut-Col G. B. McAndrew, Administrator to 7th August 1914.

Lieut-Gen Sir Geo. M. Bullock, KCB, Governor to 25th May 1917.

Lieut-Col W.H. Land, VD, Administrator to 2 June 1917

General Sir James Willcocks, GCB, GCMG, KCSI, DSO, Governor to 19th July 1919.

Lieut-Col H. B. Des Voeux, CMG, Administrator to 22nd September 1919.

General Sir James Willcocks, GCB, GCMG, KCSI, DSO, Administrator to 11th October 1920.

Lieut-Col H. B. Des Voeux, CMG, Administrator to 25th October 1920.

General Sir James Willcocks, GCB, GCMG, KCSI, DSO, Governor to 2nd August 1921.

Lieut-Col Arthur Berger, Administrator to 30th September 1921.

General Sir James Willcocks, GCB, GCMG, KSCI, DSO, Governor to 2nd June 1922.

Lieut-Col G. E. Badcock, CBE, DSO, Administrator to 9th August 1922.

Lieut-Gen Sir J. J. Asser, KCB, KCMG, KCVO, Governor to 28th July 1923.

Lieut-Col G. E. Badcock, CBE, DSO, Administrator to 7th September 1923.

Lieut-Gen. Sir J. J. Asser, KCB, KCMG, KCVO, Governor to 29th July 1924.

Lieut-Col C. W. Biggs, RE, OBE, Administrator to 22nd September 1924.

Lieut-Gen Sir J. J. Asser, KCB, KCMG, KCVO, Governor to 30th May 1925.

Lieut-Col C. W. Biggs, RE, OBE, Administrator to 11th June 1925.

Lieut-General Sir J. J. Asser, KCB, KCMG, KCVO, Governor to 15th July 1925.

Lieut-Col C. W. Biggs, RE, OBE, Administrator to 24th September 1925.

Lieut-General Sir J. J. Asser, KCB, KCMG, KCVO, Governor to 19th July 1926.

Lieut-Colonel F. B. Legh, RE, OBE, MC, Acting Governor to 19th September 1926.

Lieut-General Sir J. J. Asser, KCB, KCMG, KCVO, Governor to 1927.

Lieut-General Sir Louis Jean Bols, KCB, KCMG, DSO, 1927.

Lieut-General Sir Thomas Astley-Cubitt, KCB, CMG, DSO, 1931.

Lieut-General Sir Reginald Hildyard, KCB, CMG, DSO, 1936.

Lieut-General Sir Denis John Charles Kirwan Bernard, KCB, CMG, 1939.

The Right Hon Viscount Knollys, KCMG, MBE, DFC, 1941.

The Right Hon Lord Burghley, KCMG, 1943-1945.

The Hon William Addis, Acting Governor October 1945-May 1946.

Admiral Sir Ralph Leatham, (RN) KCB, arrived 9th May 1946.

Lieut-General Sir Alexander Hood, GBE, KCB, KCVO, 1949.

Lieut-General Sir John Woodall, KCMG, KBE, CB, MC, 1955.

Major-General Sir Julian Gascoigne, KCMG, KCVO, CB, DSO, 1959.

The Right Hon Lord Martonmere, PC, KCMG, Arrived June 1964.

Sir Richard Christopher Sharples, KCMG, OBE, 1972 arrival 12th October. Assassinated 10th March 1973.

The Hon. Ian Albert Clark Kinnear, Acting Governor from 10th March 1973.

His Excellency, Sir Edwin Hartley Cameron Leather, KCMG, b.22 May 1919, in Hamilton, Ontario, Canada; former conservative M.P. for North Somerset, England, and Chairman of Tory Party Conference 1970, m. 1940 to Shiela, d. of Major A.H. Greenlees, also of Hamilton. Sir Edwin and Lady Leather have two daughters. Sir Edwin became Governor of Bermuda 14th July 1973 (date of arrival).

The Hon. Peter Lloyd, CMG, Acting Governor from 7th April 1977.

His Excellency, the Hon. Sir Peter Ramsbotham, GCMG, GCVO, 6th September 1977 − 30th December 1980.

Peter Lloyd, Esq., CMG, JP, Acting Governor 1st January − 24th February 1981.

His Excellency, Sir Richard Posnett, KBE, CMG, arrived 24th February 1981. He was recalled to London on 6th February 1983 and resigned the governorship by letter to the Secretary of State dated 23rd February 1983, which took effect 15th March 1983 (he not having returned to Bermuda in the meantime).

Brian Watkins, Esq., Acting Governor 6th − 14th February 1983.

His Excellency, Mr. Mark Herdman, MVO, despatched by the Foreign & Commonwealth Office, became Acting Governor from 14th February 1983, since Britain is responsible for Bermuda's defence, internal security and foreign affairs − all of which are the prerogative of the Governor.

His Excellency, Viscount Dunrossil, appointed 9th May 1983 to be Governor of Bermuda in succession to Sir Richard Posnett (resigned), the appointment to take effect in July 1983. Viscount Dunrossil arrived Sunday 17th July and was officially welcomed by Acting Governor, Mr. Mark Herdman who introduced him to the waiting officials, including Premier John Swan. 18th July 1983 Lord Dunrossil was sworn in as Governor by Mr. Mark Herdman, who, as Deputy Governor, now has official residence at Montpelier, Devonshire.

THE CONSTITUTION OF BERMUDA, 1981

The Constitution of Bermuda published in 1981 incorporated the vast political changes which affected the Designation and convening of local political parties and Bermuda's entire political history.

It stated that **THE LEGISLATURE OF BERMUDA** consists of

HER MAJESTY THE QUEEN
Represented by a despatched Governor or Acting Governor.

THE SENATE
(A new Designation from December 1980, of 11 members of an Upper House which meets in its own Chambers in the Cabinet Office). Members are appointed by the Governor with advice from the Premier, (a local politician). The Secretariat Building had been renamed the Cabinet Building in March 1978. There is also a Governor's Council for His Excellency's specific consultation which also meets at Special Chambers of the Cabinet Building.

THE HOUSE OF ASSEMBLY
Consists of 40 members elected by universal adult franchise which convenes in the Sessions House, Parliament Street, Hamilton, to enact Bermuda's laws which affect the islands socially, racially, politically and provide equal opportunity for everyone.

Succession of Bishops : 1612-1982

Bermuda with London	*Bermuda with Newfoundland*
1612 John King	1839 Aubrey George Spencer
1621 George Mountain	(formerly Archdeacon of Bermuda)
1628 William Laud	1844 Edward Feild, assisted from
1633 William Juxon	1867 by Coadjutor Bishop
1660 Gilbert Sheldon	James Butler Kelly
1663 Humphrey Henchman	1879 Llewellyn Jones
1675 Henry Compton	1917-Occasional visits by
1714 John Robinson	1925 Archbishop Clare Worrell
1723 Edmund Gibson	of Nova Scotia
1748 Thomas Sherlock	
1761 Thomas Hayter	*Bermuda Alone*
1762 Richard Osbaldeston	1925 Arthur Heber Browne
1764 Richard Terrick	1949 John Arthur Jagoe
1777 Robert Lowth	1956 Anthony Lewis Elliott
1787 Beilby Porteus	Williams
1809 John Randolph	1963 John Armstrong
1813 William Howley	1969 The Right Revd Eric Joseph
	Trapp
Bermuda with Nova	1976 The Right Revd & Right Hon.
Scotia	Robert Stopford
1825 John Inglis	1977 The Right-Revd Anselm Genders,
	resigned 15th August 1982 due to
	ill health.

This list of Bishops shows that there are four distinct periods in the history of the episcopate of Bermuda — the first and longest being a two-hundred year association with the Diocese of London, a short period under Nova Scotia, some seventy odd years under Newfoundland's Bishop and since 1925 with its own Bishop.

Appendix IV

Principal Consular Officers of the United States in Bermuda

(From the State Department Washington, and kindly supplied to us by Mr George Willmot Renchard, American Consul-General, Bermuda on 6th November 1961.)

Date of Establishment of Consulate 1818 (The Consular Office was at St George's Prior to May 1872 and has been at Hamilton since that date.)

WILLIAM R. HIGINBOTHOM of Maryland. Appointed Agent for Commerce and Seamen 10th July 1818; acknowledged receipt of his appointment at his post, 20th August 1818; died at his post 25th July 1832. (Had been a resident of Bermuda 24 years. See *Bermuda Gazette* 31st July 1832.)

WILLIAM TUDOR TUCKER of Bermuda. Ad interim in charge from 26th July 1832; appointed Consular Commercial Agent, 5th September 1832; commissioned Consul 5th July 1838; retired February 1846.

ALEXANDER J. BERGEN of New York. Commissioned Consul, 1st August 1845 (recess of the Senate); declined 2nd October 1845.

FREDERICK B. WELLS of New York. Commissioned Consul 22nd November 1845 (recess of the Senate); assumed charge February 1846; recommission 2nd April 1846; left his post 20th June 1850.

JOHN ADAMS of Maryland. Commissioned Consul 18th June 1849 (recess of the Senate;) declined.

WILLIAM C. HYLAND of St George's. Ad interim in charge at Well's direction 20th June-10th July 1850.

WILLIAM TUDOR TUCKER of Bermuda. Commissioned Consul 19th June 1850; assumed charge 11th July 1850; retired 23rd August 1853.

JOHN W. HOWDEN of Ohio. Commissioned Consul 24th May 1853 (recess of the Senate); assumed charge 23rd August 1853; died at his post 11th September 1853. (In the letters recommending him to this post it was stated that he was "now seriously affected with a disease of the lungs from which, unless arrested by change of residence, we fear fatal results." A communication from William Tudor Tucker to the Department stated 13th September 1853, includes the following passage: "It becomes my duty to report to you the death on the 11th inst of J. W. Howden, Esq., U.S. Consul for this Island, by the prevailing epidemic of Yellow Fever, which has been a scourge to this place for the last fortnight." His grave is in the graveyard of St Peter's Church, St George's, Bermuda, in the north-east corner consecrated to

Christian burial since 1612. See *Bermuda Royal Gazette* for 13th September 1853.)

WILLIAM TUDOR TUCKER of Bermuda. Ad interim in charge 11th September 1853-December 1854.

FREDERICK B. WELLS of New York. Commissioned Consul 23rd February 1853; assumed charge December 1853; left his post June 1856; resigned in the United States 27th June 1856.

HENRY B. BROWN of Massachusetts. Ad interim in charge at Wells' direction from June 1856; commissioned Consul 31st July 1856; retired 17th October 1859.

FREDERICK B. WELLS of New York. Commissioned Consul 6th August 1859 (recess of the Senate); assumed charge 17th October 1859; recommissioned 10th January 1860; retired 14th November 1861.

EDWARD TROWBRIDGE of Connecticut. Commissioned Consul 19th June 1861 (recess of the Senate); declined.

CHARLES MAXWELL ALLEN of New York. Commissioned Consul 7th August 1861 (recess of the Senate); assumed charge 15th November 1861; recommissioned 14th April 1862; died at his post 24th December 1888. Funeral from his home, Wistowe, Flatts, Bermuda, to Smith's Parish Church attended by H. E. The Governor, Lieut-General Edward Newdigate Newdegate, and representatives of the Royal Navy, the Army and the Civil Service.

JAMES B. HEYL of Pennsylvania (Vice & Deputy Consul). Ad interim in charge 25th December 1888-20th February 1889. (He had been appointed Vice and Deputy Consul at Hamilton 19th June 1878 and served till March 1902.)

HENRY W. BECKWITH of Illinois. Commissioned Consul 19th January 1889; assumed charge 20th February 1889; left his post July 1891; died in Chicago, Illinois, 20th August 1891.

JAMES B. HEYL of Pennsylvania (Vice and Deputy Consul). Ad interim in charge July-25th December 1891.

WILLIAM K. SULLIVAN of Illinois. Commissioned Consul 25th November 1891 (recess of the Senate); recommissioned 16th December 1891; assumed charge 26th December 1891; left his post 7th July 1892; resigned in Chicago, Illinois, 18th November 1892.

JAMES B. HEYL of Pennsylvania (Vice and Deputy Consul). Ad interim in charge 7th July 1892-15th February 1893.

JOHN H. GROUT, Jr., of Massachusetts. Commissioned Consul 14th January 1893; assumed charge 16th February 1893; retired 26th January 1894.

MARSHALL HANGER of Virginia. Commissioned Consul 10th October 1893; assumed charge 27th January 1894; retired 19th February 1898.

M. MAXWELL GREENE of Rhode Island. Commissioned Consul 14th January 1898; assumed charge 20th February 1898; resignation effective 30th April 1915; died at East Greenwich, Rhode Island, 25th August 1920.

1913-15 WILLIAM H. ALLEN, Vice Consul in charge.

1915-17 EARL LOOP of Indiana, Consul.
1917-18 STILLMAN WITT ELLIS of Ohio, Vice Consul.
1918 ETHELBERT WATTS of Pennsylvania, Consul.
1818-19 DIGBY NILLSON, Vice Consul in charge.
1919-22 COL. ALFRED N. SWALM, of Iowa, Consul.
1922-23 EDWIN CLAY MERRELL, Vice Consul in charge.
1923-24 WILLIAM PATTON KENT, of Virginia, Consul.
1924-27 ROBERTSON HONEY, of New York, Consul.
1930-34 GRAHAM J. KEMPER, of Va., Consul.
1934-36 CHARLES H. HEISLER, of Delaware, Consul.
1937-39 HAROLD L. WILLIAMSON Consul.
1939-45 WILLIAM H. BECK, Consul.
1945-49 EDWIN CLAY MERRELL, Vice Consul in charge.
1949 HOWARD BOWMAN, Consul.
1949-50 JOHN C. POOL, Consul.
1950-51 EDWIN CLAY MERRELL, Consul.
1951-53 E. PAUL TENNEY, Consul General.
1953-55 ROBERT B. STREEPER, Consul General.
1955-57 THOMAS J. MALEADY, Consul General.
1957-60 SIDNEY K. LAFOON, Consul General.
1960-67 GEORGE W. RENCHARD, Consul General.
1967-72 CHARLES NELMS MANNING, Consul General.
1972- DONALD BRENTON McCUE, Consul General.
1976- RICHARD RAND, Consul General.
1980- JOHN P. OWENS, Consul General.
1982- MAX FRIEDERSDORF, Consul General.

Bermuda's Forts

1. Fort Scaur.
2. Wreck Hill Fort.
3. Whale Bay Fort.
4. Fort Langton.
5. Fort Hamilton.
6. Devonshire Fort.
7. Fort St. Catherine.
8. Fort Albert.
9. Fort Victoria.
10. Fort George.
11. Gates Fort.

12. Alexander Battery.
13. Fort Cunningham.
14. St. David's Battery.
15. Old Fort.
16. Old Fort.
17. Old Fort.
18. Martello Tower.
19. Gun mountings.
20. King's Castle.
21. Charles Fort.
22. Old Battery.

Appendix V

Forts and Batteries

For the many visitors who are fascinated by the era when Bermuda was heavily fortified so that not a yard of the seas around her but was covered by the range of guns, here is a list of some fortifications, now in various stages of ruin or reconstruction. Many are well worth visiting.

Starting at the west, we have:

DOCKYARD — heavy artillery defences mounted on walls and in bastions

FORT SCAUR — east coast of Somerset Is., built in nineteenth century to protect dockyard

WRECK HILL FORT — northern point of Main Is. in Sandys Parish

WHALE BAY FORT — SW shore Southampton Parish

FORT HAMILTON — east of the city overlooking Hamilton Harbour

FORT LANGTON — NNE of Fort Prospect in Devonshire, to command north shore

FORT PROSPECT — highest point in central Devonshire; moat converted to reservoir

DEVONSHIRE FORT — south coast of Devonshire Parish

FORT ST CATHERINE — NE point of St George's Island

FORT ALBERT — NE coast of St George's Island

FORT VICTORIA — N central of St George's Island

FORT GEORGE — NW guarding St George's town

GATES FORT — SE point of St George's Island

ALEXANDRA BATTERY — slightly NW of Gates

FORT CUNNINGHAM — on Paget Island, a nineteenth century fort. At extreme SE corner of this island are evidences of 1612 fortifications

ST DAVID'S BATTERY — east coast St David's Island, and remains of an old fort slightly NW of this

KING'S CASTLE — on Castle Island east of Tucker's Town Point. Each of the tiny islands lying across the entrance to Castle Harbour was fortified from 1612

CHARLES' FORT — also defending Castle Harbor from 1612, built on Charles Island and named for the prince who became Charles I

BRANGMAN'S FORT — on the island between Castle Island and Nonsuch, fortified 1612

FORT WILLIAM — N of St George's town and now designated Gunpowder Cavern though not used as a gunpowder magazine till late nineteenth century, was also known as Warwick Redoubt.

On the SW tip of St George's Is. (the point least visited to-day) are the remains of an ancient fort from early colonial days and a Martello Tower dating from 1823 built to defend the north shore.

Both St George's Harbour and Castle Harbour had defensive fortifications on the small islands at their mouths from very early days – 1612.

As Colonel Roger Willock puts it in his invaluable *Bulwark of Empire*:

> Generally speaking, Bermuda's complex system of fortifications may be arbitrarily grouped into four consecutive, chronological divisions: those dating from the earliest years of the Colony's history through the American Revolution (the period of the old Empire); the works constructed between the outbreak of the Napoleonic campaigns and the close of the Crimean War; the large additional undertaking throughout the mid-Victorian cycle (1866-1889); and the extensive and elaborate modernization program effected after 1890 which was to continue with varying degrees of intensity as late as the Second World War.

Appendix VI

Sightseeing

PLACES OF INTEREST

All places closed on Christmas Day unless stated otherwise.

* Denotes places which close at 12 noon on Thursdays.

Place & Location	Days Open	Hours
AQUARIUM, MUSEUM & ZOO Flatts Tel. 3-0104	Daily Incl. Sun. & Holidays	9.00am-5.00pm
ART GALLERY (CITY HALL) Church Street Hamilton Tel. 1-1082	Daily Closed Sat, Sun. & Holidays	10.30am-4.30pm
BERMUDA HISTORICAL SOCIETY MUSEUM Queen Street Hamilton Tel. 2-1985	* Daily Closed Sun. & Holidays	10.00am-1.00pm 2.00pm-5.00pm
BERMUDA LIBRARY Queen Street Hamilton Tel. 1-2905	Daily Closed Sun. & Holidays	10.00am-6.30pm
BERMUDA CATHEDRAL Church Street Hamilton	Daily Incl. Sun. & Holidays	8.00am-6.00pm
BERMUDA POTTERY Blue Hole Hill Hamilton Parish Tel. 3-2234	Daily Closed Sun. & Holidays	8.30am-5.00pm
BLUE GROTTO DOLPHINS Blue Hole Hill Hamilton Parish Tel. 3-0864	Daily Sat & Sun – 3.00pm, 4.15pm	12 noon, 1.30pm, 3.00pm, 4.15pm 10.30am, 12noon, 1.30am,
BERMUDA MARITIME MUSEUM Ireland Island. Tel. 4-1418	Daily Incl. Sun.	10.00am-5.00pm
CARRIAGE MUSEUM Water Street St George's Tel. 3-1199	Daily Incl. Sun & Holidays	9.00am-5.00pm
CITY HALL Church Street Hamilton Tel. 2-1234	Daily Closed Sat, & Holidays	9.00am-5.00pm
CONFEDERATE MUSEUM Duke of York Street St George's Tel. 3-9490	Daily	10.00am-5.00pm

CRYSTAL CAVES	Daily Incl. Sun	9.00am-5.00pm
Wilkinson Avenue	& Holidays	
Bailey's Bay Tel. 3-0640		
DEVIL'S HOLE	Daily Incl. Sun	10.00am-5.00pm
Harrington Sound Road	& Holidays	
Smith's Parish Tel. 3-2072		
DELIVERANCE (REPLICA)	Daily Incl. Sun	10.00am-3.30pm
Ordnance Island		
St George's		
FEATHERBED ALLEY PRINTING	Daily	9.30am-4.00pm
PRESS	Closed Sun.	
St George's	& Holidays	
FORT HAMILTON	Daily	9.30am-5.00pm
Happy Valley Road		
Pembroke Tel. 2-0630		
FORT ST CATHERINE	Daily Incl. Sun.	10.00am-4.30pm
St George's Tel. 3-9635	& Holidays	
FORT SCAUR	Daily Incl. Sun.	10.00am-4.00pm
Ely's Harbour	& Holidays	
Somerset		
GIBBS' HILL LIGHTHOUSE	Daily Incl. Sun	9.00am-5.00pm
Southampton Tel. 8-0524	& Holidays	
GUNPOWDER CAVERN	Daily Incl. Sun	10.00am-5.00pm
St George's Tel. 3-0818	& Holidays	(Guided Tours)
LEAMINGTON CAVES	Daily Incl. Sun	9.00am-5.00pm
Bailey's Bay Tel. 3-1188	& Holidays	
OLD DEVONSHIRE CHURCH	Daily Incl. Sun	7.30am-5.30pm
Middle Road	& Holidays	
Devonshire Tel. 2-1348		
PERFUME FACTORY	Daily	9.00am-5.00pm
Bailey's Bay Tel. 3-0627	Closed Sun & Hols.	
PEROT POST OFFICE	Daily	9.00am-5.00pm
Queen Street	Closed Sat, Sun	
Hamilton Tel. 2-1848	& Holidays	
ST DAVID'S LIGHTHOUSE	Daily	9.00am-4.00pm
St David's	Closed Sat, Sun.	
ST GEORGE'S HISTORICAL	Daily	10.00am-4.00pm
SOCIETY	Closed Sun	
St George's Tel. 3-9276	& Holidays	
ST GEORGE LIBRARY	Tues & Fri –	10.00am-1.00pm
Stuart Hall	Wed & Thur –	2.00pm-5.00pm
St George's Tel. 3-9629	Sat	9.30am-5.30pm
ST PETER'S CHURCH	Daily Incl. Sun	9.00am-5.00pm
Duke of York Street	& Holidays	Guide on duty except
St George's Tel. 3-9636		Saturdays
SESSIONS HOUSE	Daily	8.00am-4.15pm
(HOUSE OF ASSEMBLY)	Closed Sat, Sun	
Parliament Street	& Holidays	
Hamilton Tel. 1-1312		
SPRINGFIELD LIBRARY	Mon & Fri	2.00pm-5.00pm
Middle Road	Tue & Thur	10.00am-1.00pm
Somerset Tel. 4-8611	Sat.	9.30am-5.30pm
STATE HOUSE	Annual Peppercorn	
St George's	Ceremony in April	

TUCKER HOUSE	Daily	10.00am-12.00noon
St George's Tel. 3-9378	Closed Sun & Hols	1.00pm-5.00pm
TUCKER TREASURE	Daily	10.00am-5.00pm
Bermuda Maritime Museum		
Flatt's Tel. 3-0104		
VERDMONT	Daily	10.00am-12.00noon
Collector's Hill	Closed Sun	1.15pm-5.00pm
Smith's Parish	& Holidays	

LANDMARKS, PUBLIC GARDENS AND POINTS OF INTEREST

ARBORETUM, Middle Road and Montpelier Road, Devonshire
BLACK WATCH WELL, Marsh Folly and North Shore Road, Pembroke
BOTANICAL GARDENS, Point Finger Road, Paget (Conducted Tour every Tuesday and Friday at 10.30am);
BUILDING BAY, St George's
CENOTAPH, Front Street, City of Hamilton
DUCKING STOOL, Ordnance Island, St George's
GATES FORT, St George's
PALM GROVE GARDENS, South Shore Road
PAR-LA-VILLE GARDENS, Queen Street, City of Hamilton
SOMERS GARDEN, York Street, St George's
SOMERSET BRIDGE, Somerset
SPANISH ROCK AND SPITTAL POND, South Shore Road, Smith's
STOCKS & PILLORY & WHIPPING POST, King's Square, St George's
VICTORIA PARK, Victoria Street and Cedar Avenue, City of Hamilton
WALSINGHAM, Hamilton Parish

Each spring, some of Bermuda's historic houses are thrown open to the public on different fixed dates, with a small admission fee in aid of the Bermuda Garden Club or the Bermuda Historical Society.

The Visitors' Service Bureaux in Hamilton and St George's are open daily to serve tourists and to answer questions.

TRANSPORTATION

Bus and Ferry Timetables may be obtained at the above Bureaux. Ferries run frequently between Hamilton, Paget, Warwick and Somerset.

Motor-assisted cycles and pedal cycles are for hire; also carriages and taxis are available. *We drive on the left* and pedestrian crossings are indicated by black and white zebra stripes on the roads.

Speed maximum — 20 mph in open places — with 15 mph the limit in the City of Hamilton, town of St George's and village of Somerset.

LIST OF SOME BEACHES

Bermuda Beach Club (with charge) South Shore, Paget
Bermudiana Beach Club (with charge) South Shore, Warwick
Breakers Beach Club (with charge) South Shore, Smith's Parish

Chaplin Bay, South Shore, south of Warwick Camp
Church Bay, South Shore, Southampton
Devonshire Bay, South Shore, Devonshire Parish
Elbow Beach Surf Club (with charge) South Shore, Paget
Horseshoe Bay, South Shore, Southampton
Jobson Cove, South Shore, Warwick
John Smith's Bay, South Shore, Smith's Parish
Long Bay Beach, NW Sandys near Skeeters' Corner
Princess Beach Club (with charge) South Shore, Southampton
Shelly Bay Beach, North West Coast, Hamilton Parish
Stovell Bay near NW point of Pembroke Parish
Stonehole Bay, South Shore, Warwick
Tobacco Bay in St George's Island, N of St George's town
Tribe Road (Elbow Bay) South Shore, Paget Parish
Warwick Long Bay, South Shore of Warwick Parish
West Whale Bay SW coast of Southampton Parish
Whalebone Bay western end of St George's Island

GOLF COURSES
Port Royal Golf Course (Public)
Queen's Park Golf Course (Public)
Belmont Hotel and Golf Club (Private Club)
                              (Introduction required)
Castle Harbour Hotel and Golf Club (Introduction required)
Holiday Inn Hotel and Golf Club (Introduction required)
Princess Golf Club (Introduction required)
Riddell's Bay Golf & Country Club (Introduction required)
Rose Hill Golf Club (Introduction required)
Mid-Ocean Golf Club (Introduction required)

Some Hotels and Guest Houses in Bermuda

(figures refer to the number of guests)

Sandys Parish

Cambridge Beaches	127	Sugar Cane	25
Lantana	104	Teucer Place	9
Somerset Br. Apts.	24	Willowbank	91

Southampton Parish

By Faith	8	Pillar Ville	6
Munro Beach	30	Pompano Beach	146
Sandon	10	Reefs	86
Sonesta Beach	584	Royal Heights	8
Southampton Princess	1000		

Warwick Parish

Banana Beach	42	Maudadmar	6
Belmont	308	Mermaid Beach	230
Belljori	8	Pink Sands	20
Blue Horizons	8	Rick-A-Tan	10
Flamingo Beach	22	Surf Side	72
Marley Beach	65	White Heron	19

Paget Parish

Breezie Brae	18	Montgomery	70
Buena Vista	39	Newstead	100
Coral Beach	127	Paraquet	8
Elbow Beach	490	Pomander Gate	51
Fariesville	11	Pretty Penny	6
Gables	10	Que Sera	6
Glencoe	52	Rose Valley	6
Glen Folly	6	Salt Kettle	16
Glenmar	14	Sea Horse	17
Grape Bay	27	Seaward	10
Greenbank	15	Sky Top	14
Harmony Hall	144	South Capers	38
Highland	11	South Sea	8
Horizons	79	Sunny Isle	59
Inverurie	268	Underwood	14
Loughlands	41	Valley Cott	19
Middleton	15	White Sands	80

Pembroke Parish

Archlyn Villa	29	Pleasant View	6
Bayridge	10	Princess	936
Belle Terre	6	Ripleigh	10
Bermudiana	478	Rosedon	57
Canada Villa	14	Rosemont	56
Edgehill	18	Sherwood's	86
Fordham Hall	15	Silverleaf	19
Hi-Roy	7	Tallent Villa	9
Imperial (comm.)	14	Waterloo	66
Kimbar Terr	6	Willows	17
Mazarine	14	Woodbourne/Inverness	20
Oxford House	20		

Devonshire Parish

Ariel Sands	88	Grandview	8
Ashley Hall	9	Kennington	6

Smith's Parish

Arlington Heights	34	Masterview	12
Cabana	16	Palmetto Bay	84
Capistrano	12	Pink Beach	86
Harringay	10	Seamont	8
Deepdene	89	Seven Arches	11

Hamilton Parish

Coral Island	164	Grotto Bay	268
Gayview	12	Sterling Rock	10

St George's Parish

		Holiday Inn	800
Castle Harbour	620	Mid Ocean Club	77
Hillcrest	15	Wainwrights	6

Abridged Bibliography

So much has been written on every aspect of the Bermuda scene that it is impossible to list everything. Some of the following are out of print but all are available for study at the Bermuda Library.

Acts of the Legislature of the Islands of Bermuda (various compilations)

Annual Registers (British) eighteenth and nineteenth centuries

Arton, Mary Alicia Juliette, *Trade and Commerce of Bermuda 1515-1839*, Island Press 1965

Beebe, Dr William, *Field Book of the Shore Fishes of Bermuda*, G. P. Putnam's Sons, N.Y. 1933

 Half Mile Down, Harbourt Brace, N.Y., 1934 (Adventures in the Bathysphere)

 Nonsuch; Land of Water, Brewer, Warren & Putnam, 1932

Bell, Euphemia Young, *Beautiful Bermua*, 10th ed., 1947

Benbow, Colin, *Boer Prisoners of War in Bermuda*, Bermuda His. Society, 1962

Bermuda Almanacks from 1844

Bermuda Churchman, Church of England Monthly

Bermuda Historical Quarterly from 1944 to date

Bermuda Welfare Society (Warwick Branch) *Bermuda's Best Recipes* (700) 7th ed., 1970

Bermudian Magazine from 1930 to date, The Bermudian Publishing Co. Ltd., Hamilton, Bermuda. Ed. by Ronald J. Williams

Britton, Nathaniel Lord, *Flora of Bermuda*, Scribner N.Y. (The standard work on Bermuda botany.)

Brockman, Paymaster-Lieut W. E., *Bermuda, Growth of a Naval Base*

Brown, Alexander, *Genesis of the United States*, Cambridge, Mass., 1890

Bushell's Handbook, The Standard Year Book for thirty years, 1939 being the 30th edition. Ed. by John J. Bushelll

Cole, George Watson, *Bermuda in Periodical Literature*, 275 pp., Conn., 1907 (A comprehensive bibliography)

Colonial State Papers

Cox, William M., M.A., *Bermuda's beginning: Simplified geology*, 24 pp., Tinling, London, 1959

 Bermuda constitutional documents, Hamilton, 1970

Craven, Wesley Frank, Introduction to the *History of Bermuda* by the Associate Professor of history at N.Y. University, 1938

Department of Agriculture and Fisheries, Monthly Bulletin from January 1925

Department of Tourism, Directed by W. James Williams, O.B.E. Pamphlets, photographs, mapss

Dyer, H. Thornley, F.R.I.B.A., *The next 20 years; a report on the development plans for Bermuda*, Bermuda Press, 1963

Fodor, Eugene, (Editor) *Fodor's Guide to the Caribbean*, Bahamas, Bermuda

Godet, T. L., M.D., *Bermuda*, 1860

Hakluyt, Richard, *Hakluyt's Voyages*

Hannau, Hans W., *Bermuda in full colour*, Doubleday, N.Y., 1970

Hayward, Walter Brownell, *Bermuda Past and Present*, Dodd Mead, N.Y., 1910

Henderson, Dwight Franklin, (Editor) *The private journal of Georgiana Gholson Walker, 1862-65*, Confederate Press, 1963

Heyl, Edith Stowe Godfrey, *Bermuda through the camera of James B. Heyl* 1868-97. Robt. MacLehose & Co. Ltd., 1951
    Bermuda's Early Days, 1511-1684, Bermuda Dept. of Ed. 1959

Humphreys, John S., *Bermuda houses*. Marshal Jones, Boston, 1923 (The evolution and types of Bermuda architecture with excellent illustrations and plans))

Hyde, Bryden B., *Bermuda's Antique Furniture & Silver 1612–1830*, Bermuda National Trust, 1971; 460 illus

Journals of the House of Assembly

Kennedy, Sister Jean de C., *Bermuda's Sailors of Fortune*, Baxter's Book Shops, 1962, 1969
    Biography of a Colonial Town: Hamilton 1700-1897, Bermuda Book Stores, 1961
    Frith of Bermuda; Gentleman Privateer, The Bermuda Book Stores, Hamilton, 1964
    Isle of Devils: Bermuda Under the Somers Island Co., Collins, 1971

Kerr, Wilfred Brenton, *Bermuda and the American Revolution*, Princeton Univ. Press, 1936

Lefroy, Lieut-Gen. Sir John Henry, *Constitutional History of Bermuda Memorials of the Discovery and Early Settlement of the Bermudas or Somers Islands 1511-1687 compiled from the Colonial Records and other Original Sources*, in II Vols, Longmans Green, 1877 & 1879, Reprinted Jan. 1932

Livingston, William, *A Million Years on Mount Bermuda*, Bermuda Book Store, Hamilton, Bermuda, n.d. (A 36-p. pamphlet of geology)

Lloyd, Susette Harriet, *Sketches of Bermuda*, London, Cochrane & Co., 1835

Lucas, Sir C.P., *Historical Geography of the British Colonies*, Oxford, 1888

Ludington, Morris H., *Bermuda, the Post Office, Postal Markings and Adhesive Stamps*, London, Robson Lowe, 1962 (An authoritative work on Philately.) Supplement to above, Robson Lowe, 1968

McCallan, E. A., *Life on Old St David's, Bermuda*, Bermuda Historical Monuments Trust 1948

Mayer, Lloyd, *Colonel Tom Dill, O.B.E.*, Bermuda Book Store, 1964

Minutes of H.M. Council

Mitchell, John, *Jail Journal*

Moore, Thomas, *Poems*

Norwood, Richard, *Journal of Richard Norwood*, Scholar's Facsimiles and Reprints, 1945 (The publication of this diary of the seventeenth century surveyor was an important literary event.)

Purchas, Samuel, *Purchas his Pilgrims*, London 1625, Reprinted for the Hakluyt Society in 1905 by Glasgow Univ. Press

Rider's Guide Book of Bermuda

Robinson, Kenneth Ellsworth, *The Berkeley Educational Society's Origins and Early History*, Berkeley Educational Society, Bermuda, 1962

Sayles, Professor Robert W., *Bermuda During the Ice Age*, American Academy of Arts and Sciences, Boston, 1931 (An important work by the Professor of Geology at Harvard.)

Smith, Captain John, *General History of Virginia, New England and the Summers Islands*, London 1624. Reprinted Glasgow 1907

Smith, Louise Hutchings, *Bermuda's Oldest Inhabitants: tales of plant life*, Salmon, Sevenoaks, 1934

Stark, James H., *Stark's Illustrated Bermuda Guide*, Boston, 1897

Strode, Hudson, *Story of Bermuda*, Smith, N.Y., 1932 and 1946

Trollope, Anthony, *West Indies and the Spanish Main*, 1860

Tucker Letters (eighteenth-century.) As preserved in Williamsburg, Va. – copies in Bermuda Archives and reprinted in Bermuda Historical Quarterlies

Tucker, Terry, *Bermuda and the Supernatural; superstitions and beliefs from the seventeenth to the twentieth centuries*, Glasgow Univ. Press, 1968

    Bermuda's Story – 1609-1970, (First commissioned by the Dept. of Education and published by them in 1959 this over-all history, now in its seventh printing by Glasgow University Press, is put out by the Island Press and regularly kept up to date)

    Beware the Hurricane! (The complete story of the gyratory tropical storms that have struck Bermuda and the Islanders' folk-lore regarding them 1609-1970) Appendix of Wrecks and Earthquake Shocks, 2nd ed., Island Press, 1972; Illus.

    The Islands of Bermuda (each isle and islet's separate story with individual illustrations and an index of the 172 names given the approx. 120 islands of the group). Maps; Island Press, Hamilton, 1970; 2nd edition 1979.

Beyond the Rubber Tree: story of Par-la-ville and the Perot family, Bermuda Historical Society, 1961

Bermuda' Crime and Punishment, Seventeenth-century Style, Island Press, 1974

Vandiver, Frank E., *Confederate Blockade-running through Bermuda 1861-65*, Univ. of Texas Press, 1947

Verrill Addison E., *Bermuda Islands* (An account of their scenery, productions, physiography, natural history and geology, with sketches of their discovery and early history and the change in their flora and fauna due to man) New Haven, Conn., 1902

Voorhis, Harold V.B., *Freemasonry in Bermuda*, by the Secretary and Past Master of the American Lodge of Research, Free and Accepted Masons, N.Y.

Wardman, Elfrida L., (Editor) *The Bermuda Jubilee Garden* (A 350-page magnificent production of the Garden Club of Bermuda)

Warmke, Germaine, and Abbott, R. Tucker, *Caribbean Sea Shells*, Livingston, Pa., 1961

Waterston, Dr J.M., (Plant Pathologist) *The Fungi of Bermuda*, Dept. of Agriculture, 1947

Watlington, Hereward Trott, *Bermuda Historical Monuments Trust: The First Thirty Years 1937-1966* (Brief record of the work of a devoted body of local men and women which led to the formation of the Bermuda National Trust)

Watson, James Wreford, (Professor of Geography, Edinburgh University) with Catherine Foggo and John Oliver, *A Georgraphy of Bermuda*, Dept. of Education, Bermuda, 1965

West Indies and Caribbean Year Book, Section on Bermuda. Published annually by Thos. Skinner Directories, Croydon, England

Whitney, Christine M., (Editor), *The Bermuda Garden*, The Garden Club of Bermuda, 1955 2nd ed., 1969

Whittingham, Col. F., *Bermuda, a Fortress, a Colony, and a Prison*, 1860

Wilkinson, Henry C., *The Adventurers of Bermuda: a history of the island from its discovery until the dissolution of the Somers Island Company in 1684*, London, Oxford Univ. Press, 1933 and 1958

Bermuda in the Old Empire, 1684-1784, London, Oxford Univ. Press, 1950 (Dr Wilkinson's two volumes remain the standard history of the lengthy period they cover.)

Bermuda from Sail to Steam. The history of the Island 1784-1901. In Two Vols, Oxford University Press, 1973

Williams, Ronald John, *Bermudiana*. With 200 photographs by Walter Rutherford, (Intro. by Hervey Allen) Rhinehart & Co. Inc., N.Y., 1936, 1946

Williams, William Frith, *An Historical Account of the Bermudas*, Newby, London, 1848

Willock, Col Roger, *Bulwark of Empire: Bermuda's Fortified Naval Base 1860-1920*, Princeton 1962

Wingate, David B., (Editor) Checklist of the birds, mammals, reptiles and amphibians of Bermuda as compiled by the Bermuda Audubon Society, 1959

Zuill, William E. S., (Senior) *Bermuda Journey: a leisurely guidebook*, Coward-McCann Inc., N.Y., 1946. Bermuda Book Store 6th Imp. 1969

   Bermuda Sampler 1815-1850, Bermuda Book Store 1937 (Notes, illustrations and extracts from newspapers over 35 years)

   Tom Moore's Bermuda Poems (and notes, with comment) Bermuda Book Stores, Hamilton

Zuill, Mrs W. E. S. and Burland, Mrs Barbara, *Old Bermuda Recipes* (Small mimeographed pamphlet of old Bermuda dishes)

Zuill, Kitty (Mrs W. E. S.,) *Bermuda Kettle of Fish* (19 pp. of methods for cooking all types of Bermuda fish) Bermuda Book Store, Hamilton

Zuill, William Sears and Baxter, Ford, *Bermuda To-day* (Small useful guide for tourists) 1958

Zuill, William Sears, *The Story of Bermuda and Her People*, Macmillan, 1973

Also: File of Bermuda Newspapers 1784 onwards

Various Reports and Recommendations made by experts brought in during the 1960s and later:

Deutsch, Dr J.J., advised Finance Committee of House of Assembly on Taxation

Dyer, Thornley, wrote *The Next 20 Years* (1963) and advised on extension of land areas

Houghton Report — on total re-organization of educational system

Richardson, Professor J. Henry (1963) — economies for the banks and business community

Tressider, James (1962) — Traffic expert — proposed ban in all private cars by 1965

Urwick-Currie Report — 17 major recommendations on the re-organization of government and administration

Pitt Report on 1977 Riots

MS Material preserved in Bermuda Archives include:—

Colonial Records 1612-1713 (much from these great MS volumes was published by Sir John Henry Lefroy, q.v., to whom we owe their preservation.)

Books of Wills 1640-1812.

Inventories, Administration, Guardianship (Intestacy)

Early Compilations of Laws, Acts, Resolves.

Attorney Generals' Reports.

Journals of the House of Assembly.

Minutes of Council.

Executive and Legislative Council Minutes.

Legco Sessional Papers.

Slave Registers and Petitions.

Police Journals.
Jail Journals.
Admiralty Prize Court.
Births, Marriages, Deaths.
Customs Records.

Among Historical MSS preserved by the Bermuda Historical Monuments Trust are the following:—

Transcript of Register of Baptisms, Marriages & Burials 1743-1780 made by the Revd. John Alexander Moore (an invaluable genealogical record).

Register of Baptisms, Marriages & Burials 1755-1802 made by the Revd. Alexander Richardson.

Transcript of Private Register of Baptisms 1793-1796, St Mary's Church, Warwick.

Transcript of old Register of St Anne's Church, Southampton, from 1619 (incomplete).

John Harvey Darrell's Note-book and Letters.

Daniel Robert Tucker, Diary December 1850-January 1858.

Journal of Richard Norwood.

Hyland Diaries (On loan to the Trust from the Hyland family). 1860-1893.

Six boxes of eighteenth century Tucker Letters from the Trustees of Colonial Williamsburg.

Family Trees of:— Brown, Godet, Gray, Kempe, Tucker.

Also many eighteenth and nineteenth century water-colour sketches, and maps and plans seventeenth, eighteenth and nineteenth centuries.

Manuscript Map of Bermuda, by Sir George Somers, 1609.

Index

BOOKS ABOUT BERMUDA HISTORY

By Terry Tucker, local author and editor of the Bermuda Historical Quarterly

BERMUDA: Today and Yesterday, 1503-1978, Robert Hale Limited, London. Fully illustrated. "Here is the history of a once-isolated group of islands told with the continuity and excitement of an adventure story". (Hale, London). "This is a remarkable book." (Contemporary Review, London.) "This could easily be the one history locals will be recommending to visitors wanting to know more about their island . . . and (this is a big plus) it is an easy read to boot". (John Barritt in Royal Gazette.)

BERMUDA'S STORY. A *simplified* comprehensive history, first written at the request of the Board of Education, this book has gone through eight impressions and is now published as a paper back by popular request — brought up to date (1976) and illustrated with 30 line drawings by the author. "The WHY of everything here is indicated, along with the WHAT, WHERE and WHEN — a most absorbing and suspenseful narrative" (Marian Robb in Mid Ocean News).

BERMUDA & THE SUPERNATURAL: Superstitions & Beliefs from 17th-20th Centuries. "Ghosts and a ghoul, gnomes that cause earthquakes, buried treasure, witches, love potions — these are some of the ingredients for compelling reading — I found it impossible to put this book down" (Bob Taylor in Bermuda Sun.)

BEWARE THE HURRICANE! The story of the gyratory tropical storms that have struck Bermuda from 1609-1971. A complete compendium of all the hurricanes that have struck Bermuda together with the islanders' growing awareness of their origins. "(This book) contains a vast amount of fascinating information and draws hurricanes into the general history of Bermuda". (William S. Zuill in the Royal Gazette.)

THE ISLANDS OF BERMUDA — the separate and indiviaul story of each of the 120-odd isles and islets that form the Bermuda group, together with reasons for place names, and individual photographs.

BERMUDA'S CRIME & PUNISHMENT, 17th CENTURY STYLE — a study of how offences were punished — and exactly what offences were then considered serious violations of the law; often a grimly humorous story.

RENDEZVOUS WITH DESTINY; the Radio play of Somers' shipwreck, written and performed to be broadcast on Somers' Day, 28th July.

BEYOND THE RUBBER TREE. The story of Par-la-Ville and the famous Perot stamps. Illustrated with the author's sketches.

BERMUDA — UNINTENDED DESTINATION. Eight contemporary accounts of the apparently disastrous voyage of the 'Sea Venture" whose accidental arrival on these shores led to Bermuda becoming an inhabited place. With modern comments and research on the personalities involved.

AND TWO HISTORICAL NOVELS WITH BERMUDA BACKGROUNDS:-

HANG THE WITCH HIGH! A love story against the background of witchcraft trials.

WHAT'S BECOME OF ANNA? A famous murder mystery.